Universal Health Coverage in China – A Health Economic Perspective

Inauguraldissertation

zur

Erlangung des Grades eines Doktors der Wirtschaftswissenschaft

der

Universität Witten/Herdecke gGmbH

im

Bereich der Wirtschaftswissenschaft

Vorgelegt von:

Dr. rer. pol., Dr. med. David S. Weis

aus Mainz

Jahr der Einreichung
2015

i

Erstgutachter:

Professor Doktor Birger P. Priddat

Zweitgutachter:

Professor Doktor Markus Taube

Tag der Disputation:

03. Mai 2016

Danksagung:

Mein Dank gilt zuvorderst meinem Erstbetreuer, Herrn Professor Birger P. Priddat, der es mit seiner unvergleichlich, unkomplizierten Art geschafft hat, Unterstützung bei auftauchenden Problemen zu leisten und Lösungswege aufzuzeigen. Über sein Problemlösungstalent hinaus verfügt Herr Priddat über eine außergewöhnlich motivierende Menschenführung, von der ich als Doktorand profitieren durfte.

Auch meinem Zweitbetreuer, Herrn Professor Markus Taube, bin ich zutiefst dankbar, da er mit seiner wissenschaftlichen und praktischen China-Erfahrung während wichtiger Arbeitsschritte immer wieder wertvolle und stets fundierte Hilfestellungen gegeben hat.

Frau Juliane Slotta danke ich herzlichst für das kompetente und engagierte Lektorat.

Nicht weniger dankbar bin ich auch all denjenigen Menschen, die außerhalb der wissenschaftlichen Arbeit wichtige Unterstützung geleistet haben. Dazu zählt zu allererst meine Familie, die mir nicht nur auf persönlicher, sondern auch auf ganz pragmatisch organisatorischer Ebene immer eine wertvolle Unterstützung war. Nicht zuletzt danke ich allen Freunden, die mich in schwierigen Zeiten unterstützt und in leichten begleitet haben, sowie alle vergangenen und gegenwärtigen Philosophen mit denen ich in Diskurs treten durfte.

Vielen Dank einem jeden oben Erwähnten, und auch einem jeden Unterschlagenen. Ohne Ihre und Eure Unterstützung wäre diese Arbeit nicht möglich gewesen.

Table of Contents

Table of Contents...i
Table of Figures...iii
List of Tables v
List of Abbreviations.. viii
1   Introduction 1
  1.1   Historical background 1
  1.2   Status quo and recent development.. 3
  1.3   Reasons to aim for UHC 4
  1.4   Status quo of health insurance coverage in China 7
  1.5   Contributions to the scientific literature and structure of this thesis 7
2   Definition and concept...13
  2.1   Height: "What proportion of the costs is covered?"......................15
    2.1.1   Theoretical views on cost-sharing in health insurance systems 15
    2.1.2   Practical approaches concerning cost-sharing in health insurance systems 17
  2.2   Depth: "Which benefits are covered?"...24
    2.2.1   Theoretical views on services in health insurance systems................................24
    2.2.2   Practical approaches concerning services in health insurance systems..............31
  2.3   Breadth: "Who is insured?" 33
  2.4   Overall findings 35
3   The situation in the People's Republic of China 37
  3.1   The height dimension in China...39
    3.1.1   Low user fees and OOP...39
    3.1.2   Benefit distribution according to the need 42
    3.1.3   Payments according to the ability to pay.......................................47
    3.1.4   Intermediate findings and interpretation 53
  3.2   The depth dimension in China 55
    3.2.1   The situation of appropriate health care in China 55

i

3.2.2   Relevance of the NCD-topic..61

3.2.3   What are possible health interventions to reduce this burden? 67

3.2.4   Making health effects comparable: cost-effectiveness and cost-benefit 75

3.2.5   Conclusion...96

3.3   The breadth dimension in China 98

3.3.1   Overview of literature: Does marginalization of migrant workers matter in the context of health?...98

3.3.2   Health Insurance Coverage in China – 2011 and 2020 107

4   Summary and conclusion...130

5   Boundaries and discussion 139

5.1   Analysis of the first dimension (height)...139

5.2   Analysis of the second dimension (depth)...140

5.3   Analysis of the third dimension (breadth) 142

6   Outlook 143

6.1   New aspects 143

6.2   International context...144

Bibliography 149

Annexes..171

Annex 1: Housing Choices for temporary migrants 171

Annex 2: Housing conditions for temporary migrants..172

Annex 3: Migration paths in China 173

Annex 4: Total Economic Value (TEV)..174

Annex 5: VSL and Equity...176

Annex 6: The Chinese situation in comparison with Europe and the USA 183

Annex 7: GDP, VSL and Correlations 186

Annex 8: Explanation of economic values used for calculations 187

Annex 9: Proposed targets and indicators for SDG goal 3.8...............................188

Table of Figures

FIGURE 1: "YEAR OF UHC LEGISLATION AND LEVELS OF GDP PER CAPITA", (STUCKLER ET AL., 2010, P. 17)......2

FIGURE 2: "RURAL AND URBAN HEALTH INSURANCE COVERAGE IN CHINA, BY PROGRAM, 1993-2011" (MENG ET AL. 2012A) 8

FIGURE 3: "THREE DIMENSIONS OF UNIVERSAL COVERAGE" (WHO, 2014, P. 5, 2010, P. XV; WHO AND LERBERGHE 2008, P. 26)......14

FIGURE 4: "CATASTROPHIC EXPENDITURE RELATED TO OUT-OF-POCKET PAYMENT AT THE POINT OF SERVICE" (WHO AND LERBERGHE, 2008, P. 24) 18

FIGURE 5: "NUMBER OF HOUSEHOLDS IMPOVERISHED BY OUT-OF-POCKET PAYMENT FOR HEALTH SERVICES IN THAILAND" (1996–2010) (WHO, 2014, P. 33). 19

FIGURE 6: "BIRTHS ATTENDED BY MEDICALLY TRAINED PERSONNEL (PERCENTAGE), BY INCOME GROUP" (WHO AND LERBERGHE, 2008, P. 28). 20

FIGURE 7: "IMPACT OF ABOLISHING USER FEES ON OUTPATIENT ATTENDANCE IN KISORO DISTRICT, UGANDA: OUTPATIENT ATTENDANCE 1998–2002" (WHO AND LERBERGHE, 2008, P. 27)......21

FIGURE 8: "SOCIOECONOMIC INEQUALITIES IN COVERAGE RATES IN THREE COUNTRIES", DATA FOR ETHIOPIA FROM 2011, FOR INDIA AND COLUMBIA FROM 2014 (WHO, 2014, P. 25). 34

FIGURE 9: "OUT-OF-POCKET HEALTH EXPENDITURE (% OF TOTAL EXPENDITURE ON HEALTH) IN CHINA" (WORLD BANK, 2014)......40

FIGURE 10: "OVERALL ADMINISTRATIVE STRUCTURE OF HEALTH SECTOR" (LIU AND YI 2004, P. 14). 48

FIGURE 11: "TOP 10 CAUSES OF DEATH IN HIGH INCOME COUNTRIES, 2012" (WHO 2014A)......61

FIGURE 12: "TOP 10 CAUSES OF DEATH IN LOWER-MIDDLE INCOME COUNTRIES, 2012" (WHO 2014A)......61

FIGURE 13: "WELFARE COSTS (IN MILLION USD) OF THE 'DEADLY QUARTET' IN CHINA", PER 100,000 INHABITANTS, 1990-2010 DATA, HEALTH DATA FROM IHME (IHME, 2014A), AUTHOR'S CALCULATIONS. 64

FIGURE 14: "WELFARE COSTS (IN MILLION USD) OF THE 'DEADLY QUARTET' IN CHINA", PER 100,000 INHABITANTS, 2005-2010 DATA, HEALTH DATA FROM IHME (IHME, 2014A), AUTHOR'S CALCULATIONS. 64

FIGURE 15: "SURVIVAL FROM AGE 35 FOR CONTINUING CIGARETTE SMOKERS AND LIFELONG NON-SMOKERS AMONG UK MALE DOCTORS BORN 1900-1930, WITH PERCENTAGES ALIVE AT EACH DECADE OF AGE" (DOLL 2004). 70

FIGURE 16: "PROPORTION OF PATIENTS WITH DECREASED (I) AND INCREASED (II) VALUES. VARIABLE PERCENTAGE REFERS TO MINIMUM DECREASE (I) OR INCREASE (II) FROM BASELINE TO 3 YEARS. THERE WAS NO STATISTICALLY SIGNIFICANT DIFFERENCE BETWEEN THE STUDY GROUPS. SRA, SELF-REPORTED ALCOHOL CONSUMPTION; CDT, CARBOHYDRATE-DEFICIENT TRANSFERRIN; GGT, GAMMA-GLUTAMYLTRANSFERASE" (AALTO 2001). 74

FIGURE 17: "FRAMEWORK FOR INTEGRATING COST-EFFECTIVENESS WITH OTHER CRITERIA WHEN SELECTING SERVICES", COST PER HEALTHY LIFE YEAR AS A MULTIPLE OF GDP PER CAPITA, (WHO 2014C, P. 21). 85

FIGURE 18: "COST-EFFECTIVENESS OF SERVICES TARGETING HIGH-BURDEN CONDITIONS" (WHO 2014C, P. 14). 86

FIGURE 19: "INCLUSION OF THE "DEADLY QUARTET" AND ASSOCIATED PHYSIOLOGICAL RISK MARKERS INTO THE
FRAMEWORK FOR INTEGRATING COST-EFFECTIVENESS WITH OTHER CRITERIA WHEN SELECTING SERVICES"
(WHO 2014C, P. 21), AUTHOR'S ADAPTATION. 87
FIGURE 20: "INCLUSION OF THE 'DEADLY QUARTET' AND ASSOCIATED PHYSIOLOGICAL RISK MARKERS INTO THE
RANKING OF COST-EFFECTIVENESS OF SERVICES TARGETING HIGH-BURDEN CONDITIONS" (WHO 2014C, P.
14), AUTHOR'S ADAPTATIONS. 89
FIGURE 21: "INSURANCE STATUS INCLUDING MIGRANT WORKERS." AUTHOR'S INVESTIGATION. 117
FIGURE 22: "POPULATION DEVELOPMENT IN CHINA 1980-2050" (WORLD BANK 2014). 119
FIGURE 23: "URBAN INSURANCE STATUS INCLUDING MIGRANT WORKERS.", AUTHOR'S INVESTIGATION. 121
FIGURE 24: TOP 50 CROSS-PROVINCIAL POPULATION MIGRATION PATHS IN CHINA, BASED ON POPULATION CENSES
IN 1990 AND 2000, AND THE 1% POPULATION SAMPLING SURVEY IN 1985, 1995 AND 2005.3 BACKGROUND
SHADING REPRESENTS THE TOTAL IMMIGRATION TO EACH PROVINCE DURING THE INTERVAL. PATH COLORS
INDICATE THE TOTAL NUMBER OF CROSS-PROVINCIAL MIGRANTS MOVING BETWEEN PROVINCES IN DIRECTION
OF ARROW DURING THE TIME PERIOD. THE PATHS SHOWN ACCOUNTED FOR 31%, 50%, 66% AND 67% OF
THE TOTAL MIGRATION THAT OCCURRED IN THE FOUR TIME PERIODS, RESPECTIVELY. DATA FROM WANG, LI
ET AL. 2011 (GONG ET AL., 2012B). 173
FIGURE 25: ECONOMIC VALUATION OF TOTAL HEALTH COSTS BY COI AND WTP (WHO, 2008C, P. 25). 175
FIGURE 26: WELFARE COSTS (IN MILLION US$) OF TOBACCO AND ALCOHOL USE 1990-2010, HEALTH DATA FROM
IHME (IHME, 2014B), AUTHOR'S CALCULATIONS. 184
FIGURE 27: WELFARE COSTS (IN MILLION US$) OF DIETARY RISKS 1990-2010, HEALTH DATA FROM IHME (IHME,
2014B), AUTHOR'S CALCULATIONS. 184
FIGURE 28: WELFARE COSTS (IN MILLION US$) OF TOBACCO AND ALCOHOL USE 2005-2010, HEALTH DATA FROM
IHME (IHME, 2014B), AUTHOR'S CALCULATIONS. 185
FIGURE 29: WELFARE COSTS (IN MILLION US$) OF DIETARY RISKS AND PHYSICAL INACTIVITY 2005-2010, HEALTH
DATA FROM IHME (IHME, 2014B), AUTHOR'S CALCULATIONS. 185

List of Tables

TABLE 1: "CRITICAL DIMENSIONS AND CHOICES ON THE PATH TO UNIVERSAL HEALTH COVERAGE" (WHO, 2014A, P. 5). 15

TABLE 2: "OUT-OF-POCKET HEALTH EXPENDITURE (% OF TOTAL EXPENDITURE ON HEALTH) IN SIX COUNTRIES" (WORLD BANK, 2014). 21

TABLE 3: "ASPECTS OF EQUITY", AUTHOR'S INVESTIGATION. 24

TABLE 4: "OUT-OF-POCKET HEALTH EXPENDITURE (% OF TOTAL EXPENDITURE ON HEALTH) IN CHINA" (WORLD BANK, 2014). 39

TABLE 5: "INPATIENT REIMBURSEMENT IN THE THREE SOCIAL HEALTH INSURANCE PROGRAMS, 2008 AND 2010", NUMBERS FROM YIP ET AL., 2012, P. 835, AUTHOR'S INVESTIGATION. 44

TABLE 6: "INPATIENT REIMBURSEMENT IN THE THREE REGIONS, 2008 AND 2011", NUMBERS FROM MENG ET AL. 2012B: 809, AUTHOR'S INVESTIGATION. 46

TABLE 7: "RATIOS OF INPATIENT REIMBURSEMENT RATES BETWEEN LESS ADVANTAGED AND MORE ADVANTAGED COMPARISON GROUPS, 2008 AND 2011", NUMBERS FROM MENG ET AL. 2012B, P. 810, AUTHOR'S INVESTIGATION. 46

TABLE 8: "SUMMARY OF THREE SOCIAL HEALTH INSURANCE PROGRAMS" (YIP ET AL. 2012, P. 835). 51

TABLE 9: "INDIVIDUAL CONTRIBUTION IN THE THREE SOCIAL HEALTH INSURANCE PROGRAMS, 2010", NUMBERS FROM YIP ET AL. 2012 P. 835, AUTHOR'S INVESTIGATION. 52

TABLE 10: "THE 10 LEADING RISK FACTORS FOR DEATH IN MIDDLE INCOME COUNTRIES", 2004 DATA (NARAYAN ET AL. 2010, P. 1197). 62

TABLE 11: "THE 'DEADLY QUARTET' IN CHINA", 2010 DATA (IHME 2014A), AUTHOR'S CONTRIBUTION. 63

TABLE 12: "WELFARE COSTS OF THE "DEADLY QUARTET" IN CHINA (PER 100,000 INHABITANTS)", 1990-2010 DATA, IN 2010 MILLION USD, HEALTH DATA FROM IHME (IHME 2014A), AUTHOR'S CALCULATIONS. 65

TABLE 13: "WELFARE COSTS OF THE 'DEADLY QUARTET' IN CHINA", 2010 DATA, TOTAL POPULATION, IN 2010 MILLION USD, HEALTH DATA FROM IHME (IHME 2014A), AUTHOR'S CALCULATIONS. 66

TABLE 14: "WELFARE COSTS OF THE "DEADLY QUARTET" AND THE PHYSIOLOGICAL RISK MARKERS IN CHINA", 2010 DATA, TOTAL POPULATION, IN 2010 MILLION USD, HEALTH DATA FROM IHME (IHME 2014A), AUTHOR'S CALCULATIONS. 66

TABLE 15: "SUMMARY OF INTERVENTIONS INCLUDED IN THE CORE SCALING-UP COSTING SCENARIO" (CHISHOLM ET AL., 2011, P. 12). 67

TABLE 16: "DISTRIBUTION OF BODY MASS INDEX (BMI) IN CHINA", 2000 DATA, ADAPTED TO A 10 KG REDUCTION SCENARIO, DATA OF THE FIRST THREE ROWS FROM ERDMANN ET AL. (ERDMANN ET AL. 2008), FURTHER DATA ENTRIES ARE AUTHOR'S CALCULATIONS. 73

TABLE 17: "SUMMARY OF HEALTH RESULTS OF MEDICAL INTERVENTIONS TO REDUCE THE IMPACT OF THE 'DEADLY QUARTET' IN CHINA", AUTHOR'S INVESTIGATION. 78

TABLE 18: "NEED FOR INTERVENTIONS AND ACTUAL DEATH RATE OF THE 'DEADLY QUARTET' AND THE PHYSIOLOGICAL RISK MARKERS IN CHINA", 2010 DATA, AUTHOR'S INVESTIGATION. 80

TABLE 19: "NEED FOR INTERVENTIONS (TOTAL AND WILLING TO CHANGE GROUP) TO MANAGE THE 'DEADLY QUARTET' AND THE PHYSIOLOGICAL RISK MARKERS IN CHINA", 2010 DATA, AUTHOR'S INVESTIGATION....... 80

TABLE 20: "COSTS PER PERSON FOR THE MEDICAL INTERVENTIONS TO REDUCE THE IMPACT OF THE 'DEADLY QUARTET' IN CHINA", IN 2010 USD, AUTHOR'S INVESTIGATION. 82

TABLE 21: "TOTAL COSTS FOR THE MEDICAL INTERVENTIONS TO REDUCE THE IMPACT OF THE 'DEADLY QUARTET' IN CHINA", IN 2010 USD, AUTHOR'S INVESTIGATION. 83

TABLE 23B: "BENEFITS IN DALYS FOR REDUCING THE RISK FROM UNHEALTHY DIETS, PHYSICAL INACTIVITY AND ASSOCIATED PHYSIOLOGICAL RISK MARKERS IN CHINA", TOTAL POPULATION, IN 2010 USD, HEALTH DATA FROM IHME (IHME 2014A), AUTHOR'S CALCULATIONS. 90

TABLE 23A: "BENEFITS IN DALYS FOR REDUCING THE RISK FROM THE 'DEADLY QUARTET' IN CHINA", TOTAL POPULATION, IN 2010 USD, HEALTH DATA FROM IHME (IHME 2014A), AUTHOR'S CALCULATIONS........... 90

TABLE 24: "COUNTRY-SPECIFIC VSLS: EXPLANATION OF ADJUSTMENT FACTORS", CONTENT FROM (OECD, 2014A, PP. 54–55), SLIGHTLY MODIFIED BY THE AUTHOR. 92

TABLE 25: "BENEFITS FROM REDUCING THE WELFARE COSTS OF THE 'DEADLY QUARTET' IN CHINA", TOTAL POPULATION, IN 2010 MILLION USD, HEALTH DATA FROM IHME (IHME 2014A), AUTHOR'S CALCULATIONS. 93

TABLE 26: "BENEFITS FROM REDUCING THE WELFARE COSTS OF THE 'DEADLY QUARTET' AND ASSOCIATED PHYSIOLOGICAL RISK MARKERS IN CHINA", TOTAL POPULATION, IN 2010, MILLION USD, HEALTH DATA FROM IHME (IHME 2014A), AUTHOR'S CALCULATIONS. 94

TABLE 27: "CBA RESULTS FOR REDUCING THE RISK FROM THE 'DEADLY QUARTET' IN CHINA", TOTAL POPULATION, IN 2010 USD, HEALTH DATA FROM IHME (IHME 2014A), AUTHOR'S CALCULATIONS. 94

TABLE 28: "CBA RESULTS FOR REDUCING THE RISK FROM PHYSIOLOGICAL RISK MARKERS IN CHINA", TOTAL POPULATION, IN 2010 USD, HEALTH DATA FROM IHME (IHME 2014A), AUTHOR'S CALCULATIONS........... 95

TABLE 29: "INSURANCE STATUS 2020 INCLUDING MIGRANT WORKERS.", DATA FROM THE NATIONAL BUREAU OF STATISTICS OF CHINA (NBSC 2012) AND THE WORLD BANK (WORLD BANK 2014), AUTHOR'S INVESTIGATION. 122

TABLE 30 "INSURANCE STATUS 2011 INCLUDING MIGRANT WORKERS.", DATA FROM THE NATIONAL BUREAU OF STATISTICS OF CHINA (NBSC 2012), AUTHOR'S INVESTIGATION. 122

TABLE 31: "NUMBER OF DE JURE (IP) AND DE FACTO (IP_{MW}) INSURED PEOPLE IN THE PRC IN 2011", DATA FROM THE NATIONAL BUREAU OF STATISTICS OF CHINA (NBSC 2012), AUTHOR'S INVESTIGATION.................. 123

TABLE 32: "NUMBER OF DE JURE (IP) AND DE FACTO (IP_{MW}) INSURED PEOPLE IN THE PRC IN 2020.", DATA FROM THE NATIONAL BUREAU OF STATISTICS OF CHINA (NBSC 2012) AND THE WORLD BANK (WORLD BANK 2014), AUTHOR'S INVESTIGATION. 123

TABLE 33: "INCREASE OF UNINSURED CHINESE CITIZENS 2011-2020.", DATA FROM THE NATIONAL BUREAU OF STATISTICS OF CHINA (NBSC 2012) AND THE WORLD BANK (WORLD BANK 2014), AUTHOR'S INVESTIGATION. 124

TABLE 34: "GAPS TO REACHING THE 90% AND 100% GOAL IN 2011 AND 2020.", DATA FROM THE NATIONAL BUREAU OF STATISTICS OF CHINA (NBSC 2012) AND THE WORLD BANK (WORLD BANK 2014), AUTHOR'S INVESTIGATION. 124

TABLE 35: "NUMBER OF *DE JURE* (IP) AND *DE FACTO* (IP$_{MW}$) INSURED URBAN CITIZENS IN 2011.", DATA FROM THE NATIONAL BUREAU OF STATISTICS OF CHINA (NBSC 2012) AND THE WORLD BANK (WORLD BANK 2014), AUTHOR'S INVESTIGATION. 125

TABLE 36: "COMPARISON OF UNINSURED MIGRANT WORKERS IN CITIES (UM) AND UNINSURED URBAN RESIDENTS (UU)", AUTHOR'S INVESTIGATION. 125

TABLE 37: "NUMBER OF *DE JURE* (IP) AND *DE FACTO* (IP$_{MW}$) INSURED URBAN CITIZENS IN 2020.", DATA FROM THE NATIONAL BUREAU OF STATISTICS OF CHINA (NBSC 2012) AND THE WORLD BANK (WORLD BANK 2014), AUTHOR'S INVESTIGATION. 126

TABLE 38: "GAPS TO REACHING THE 90% AND 100% GOAL IN 2011 AND 2020 IN URBAN AREAS.", DATA FROM THE NATIONAL BUREAU OF STATISTICS OF CHINA (NBSC 2012) AND THE WORLD BANK (WORLD BANK 2014), AUTHOR'S INVESTIGATION. 126

TABLE 39: "GAPS TO REACHING THE 90% AND 100% GOAL IN 2011 AND 2020 AS A COMPARISON OF THE TOTAL AND THE URBAN AREA.", DATA FROM THE NATIONAL BUREAU OF STATISTICS OF CHINA (NBSC 2012) AND THE WORLD BANK (WORLD BANK 2014), AUTHOR'S INVESTIGATION. 127

TABLE 40: "SUMMARY OF BENEFIT RELATED EQUITY ISSUES IN THE CHINESE HEALTH INSURANCE SYSTEM", AUTHOR'S INVESTIGATION. 133

TABLE 41: "SUMMARY OF PAYMENT RELATED EQUITY ISSUES IN THE CHINESE HEALTH INSURANCE SYSTEM", AUTHOR'S INVESTIGATION. 134

TABLE 42: "HOUSING CHOICES FOR TEMPORARY MIGRANTS", (WU, 2002, P. 105). 171

TABLE 43: "HOUSING CONDITIONS OF TEMPORARY MIGRANTS COMPARE VERY UNFAVORABLY AGAINST THOSE OF LOCAL RESIDENTS ACROSS GEOGRAPHICAL LOCATION (IN PERCENTAGE)" (WU, 2002, P. 107). 172

TABLE 44: "GDP AND VSL CORRELATION", AUTHOR'S CALCULATIONS. 178

TABLE 45: "WELFARE COSTS OF THE 'DEADLY QUARTET', 1990-2010", PER 100.000 INHABITANTS, IN 2010 MILLION US$, HEALTH DATA FROM IHME (IHME, 2014B), AUTHOR'S CALCULATIONS. 183

TABLE 46: "DATASET: GROSS DOMESTIC PRODUCT (GDP) AND VALUE OF STATISTICAL LIFE (VSL) VALUES", (OECD, 2014B, 2014C) AND AUTHOR'S CALCULATIONS. 186

TABLE 47: "EXPLANATION OF ECONOMIC VALUES USED FOR CALCULATIONS.", (OECD, 2014A; WHO AND OECD, 2015), AUTHORS' ADJUSTMENTS. 187

List of Abbreviations

B	benefits
C	costs
CBA	cost-benefit analysis
CEA	cost-effectiveness analyses
CMS	Cooperative Medical Scheme
COI	cost of illness
CPI	consumer price index
CULS	China Urban Labor Survey
DALY	disability adjusted life year
GBD	Global Burden of Disease
GDP	Gross Domestic Product
GP	general practitioner
GIS	Government Insurance System
HED	Heavy Episodic Drinking
LIS	Labor Insurance System
MAP	Medical Assistance Program
MOHRSS	Chinese Ministry of Human Resources and Social Security
NB	net benefit
NCD	non-communicable disease
NCMS	New Rural Cooperative Medical Scheme
NHSS	National Health Services Survey
OOP	out of pocket payments
PPP	purchasing power parity

PRC	People's Republic of China
R	ratio
RAND HIE	RAND Health Insurance Experiment
SHI	social health insurance
TEV	total economic value
UEBMI	Urban Employee Basic Medical Insurance
UHC	universal health coverage
UN	United Nations
URBMI	Urban Resident Basic Medical Insurance
URS	Urban Resident Scheme
USD	United States Dollar
VSL	value of a statistical life
WHA	World Health Assembly
WHO	World Health Organization

Health economic theory section (2.2.1)

M, iM, aM	medical care, inappropriate medical care, appropriate medical care
u_{iM}, u_{aM}	utility from inappropriate and appropriate medical care
EU	expected utility
π_u, π_i	probability for health care consumption for uninsured and insured
C_M	cost of medical care
w, W	disposable wealth and gross wealth
P	insurance premium
I	insurance payoff

Health insurance coverage section (3.3.2)

tp total Chinese population

ud, ud_{mw} total urban dwellers (excluding and including migrant workers)

mw, mw_{up}, mw_{ip} migrant workers (within the *de jure* uninsured and insured group)

up, ip *de jure* uninsured and insured people

uu, iu *de jure* uninsured and insured urban residence holder

um, im *de jure* uninsured and insured migrant workers

ip_{mw} *de facto* insured citizens

uu_{mw}, iu_{mw} *de facto* uninsured and insured urbans

um_{up}, um_{ip} *de facto* uninsured migrants (within *de jure* uninsured and insured)

im_{up}, im_{ip} *de facto* insured migrants (within the *de jure* uninsured and insured)

1 Introduction

1.1 Historical background

It has long been known that social security and health status are closely linked. Already during the Middle Ages, when craftsmen were working independently and self-employed, insurance systems were set up against the consequences of sickness. In the 16th and 17th century, it was the guilds that collected a certain contribution from their members to protect the sick from medical payments and loss of income. These supporting networks had come to an end by the 18th and 19th century, after the industrial revolution had taken place and workers were no longer organized in guilds but became employed at factories. In this working environment, sickness caused a double hardship for the individual. On the one hand medical services had to be financed and on the other hand wages were terminated. As it was well understood that the event of sickness cannot be predicted for an individual but only for large groups, hundreds of sickness funds were developed in Germany to pool the health risks of their members. Already in 1854, one of the 30 German member states (Prussia) enacted a law that forced low-wage workers to contribute a certain percentage of their income to a health insurance system – an equal sum had to be paid by the employer. This system, where employer and employee pay the same amount to the sickness fund, was taken up again in the 1880s after the German chancellor Bismarck unified the formerly warring German states. After a long lasting political discussion, a bill was finally passed in 1883 that required employers with low income to join one of the numerous sickness funds. Contributions were shared between employers (2/3) and employees (1/3). The benefits included partial wage payment (about 50%) and covered medical care (usually general practitioners and drugs), maternity benefits and funeral costs (Roemer, 1993, p. 91). Although the definition of universal health coverage (UHC)[1] is ambiguous, most scholars see the reforms described above as the first achievement of UHC (e.g. Stuckler et al., 2010).

---

[1] UHC is sometimes called universal coverage (Kieny and Evans, 2013, p. 305; WHO, 2010a, p. ix). Universal access and universal health care are components of UHC (WHO, 2014a, p. 1).

1

Norway is said to be the second Nation that implemented UHC (around 1910) (Stuckler et al., 2010, p. 17) and Russia followed in 1937 by joining its system for the working population in cities with its system for the rural population (Roemer, 1993, p. 95) (not shown in Figure 1 below). The first country to cover its entire population thereafter was New Zealand, where the Ministry of Health installed a medical insurance system nearly from scratch in 1939 (Roemer, 1993, p. 95) (also not shown in Figure 1 below). Although neither Russia nor New Zealand are included in Figure 1 below, it can clearly be seen, that only a few countries initiated UHC before the 1950s and the largest share of UHC implementation happened after the Second World War (Stuckler et al., 2010, p. 17; WHO and Lerberghe, 2008, p. 26).

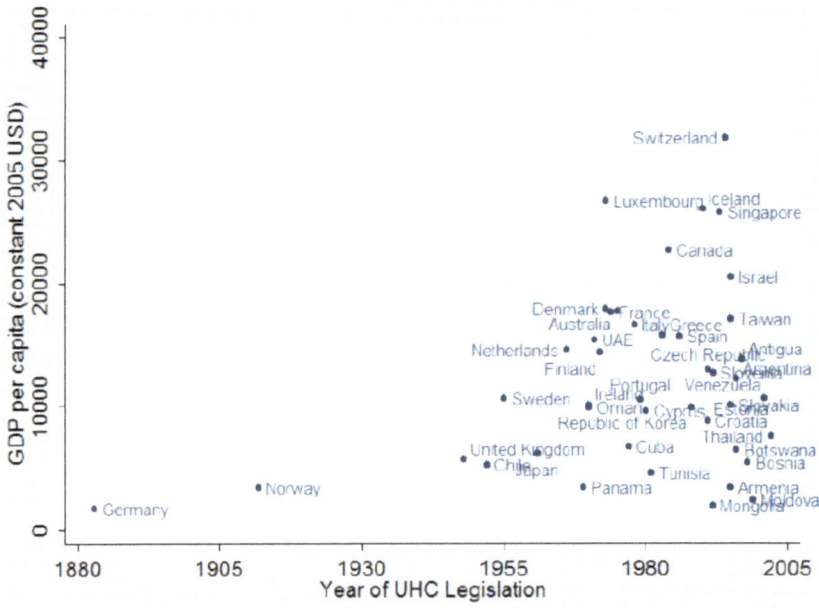

Figure 1: "Year of UHC Legislation and levels of GDP per capita" (Stuckler et al., 2010, p. 17).

In 1948, the United Kingdom installed its National Health Service (MoH UK, 1948), Sweden passed a relevant law in 1946 and put it into practice in 1955 (Glenngård et al., 2005, p. 16), Iceland and Norway followed in 1956,[2] Denmark in 1960, Finland in 1963 (Kuhnle and Hort, 2004, p. 7) and Belgium in 1969 (Corens, 2007, p. 17). Outside of Europe, Japan was among the earliest countries to reach UHC (1961) (Rodwin, 1994). Canada passed the crucial law in 1968 (Maioni, 1998, p. 135), Australia followed in 1975 (Hilless and Healy, 2001, p. 15), Korea in 1989 (Bärnighausen and Sauerborn, 2002, p. 1568), Taiwan (NHI, 2012) and Israel in 1995 (Woolf, 2011, p. 5). Quite a large number of European countries only reached UHC in the late 1970s or even in recent years. Among them are: Italy in 1978 (Donatitini, 2013, p. 66), Austria in 1978 (Austrian Information, 2012), Portugal in 1979 (Pedro et al., 2011, pp. xv, 15), Greece in 1983 (WHO, 1996, p. 67), Spain in 1986 (Lopez et al., 2004), Switzerland in 1996 (Camenzind, 2013, p. 119), France in 2000 (Durand-Zaleskiki, 2013, p. 45) and the Netherlands in 2006 (Daley et al., 2013).

1.2 Status quo and recent development

Drawing from experiences of these and other countries, low- and middle-income countries like Costa Rica, Mexico, Thailand and Turkey are moving significantly faster towards UHC than industrialized countries did in the past (WHO and Lerberghe, 2008, pp. 25, 26). According to WHO, the way to UHC requests three steps: 1. raising funds, 2. reducing direct payments, 3. improving efficiency and equity. In all three aspects, countries like Brazil, Chile, China, Mexico, Rwanda and Thailand have been attested remarkable progress (WHO, 2010a, p. xi).

For further investigation of today's situation and future development, the international treaties of the WHO and the UN are most useful as they reflect the consensus of all member states. A central document in this context is the World Health Assembly (WHA) document 58.33. It points out how "Sustainable health financing, universal coverage and social health insurance" (WHO, 2005) can best be managed. In this document, UHC is endorsed as a central goal and it is stated that everyone should be able to

---

[2] As this section aims to give a brought overview on the development of UHC, the different classifications made by different authors are not investigated further.

access health services and not be subject to financial hardship in doing so (WHO, 2014a, pp. vii, x, 2010a, p. x). Furthermore, the WHA document 64.9, "Sustainable health financing structures and universal coverage" (WHO, 2011a), has strengthened the importance of UHC and was one of the major forces in the process of initiating the report, "Making fair choices on the path to universal health coverage" by the "WHO Consultative Group on Equity and Universal Health Coverage" (WHO, 2014a). In addition, the World Health Report 2013, "Research for Universal Health Coverage", emphasized the need for progress towards UHC and pointed out several means to achieve this goal (WHO, 2014a, p. viii, 2013). Further activities – within the 12th general program of work for the 2014-2019 period and the post-2015 development agenda – have set priority to UHC as a central theme (WHO, 2014a, p. viii). These goals are supported by other UN organizations as can be seen through the adoption of a resolution by the United Nations General Assembly (UN, 2012a, 2012b) which emphasizes the responsibility of governments to increase their efforts to "accelerate the transition towards universal access to affordable and quality health-care services" (WHO, 2014a, p. viii). The documents mentioned above show clearly that UHC enjoys a high priority on the political agenda – not only, but especially regarding health effects.

1.3 Reasons to aim for UHC

Among the reasons to promote UHC are numerous benefits for the individual as well as society. They include an increase of quality of life, economic and social development and peace (Bai and Wu, 2014; Brown et al., 2007; Cheng et al., 2014; Chen and Jin, 2012; Hou et al., 2012; Jung and Liu, 2011; Marten et al., 2014; Moreno-Serra and Smith, 2012; WHO, 2011a, 2010a, 1978). More specifically, benefits can be located in the following five areas: 1. service utilization, 2. affordable access, 3. distributional effects, 4. economic and social development and 5. international law.

(1) Benefits from "service utilization" are gained through the consumption of health services and the possibility to access them. An underlying assumption is that the possibility to access medical services leads to higher health levels of the population. The importance that is given to UHC in this context becomes obvious as universal

4

coverage is "one of the four key pillars of primary health care and services through patient centered care, inclusive leadership and health in all policies" (WHO, 2011a, p. 1). Achieving health is also seen as valuable in itself, especially due to its importance for overall well-being and the capabilities and opportunities that arise from it (WHO, 2014a, p. 2).

(2) "Affordable access" refers to the personal financial situation of the health care consumer. A health care system that includes large out-of-pocket payments (OOP) for medical services often suffers from several negative effects: (i) The well-being of people is severely limited. (ii) In case of financial problems, psychological pressure can affect people's health. (iii). Economic opportunities are limited through enforced or anticipated health costs. All of these problems do not only affect the individual patient but also his or her family that might have to support the ill person financially. As affordable access to medical treatments therefore leads to financial protection, it overlaps with the following points "distributional effects" and "economic and social development".

(3) "Distributional effects" can be observed, if health-financing systems include a mode for prepayment of health costs and a risk pooling mechanism that disconnects the need for health care from the ability to pay for it. As a result, the individual risk is shared among the population and catastrophic health expenditure 3 and impoverishment of individuals can be avoided (Kieny and Evans, 2013). As low health insurance coverage mostly excludes the poorest people of a society from medical care, UHC can promote a fairer distribution of health and well-being by improving coverage for the underprivileged (WHO, 2014a, p. 2).

(4) The "economic and social development" of a country can be affected in a direct as well as in an indirect way. Directly, a higher health status of the population leads to a better working and learning capacity and thereby improves the general economic situation. This aspect can be captured in the statement: "Healthy children are better able to learn and a healthy population facilitates economic growth" (WHO, 2014a, p. 2). Indirectly, a higher level of education empowers people to protect their own

---

[3] Catastrophic health (also "catastrophic out-of-pocket expenditures/payments") are defined by WHO as health expenditures that surpass a threshold share of 40 percent of nonfood household expenditure (WHO, 2014a, p. 31).

health. This includes the use of preventive services before a possible disease manifests. In the case of illness, they might choose the right health service at the right time (Kieny and Evans, 2013, p. 305). Consuming the right services at the right time and consuming preventive care both make health systems more cost-effective and therefore have a positive effect on the economy and the social development opportunities of a nation (Kieny and Evans, 2013, p. 305; WHO, 2014a, p. 2).

(5) "International laws" are important in so far as every country has ratified at least one treaty which specifies obligations to meet the right to health. Among those treaties is the Universal Declaration of Human Rights which supports "the enjoyment of the highest attainable standard of physical and mental health" (WHO, 2014a, p. 2) or more specific, in article 25.1, "the right to a standard of living adequate for the health and well-being of himself and of his family, including food, clothing, housing and medical care and necessary social services, and the right to security in the event of unemployment, sickness, disability, widowhood, old age or other lack of livelihood in circumstances beyond his control" (WHO, 2011a, p. 1). Furthermore, a large number of the WHO treaties make a strong statement for the importance of health being a social value, such as the WHO constitution which proclaims that the "enjoyment of the highest attainable standard of health is one of the fundamental rights of every human being without distinction of race, religion, political belief, economic or social condition" (WHO, 2006, p. 1). It is clear that UHC by itself is insufficient to ensure all the aims formulated within these and other international treaties, but reaching UHC in a country is evidently an important part of this strategy. Overall, the international community agrees about providing UHC being one of the core obligations of any government that strives to develop a modern society (WHO and Lerberghe, 2008, p. 25).

As mentioned above, implementing UHC is associated with many positive effects for society. Among them are the just presented five specific points, but also broader benefits such as increase of quality of life, economic and social development as well as peace (Bai and Wu, 2014; Brown et al., 2007; Cheng et al., 2014; Chen and Jin, 2012; Hou et al., 2012; Jung and Liu, 2011; Marten et al., 2014; Moreno-Serra and Smith, 2012; WHO, 2011a, 2010a, 1978). It is hence not surprising that people in most

6

countries rate health as one of their highest priorities, even higher than economic concerns such as employment status, wage levels and cost of living standards (WHO, 2010a, p. ix). Against this background it is most interesting for this study to understand the specific situation in the People's Republic of China before the detailed analysis is undertaken.

1.4 Status quo of health insurance coverage in China

The Chinese health insurance system was established in the 1950s and, at this point, included three different schemes: firstly, the Cooperative Medical Scheme (CMS) for the rural population; secondly, the Labor Insurance System (LIS) for urban employees and their dependents of state-owned enterprises and collectively-owned enterprises; thirdly, the Government Insurance System (GIS) for Government staff, retired government staff and university students. This structure, which offered a somewhat universal coverage, collapsed between 1978 and 1998, when only 12.7% of rural residents and 55.9% of urban citizens still enjoyed health coverage (Liu and Yi, 2004; Meng et al., 2012a, pp. 7–8). In the course of the 2000s this development was targeted by introducing the New Rural Cooperative Medical Scheme (NCMS), the Urban Employee Basic Medical Insurance (UEBMI) and the Urban Resident Basic Medical Insurance (URBMI). As a result, the recent Chinese coverage rate is regarded to be 97.4% for the rural and 90.9% for the urban population (numbers for 2011, compare Figure 2 below) (Meng et al., 2012a).

7

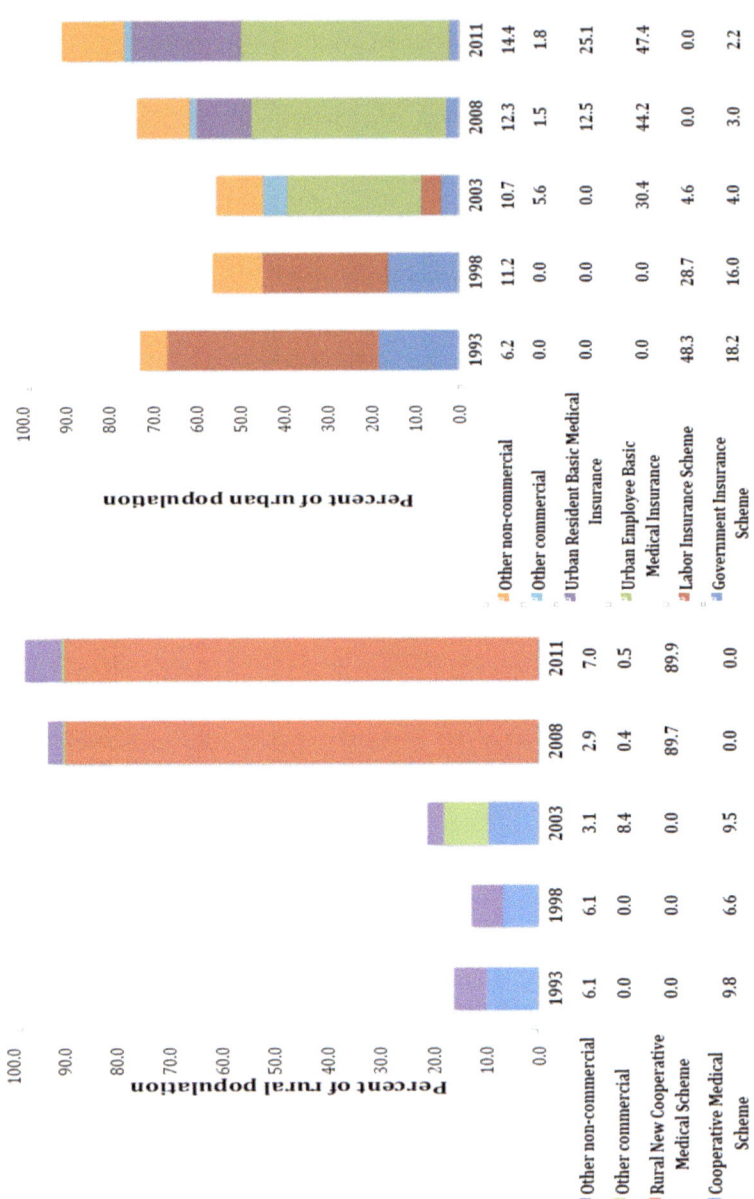

Figure 2: "Rural and urban health insurance coverage in China, by program, 1993-2011" (Meng et al. 2012a).

8

In addition to this positive tendency, the relevant Five-Year Plan for this study (2011-2015) marks another important step of the development of the Chinese health care reform. Contrary to the previous Five-Year Plans, this one does not merely emphasize economic growth but also the improvement of overall welfare of society (Casey and Koleski, 2011, p. 2).

Among other sectors of health reform, the development of a comprehensive insurance system is a major task of the 12th Five-Year Plan. Subordinate to this objective is the achievement of medical insurance for the whole population, the increase of the coverage rate, more financial support for medical expenses as well as the improvement of the payment and the reimbursement system (Dong, 2011, p. 3). For the first time in the history of Chinese Five-Year Plans, the 2011-2015 plan explicitly targets the well-being of individuals: It is planned to increase the average life expectancy of the Chinese people by one year between 2011 and the end of 2015 (Casey and Koleski, 2011, p. 4). Overall it can be stated that this Five-Year Plan is aiming towards a fairer income distribution (Chinese Embassy, 2011), a greater insurance level of the people (Dong, 2011, p. 3) and the increase of the well-being of society (Casey and Koleski, 2011, p. 4).

Also with regard to positioning, the described content is highlighted due to the impact of the Five-Year Plan on Chinese politics. Achieving the goals of the Five-Year Plan is an important precondition for the career of provincial politicians: "Meeting targets for a city, region or province, for example, is the path to advancement for officials in the Party. Those who do a superlative job get chosen for prime leadership positions. Those who fail to meet those targets get sidetracked. So the motivation is really quite powerful" (Shih, 2011).

Given the positive development since the 2000s and the current political will of the Chinese Communist Party to further reform the health insurance system, expectations for the implementation of UHC in China are set high. It is on this high level of expectations that this study will analyze the universal health coverage in China from a health economic perspective.

1.5 Contributions to the scientific literature and structure of this thesis

This thesis first and foremost contributes to the scientific literature in three ways. As a whole, this thesis offers a first of its kind analysis of the Chinese health insurance system that focusses at the three dimensions of UHC which are identified by WHO as the main characteristics. The unique points within this investigation are the exploration of the large pool of existing literature about health insurance in China, its development of a framework that is capable to give the reader an understanding of the interlinkage between different aspects, as well as an understanding of the overall picture (the conceptual framework is described in chapter 2).

In addition to the value that this thesis adds as a complete work, several aspects within the analyses contribute new insights to the existing scientific literature. To the knowledge of the author, health economic theory has so far not investigated and modeled the appropriateness of health care. This has far reaching consequences. It is for example intuitive to regard "moral hazard" as a negative issue. However, following the definition used in health economic theory – where moral hazard is defined as increased health service usage due to lower marginal cost of care (Pauly, 1968, p. 535) – this study shows that "moral hazard" is not only the source of welfare loss, but also of welfare gain. Simply speaking, the neglected positive aspect of "moral hazard" shows when the increase of health service usage happens in appropriate medical care. Then, people are able to receive additional positive services and their utility increases. On the other hand, "access to health services" is generally seen as a positive issue. Once again, this study is able to show that the final appraisal highly depends on the appropriateness of the service that access is offered to. Only if access to appropriate medical care is granted, will the utility of the people rise and society achieve welfare gains. A last new aspect that the new appropriateness approach can offer is the inclusion of preventive care. In the new approach, the utility of the people is not modeled following the individual's state of health (sick-healthy polarity), but the appropriateness of delivered care. It is therefore possible to value the delivery of health services as positive even if they are given to healthy people. In the appropriateness approach, preventive interventions to healthy people (primary prevention) can be interpreted as an increase of utility, if provided care is appropriate (e.g. consultancy, vaccination, screening) (compare chapter 2.1 for details of the appropriateness approach). The appropriateness approach is therefore hoped to give impulses to the scientific community to focus more on the *character* of services and move away from merely taking into account the *amount* of services. A first attempt to investigate the inclusion of appropriate health services into the Chinese catalogue of benefits can be found in chapter 3.2.1 of this thesis.

The lack of focusing on preventive besides curative health interventions is not only observable in theory. The study at hand shows that behavior changing interventions are currently only taken into account in so far as they address entire populations (e.g. through tax or law interventions). The potential of individual interventions has received very little attention so far. In order to fill this gap, this study undertakes an in-depth analysis of individual health interventions targeting non-communicable diseases (NCDs) in China. To show the potential of NCD interventions targeting individuals, a literature research about the potential health effects in the areas of smoking, alcohol consumption as well as diet and physical inactivity was carried out. Building on the work that was done by other scholars, this study manages to collect the relevant literature needed to quantify the health impacts of NCD related risk factors. On this basis and referring to other data, the first cost efficient and cost-benefit analysis of individual health interventions targeting NCDs in China is undertaken (chapter 3.2). As the methodology developed for this investigation can be adapted to other countries, it is the hope of the author that other scholars will contribute to the necessary awareness raising of the potential of individual based preventive NCD interventions.

A third large aspect which is added to the state of current literature is the review of the *de facto* insurance status of migrant workers in China. A literature review was able to show that migrant workers are exposed to more health risks than their sedentary counterparts and at the same time have less access to health services. As a consequence, their health situation is found to be worse than that of comparable rural and urban residents (compare chapter 3.3.1). On the basis of this literature review, an in-depth analysis was undertaken investigating the mode of measurement of the health insurance coverage rate in China. This analysis showed that the current calculation of the coverage rate is based on household surveys and therefore excludes migrant workers – at least *de facto*. Two aims that have been set by the Chinese government, to achieve 90% coverage rate in 2011 and UHC in 2020, were therefore tested by a methodology which allows accounting for the large amount of neglected migrant workers. The result of this analysis is that the *de jure* health insurance coverage rates sharply decrease if the *de facto* rate, including migrant workers, is calculated. The lower values proposed in this thesis finally lead to the conclusion that neither of the two goals has been or will be achieved if the Chinese government does not significantly intensify its efforts towards these goals (the detailed analysis of the health insurance coverage rate can be found in chapter 3.3).

The above contributions to the scientific literature are not presented individually, but as a part of a coherent thesis. The structure which embeds the above contributions is the following: After the introductory part (chapter 1), the definition and concept of the approach of this study is explained (chapter 2). This theoretical outline is then adapted to the situation in China (chapter 3). The theory chapter (chapter 2) and the praxis chapter (chapter 3) introduce and strictly follow the three dimensions that are necessary for implementing UHC: height (chapter 2.1 and 3.1), depth (chapter 2.2 and 3.2) and breadth (chapter 2.3 and 3.3). This structure is taken up in the summary and conclusion (chapter 4), the chapter on boundaries and discussions (chapter 5) and the outlook chapter (chapter 6).

In order to ensure building on a profound scientific basis, the following chapter 2 will, as mentioned, lay out the definition and concepts that are used for the then following in-depth analysis.

2 Definition and concept

After having introduced into the historical and structural background of health insurance systems, this section will describe the methodological concept which serves as the basis of the then following analysis of the Chinese health insurance system.

Simply speaking, UHC stands for the aspiration of granting access to health services to all people without putting them at risk of suffering financial hardship (Kieny and Evans, 2013, p. 305; WHO, 2010a, p. ix). Although this definition is widely accepted, it is used in slight variations that are described in the recent WHO publication "Making fair choices on the path to universal health coverage":

> "[...] at least four types of variation should be acknowledged. First, some definitions assert that everyone must have 'access' to services as opposed to 'receiving' services. Second, some definitions refer to 'needed services', 'key services', or 'necessary services, as opposed to 'services that meet [people's] needs'. [...] Third, some definitions refer to 'financial catastrophe', 'financial ruin', or 'poverty' rather than 'financial hardship'. Fourth, not all definitions explicitly link the financial harm to payment for services." (WHO, 2014a, pp. x, 1)

Despite the slight variations of the general definition, UHC is generally thought to consist of three parts. One way of illustrating them is through the three dimensions of a cube – height, depth and breadth. The height dimension is described by the question "What proportion of the costs is covered?", the depth dimension by the question "Which benefits are covered?" and the breadth dimension by "Who is insured?" (Figure 3).

As indicated by the small green cube and the big transparent cube (Figure 3), a gap exists between what is theoretically aspired and practically feasible. To get closer to the theoretical optimum, policy makers have to reduce cost sharing (height dimension), include more services (depth dimension) and extend coverage to the uninsured (breadth dimension) (WHO, 2014a, p. 5, 2010a, p. xv; WHO and Lerberghe, 2008, p. 26).

However, resources are scarce and no country – no matter how wealthy – has yet been able to ensure access to every possible service (depth dimension) for everyone (breadth dimension) without personal contributions (height dimension) (WHO, 2010a, p. xi).

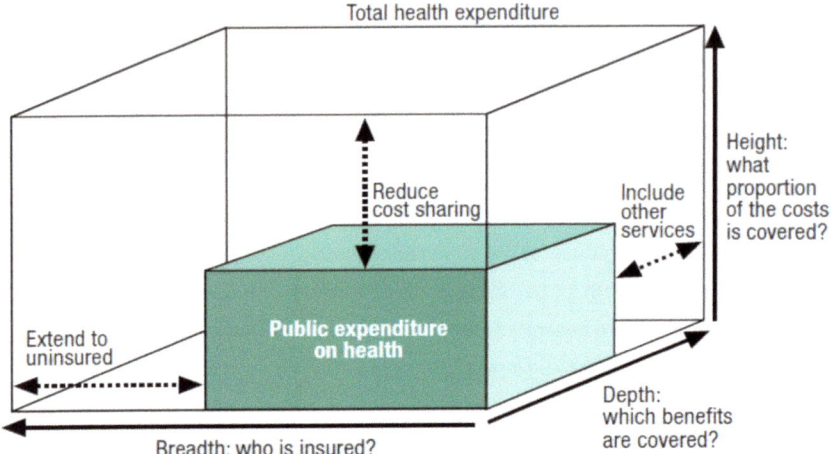

Figure 3: "Three dimensions of universal coverage" (WHO, 2014, p. 5, 2010, p. xv; WHO and Lerberghe 2008, p. 26).

The insight that resources are scarce is also important in order to understand the "need" aspect mentioned in the definitions above. It can either refer to a gap compared to the "normal" health level or to not receiving the maximum of possible health services (transparent cube in Figure 3). Due to the limitation of resources, it is evident that the definitions above can only refer to "need" in the first sense and any health system shall concentrate on the most important set of health services in order not to jeopardize other important social goals by wasting scarce resources (WHO, 2014a, pp. x, 1). As a consequence, UHC does not mean total coverage of all services for everyone at all times (WHO, 2010a, p. xvi) but rather to realize access to "key promotive, preventive, curative and rehabilitative health interventions" (WHO, 2014a, pp. x, 1).

In order to implement UHC according to the needs-definition described above, three activities were added to the three dimensions of the cube: The height dimension was paired with the call to reduce out-of-pocket payments, the depth dimension with the demand to include more people and the breadth dimension with the request to expand priority services (WHO, 2014a, pp. ix, 4, 5). Additionally, three related questions were identified that are expected to arise on the way towards UHC: (1) "How to shift from out-of-pocket payments toward prepayment?", (2) "Whom to include first?" and (3) "Which service to expand first?" (Table 1).

14

Dimensions of progress	Critical choice
Reducing out-of-pocket payments	How to shift from out-of-pocket payments toward prepayment?
Including more people	Whom to include first?
Expanding priority services	Which service to expand first?

Table 1: "Critical dimensions and choices on the path to universal health coverage" (WHO, 2014a, p. 5).

In the following chapters, these three dimensions will be analyzed in depth in order to understand how UHC can be reached. Due to internal consistency, the analysis of the definition and concept will start with the height dimension (2.1), followed by the investigation of the depth dimension (2.2) and ending with the breadth dimension (2.3). As a conclusion of chapter 2, the findings of the three former sections will be summarized (2.4). The questions raised in Figure 2 and Table 1 will be used as a guiding structure for part 2.1, 2.2 and 2.3.

2.1 Height: "What proportion of the costs is covered?"

In order to answer the crucial questions of the height dimension, "What proportion of the costs is covered?" (Figure 3) and "How to shift from out-of-pocket payment toward pre-payment?" (Table 1), this chapter will first of all look into health economic theory to outline the theoretical knowledge (2.1.1). The following chapter will present recommendations given by scholars and international institutions (2.1.2) to complement the theoretical knowledge with practical approaches.

2.1.1 Theoretical views on cost-sharing in health insurance systems

Explaining the theory of an ideal insurance, Arrow points out that it is the health outcome which is most important (Arrow, 1963, pp. 959–961). However, health as an outcome measure contains various uncertainties (Arrow, 1963, pp. 961, 964–965) and is therefore regarded as uninsurable (Dranove and White, 1987; Ma and McGuire, 1997; McGuire, 2000b, pp. 466, 499; Mooney and Ryan, 1993). As the status of health is too complex, compromises are made in order to assure measurability and insurability. One of these compromises is the assumption that the use of health care increases the probability of (re)gaining health. Hence, in a state of illness, health care will be used and financial claims accumulated. As a protection against financial risks that may arise through illness, Arrow showed the efficiency of introducing health insurance (Arrow, 1963, pp. 959–961).

In contrast to the risk protection view of Arrow, many authors value the negative welfare effects of moral hazards as strong enough to call for a reduction or rejection of health insurance (Feldman and Dowd, 1991; Feldstein, 1971; Friedman, 1974; Manning and Marquis, 1996, 1989; McGuire, 2000a, pp. 344–350; Pauly, 1968, p. 535). This view builds on, firstly, the definition of the term "moral hazard" as an increased usage of medical care resulting from lowering the cost for each unit of service (e.g. through issuing health insurance) (Pauly, 1968, p. 535). Secondly, it builds on studies that find price elasticity of demand[4] for medical care (Chandra et al., 2010; Danzon and Pauly, 2002; Feldstein, 1973; Gaynor et al., 2007; Gibson et al., 2005; Gilman and Kautter, 2008, 2007; Goldman et al., 2007; Huskamp et al., 2005, 2003; Keeler and Rolph, 1988; Landon et al., 2007; Manning and Marquis, 1996, 1989; Phelps, 2010). Directly interpreting rising demand as moral hazard is however problematic in two respects: Firstly, as de Meza has shown (de Meza, 1983) and Pauly has admitted (Pauly, 1983), a large part of rising demand also occurs when moral hazard motivation is absent. Secondly, rising demand observed at insured people might rather be motivated by the capability, not the willingness, to pay. (That is: People only get the chance to demand health care through financial support such as health insurance. Without this financial support, the consumption would not be possible (capability to pay) even if they liked to consume (willingness to pay) the health service in question.) By focusing on the outcome of insurance plans, Nyman shows that the biggest part of increased service consumption can be interpreted as a sign for improved financial access to health care services (Nyman, 1999) and thereby weakens the critique of those who see moral hazard as a reason to reject the introduction of UHC. In this view, increased service consumption is no longer necessarily negative and health insurance can be viewed as creating welfare gain by assuring access to health care.

---

[4] Building on price elasticity may be interpreted as including consumer (Zweifel and Manning, 2000) as well as supplier (McGuire, 2000b) initiated demand increase.

16

Summing up, it can be stated that health insurance theory has evolved by three main steps: Arrow has pointed out the important function of risk protection, de Meza and Pauly have identified more important reasons for the rising health consumption than moral hazard and Nyman finally pointed towards the access to health services as the most important reason for increased demand of health services. Keeping in mind minor possible risks of moral hazard, economic theory assigns two convincing benefits to the introduction of health insurance: (1) risk protection and (2) access to medical services.

2.1.2 Practical approaches concerning cost-sharing in health insurance systems

After having analyzed the theoretical background, the focus of this chapter is set on three important areas that the WHO identifies regarding the height dimension: Firstly, out-of-pocket payments should be reduced primarily for high-priority services and with a special focus on disadvantaged groups (WHO, 2014a, pp. 35, 36). Secondly, it is important to distribute benefits based solely on medical need (and not the ability to pay). Thirdly, contributions to the health insurance system should only be linked to the ability to pay (and not to medical needs) (WHO, 2014a, pp. 35, 36). These two latter areas are obviously contrary aspects – benefits and payments – of requirement: to separate the use of services from the payment for services. Similar to the first area, these two latter points are demanded to primarily focus on highly ranked health services and on vulnerable groups such as people with a low social status, low-income groups, rural populations or those living in difficult areas, ethnic minorities, sub-groups with special behavior and those intensely exposed to stress factors.

As the prioritization of services mentioned in both aspects will be addressed in detail in the depth section (2.2), the height section will concentrate on the analysis of the existence of OOP in general. The focus on disadvantaged groups will be content of the two sections discussed in the next paragraphs.) Hence, the structure of this chapter 2.1.2, will focus on a deeper analysis of (1) low user fees and OOP (2.1.2.1) as well as (2) benefits and (3) payments with a special focus on equity (2.1.2.2).

2.1.2.1 Low user fees and OOP

In the 1980s and 1990s, a tendency to market liberalism was observable in many countries, also in the field of health insurance. One example for this tendency to liberalism is the health insurance rate in China, as shown in part 1.4. More important for this chapter however is the reduction of public resources for health and the introduction of user fees. Although this tendency was supported by economic theory and large field studies which promoted user fees as a tool to embank overconsumption because of moral hazard (Newhouse, 1996; Pauly, 1968), the above overview of the health economic theory (2.1.1) showed that this issue is only minor and should not restrict

other more positive achievements of UHC. As predicted by theory, negative consequences were often observable after the introduction of liberalization policies in form of a decline in service use and an increase of catastrophic payments – especially among vulnerable groups (Doorslaer

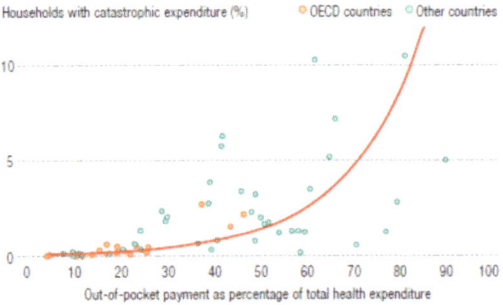

Figure 4: "Catastrophic expenditure related to out-of-pocket payment at the point of service" (WHO and Lerberghe, 2008, p. 24)

and O'Donnell, 2008, p. 9; WHO and Lerberghe, 2008, p. 26).

Catastrophic payments are generally defined as a situation where the level of OOP health expenditure surpasses 40% of nonfood household expenditure (WHO, 2014a, p. 31). In order to get the incidence rate of financial catastrophe and impoverishment to acceptable levels, the WHO recommends that OOP should not surpass 15-20% of the total health expenditures (WHO, 2014a, p. 33, 2010a, p. xiv). Looking at multiple OECD and non-OECD countries (Figure 4), it becomes obvious that a share of OOP lower than 15-20% of total health expenditure results in a very low percentage of households which experience catastrophic expenditures. Figure 4 furthermore suggests that the relationship between catastrophic payments and OOP is exponential, meaning: The more health expenditure of a country is financed by OOP, the (exponentially) more households happen to experience catastrophic payments (Figure 4). The threshold of

18

15-20%, as set by the WHO, might however be able to neutralize all negative consequences, because OOP is found to force households to sacrifice other basic needs, sell assets, indebt themselves, or be impoverished, even at a OOP rate of 10% and more (Doorslaer and O'Donnell, 2008, p. 6). Impoverishment due to OOP payments is furthermore especially precarious as it does not always show in standard measures of poverty. The reason for this hidden impoverishment is that OOP payments might raise a household's spendings above the poverty line, while at the same time resources for food, clothing and shelter are below subsistence levels (Doorslaer and O'Donnell, 2008, p. 9). It is hence not surprising that, while half of all health expenditure of the roughly 5.6 billion people in low- and middle income countries is financed through OOP, around 100 million people in these countries are pushed into poverty because of OOP each year (WHO and Lerberghe, 2008, p. 24). As a consequence, many scholars even demand OOP to be below 10% of total household expenditure (Doorslaer and O'Donnell, 2008, p. 9).

A positive example which shows the effects of reducing OOP is found in Thailand. In 2002, Thailand introduced the "UC 30 baht scheme" (UCS) which was designed to cover the 47 million citizens that were not yet covered by the "Civil Servant Medical Benefit Scheme" or the "Social Security

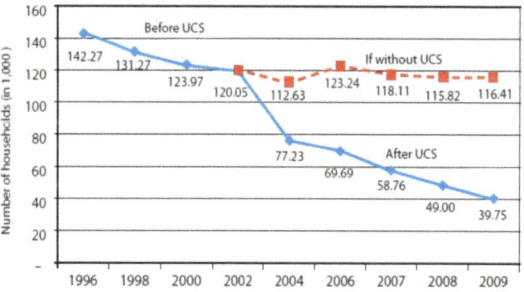

Figure 5: "Number of households impoverished by out-of-pocket payment for health services in Thailand" (1996–2010) (WHO, 2014, p. 33).

Scheme". As Figure 5 shows, its introduction in 2002 drastically reduced the number of people falling under the poverty line because of OOP. The number dropped from 120,000 to 40,000 in 2009 – a reduction of 2/3 within only six years. This drop is especially remarkable if compared to the pre-reform tendency of only slightly lowering the numbers of impoverished households and the nearly unchanged number of the projection for the development without the UCS intervention (WHO, 2014a, p. 33). This observation is strengthened by other datasets showing the share of OOP in the pre- and post-reform period of the same example. While the OOP share dropped from 42.49% in 1996 to 33.07% in 2001 (a reduction of 9.42 percentage points), the post-reform period saw a further reduction to 15.37% of OOP share (a reduction of 17.70 percentage points) (World Bank, 2014a).

It was stated above that the consequences of high user fees and OOP not only led to an increase of catastrophic payments, but also to a decline of service use (Doorslaer and O'Donnell, 2008, p. 9; WHO and Lerberghe, 2008, p. 26). And indeed, it can be observed that OOP payments seem to prevent low-income households from consuming substantial health care services, especially in low-income countries[5] (Doorslaer and O'Donnell, 2008, p. 9).

The interrelation between income and declining use of service is demonstrated in Figure 6, where the different income quintiles are matched with the percentage of births attended by medically trained personnel. It can be observed that these countries show different patterns of exclusion: While Colombia and Nicaragua (and to a lower extend Turkey) cover the largest part of their population with health services, Bangladesh, Chad and Niger show very low coverage rates and only support the richest part of their population (Figure 6).

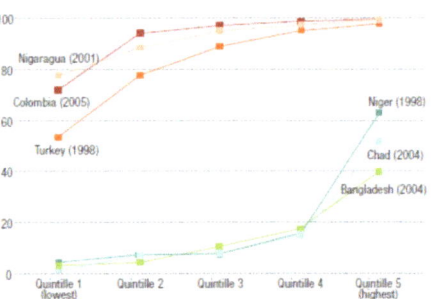

Figure 6: "Births attended by medically trained personnel (percentage), by income group" (WHO and Lerberghe, 2008, p. 28).

---

[5] In high-income economies with widespread insurance coverage, it can be observed that OOP payments consume a larger part of low-income households' resources (Doorslaer and O'Donnell, 2008, p. 9).

The finding shown in Figure 6 becomes even more telling by comparing it to the OOP health expenditure of these countries. Looking at the years considered in Figure 6, it shows that the three countries with more equal results – Nicaragua, Colombia and Turkey – are also those with the lower OOP values (below 50%) (Table 2).

Country Name	1998	2001	2004	2005
Bangladesh	56.75%	57.48%	58.72%	62.64%
Chad	66.71%	57.93%	62.25%	56.88%
Colombia	24.15%	12.59%	14.51%	17.01%
Nicaragua	49.74%	42.12%	41.09%	39.89%
Niger	68.58%	67.22%	65.36%	57.30%
Turkey	27.96%	22.85%	19.24%	22.76%

Table 2: "Out-of-pocket health expenditure (% of total expenditure on health) in six countries" (World Bank, 2014).

From longitudinal data it can furthermore be stated that user fees and OOP have a strong influence on the consumption of health care services. Abolishing the user fees for outpatient attendance in Kisoro district in Uganda clearly showed an increase of outpatient services. Have outpatient services been used by approximately 15,000 people per month while user fees were common practice, they have mounted to roughly 25,000 per month after user fees were abolished (Figure 7). (More information about the effect of user fees on health service utilization can be found in the systematic

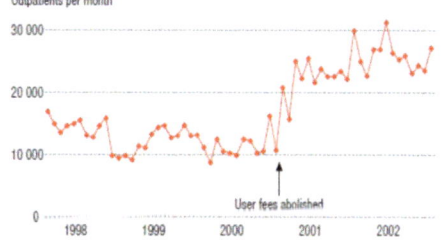

Figure 7: "Impact of abolishing user fees on outpatient attendance in Kisoro district, Uganda: outpatient attendance 1998–2002" (WHO and Lerberghe, 2008, p. 27).

literature review, "The impact of user fees on health service utilization in low- and middle-income countries: how strong is the evidence?" (Lagarde, 2008).)

2.1.2.2 Benefits and payments

In the above section the positive effects of reducing OOP were discussed and hence, indirectly, the positive effects arising from pre-payment mechanisms that are unrelated to health benefits (WHO, 2014a, p. 34, 2005, p. 139). Payments and benefits will be discussed in the following chapter by showing the importance of separating the *use* of services from the *payment* for services (WHO, 2014a, p. 36).

The statements that (1) benefits should be distributed only following medical need arguments and (2) contributions should only be raised due to the ability to pay, are the most central finding of this section. To provide a well-founded background for the analysis of these two aspects, the following paragraphs will additionally investigate background principles as well as the link to vulnerable groups and an equitable distribution.

In order to achieve the separation of service *consumption* (benefits) and service *financing* (payments), pooling people and thereby sharing the individual risk is key to success (WHO, 2014a, p. 31, 2011a, p. 2, 2005, p. 139). The reason for rather demanding large than small pools is sustainability. It was observed that those schemes which are built on larger numbers of people are more reliable while those only having a few members more frequently go bankrupt in case of expensive treatments or epidemics. Furthermore, a system that embraces the whole population avoids multiplying the administrative work (WHO, 2010a, p. xv). Pooling is furthermore demanded for the reason of equity and solidarity. While the richer and healthier people would rationally choose to exclude the poor and ill in order to lower their own costs, the often greater need and lower financial capacity of the poor and the ill calls for substitutional mechanisms (WHO, 2014a, p. 32). A mandatory health insurance scheme is therefore seen as the solution for this problem, as it automatically establishes a system of solidarity between the sick and the healthy, the young and the old as well as between the rich and the poor by raising funds according to the ability to pay and granting benefits based on medical need (Fischer et al., 2003, pp. 27–28; WHO, 2014a, p. 36, 2010a, pp. xiv, xv).

To measure the success of the benefit-payment separation and the introduction of large insurance pools including vulnerable groups, an important question is that of equality and equity (as well as their correlation) and of need. Equality was divided into the fields "equality of chances" and "equality of outcomes" by modern philosophers like John Rawls, Amartya Sen, Ronald Dworkin and John Roemer (World Bank, 2005, pp. 76–77). The difference of these two concepts and their relationships to equity becomes clear by looking at health inequalities between different age groups. The inequality of health between the young and the old (inequality in the outcomes) might not be interpreted as

22

inequity if the differences solely arise from the natural decline of health in later life years (equality in chances). Neither might inequalities between the ill and those in good health (inequality in the outcomes) be regarded as inequities, if health care will be given to those who are healthy today and at the time fall ill (equality in chances) (Fleurbaey and Schokkaert, 2011, p. 3). Equity can therefore be described as a situation where equal chances are permitted; the equality of outcomes is secondary.

Although this definition offers a general understanding of equity, it does not solve the problem of how to evaluate the equality of chances. Gravelle and colleagues try to approach this question by distinguishing between "need variables that 'ought' to affect use of health care and non-need variables that 'ought not' [to]" (Gravelle et al., 2006, p. 193). Those variables are found to depend on scientific results concerning their effect on the health of the people as well as on value judgments (Gravelle et al., 2006, p. 193). Being able to evaluate equal chances through need and non-need variables is an important step in allocating health care referring to the "need principle" (Doorslaer and O'Donnell, 2008, p. 5) mentioned above. Those need and non-need variables furthermore serve as the basis for the two theoretical concepts of horizontal and vertical equity.

> "There is horizontal inequity when use is affected by non-need variables, so that individuals with the same level of the needs variables consume different amounts of care. [...] There is vertical equity when individuals with different levels of the needs variables consume 'appropriately' different amounts of health care." [6] (Gravelle et al., 2006, p. 193)

Horizontal equity is therefore the principle that is concerned with the question of how to value outcomes of individuals with the same needs, while vertical inequity asks how to evaluate inequalities that result from different needs (Fleurbaey and Schokkaert, 2011, pp. 4–6). The different aspects of equity according to these explanations are summarized in Table 3 below.

---

[6] An encyclopedic explanation: "Horizontal equity means providing equal healthcare to those who are the same in a relevant respect (such as having the same 'need'). Vertical equity means treating differently those who are different in relevant respects (such as having different 'need')" (Wikipedia, 2012).

need	care	equity aspect
different	equal	vertical inequity
different	"appropriately" different	vertical equity
equal	different	horizontal inequity
equal	equal	horizontal equity

Table 3: "Aspects of equity", author's investigation.

2.2 Depth: "Which benefits are covered?"

The depth dimension is concerned with the questions "Which benefits are covered?" (Figure 3) and "Which services to expand first?" (Table 1). To answer these two questions, this chapter will, as done in the height section, firstly investigate the position of health economic theory (2.2.1). Secondly, also as in the height section, an additional part will look at recommendations given by scholars and international institutions (2.2.2).

2.2.1 Theoretical views on services in health insurance systems

After having analyzed the theoretical background of health insurance (2.1.1), this section 2.2.1 will spot requests coming from empiric studies (2.2.1.1). Thereafter, it will conceptualize a theoretical model that takes into account positive and negative outcomes of health interventions. With the help of this focus, the value of health insurance will be evaluated through analyzing the appropriateness of care (2.2.1.2). To show the implication for economic health insurance theory, the three theories mentioned in chapter 2.1.1 – risk protection, moral hazard and access to medical services – are explained along the lines of the new appropriateness model (2.2.1.3). Finally, a conclusion summarizes the main points of this chapter 2.2.1.4.

2.2.1.1 Overlooked empirical issues concerning the value of health insurance

As originally demanded by Arrow (Arrow, 1963, pp. 959–961) and in addition to the finding that health insurance increases the consumption of health services (Chandra et al., 2010; Danzon and Pauly, 2002; Feldstein, 1973; Gaynor et al., 2007; Gibson et al., 2005; Gilman and Kautter, 2008, 2007; Goldman et al., 2007; Huskamp et al., 2005,

2003; Keeler and Rolph, 1988; Landon et al., 2007; Manning and Marquis, 1996, 1989; Phelps, 2010), the "RAND Health Insurance Experiment" (RAND HIE) examined the impact on health outcomes. Their basic finding was that higher consumption of health services only shows marginal positive correlations with the observable health output[7] (Newhouse, 1996, p. 339). Although economic health insurance theory assumes otherwise, implicitly (Pauly, 1968) or explicitly (Arrow, 1963; Nyman, 1999), this finding suggests that the consumption of health services does not necessarily lead to an increase of health. What is the reason for this finding? By separating the participants of the RAND HIE into two groups (receiver of "inappropriate" or "unnecessary"[8] services and receiver of "appropriate" services), the conclusion was drawn that "inappropriate" care has offsetting effects to the positive health results of "appropriate" care[9] (Lohr et al., 1986; Siu et al., 1986). For a judgment of the value of health insurance, the inclusion of the appropriateness of care is therefore vitally important.

2.2.1.2 Remodeling the value of health insurance

The analysis in chapter 2.1.1, which presented the three existing theories that are only loosely linked to each other, together with the finding of above chapter 2.2.1.1 showed that remodeling health insurance theory is important regarding two academic voids: (1) merging existing theoretical models and (2) integrating the concept of appropriateness of care. To fill these voids, a new model is introduced here. It builds on the expected utility theory as developed by von Neumann, Morgenstern, Friedman and Savage (Friedman, 1974; von Neumann and Morgenstern, 1944).[10] The model will also converge to Arrows wish to finance medical services that will have a positive effect on

---

[7] Positive effects of health insurance are observed for poor adults in poor health, for the correction of far vision, for diastolic blood pressure (Keeler, 1987; Keeler et al., 1985) and for avoiding "serious symptoms" (Shapiro et al., 1986).
[8] The delivery of "inappropriate" or "unnecessary" health care can be well explained by information asymmetry (Arrow, 1963; profit maximization of physicians (Epstein et al., 1986; Glazer, 1993; Greenfield et al., 1992; Hemenway et al., 1990; McGuire, 2000b; Mitchell and Cromwell, 1982; Stearns et al., 1992; Zuckerman and Holahan, 1991), financial ownership (Bruce Hillman et al., 1992; Hillman et al., 1990; Scherer, 2000) and other reasons for malpractice (Blendon et al., 1993; Kessler and McClellan, 1996; Lawthers et al., 1992; McGuire, 2000b).
[9] It was furthermore concluded that cost sharing is not recommendable as it will equally reduce care in both groups (Newhouse, 2004; Siu et al., 1986; Swartz, 2010).
[10] The appropriateness model furthermore builds on Nyman's access theory and will therefore not mention basic concepts that were already discussed there (Nyman, 1999).

the state of health of the insured (Arrow, 1963, p. 161). Health outcomes are however, due to high measurement costs or missing data, barely verifiable. Therefore, theory assumes that health services per se result in positive health outcomes (Arrow, 1963, p. 161; Nyman, 1999, p. 143) and scientists mostly measure the utilization of medical care resources (McGuire, 2000b, p. 465). As the findings of the RAND HIE suggest that health care utilization does not necessarily lead to health outcomes (Lohr et al., 1986; Siu et al., 1986) and in order to get closer to health as an outcome measure (Arrow, 1963, p. 161), this analysis assumes that only appropriate medical care (aM)[11] has a positive, whereas inappropriate medical care (iM) has a negative effect on health and utility ($u_{iM/aM}$).

For modeling probability π, it is important to include the finding of a positive correlation between the consumption of health services and the insurance status (Nyman, 1999). This means: The probability π for health care consumption varies for insured (π_i) and uninsured (π_u) people. [12] Additionally, health services are partly consumed as inappropriate and partly as appropriate care. Therefore, π_i and π_u are defined as the probability for inappropriate care being offered (to insured (π_i) and uninsured (π_u) people); 1-π_i and 1-π_u are termed probability for appropriate care. Both, π_i and π_u, are greater than zero, but smaller than one ($0 < \pi_{i/u} < 1$).

Insurance premium (P) is calculated by the probability of consuming health care ($\pi_{i/u}$ or 1-$\pi_{i/u}$) multiplied by the cost of medical care (C_M). The insurance payoff (I) equals medical costs (C_M)[13]. The disposable wealth (w) of a person depends on gross wealth (W), medical costs (C_M), insurance premium (P) and insurance payoff (I) and can be written as:

$w = W - C_M - P + I$, or (due to $I = C_M$) $w = W - P$ (Nyman, 1999, pp. 143–145).

---

[11] Appropriateness must not be confused with quality. While the first one judges the characteristic of treatments, the second one refers for example to a doctors "diligence, care, attentiveness" (McGuire, 2000b, p. 487) and could be measured in time spent with the patient (Glazer, 1993; McCall, 1996).
[12] Values for π_i and π_u can be derived from the large amount of studies evaluating price elasticity of demand for medical care (Chandra et al., 2010; Danzon and Pauly, 2002; Feldstein, 1973; Gaynor et al., 2007; Gibson et al., 2005; Gilman and Kautter, 2008, 2007; Goldman et al., 2007; Huskamp et al., 2005, 2003; Keeler and Rolph, 1988; Landon et al., 2007; Manning and Marquis, 1996, 1989; Phelps, 2010).
[13] The costs for medical care are normalized due to the assumption that the price of medical care is fixed (Nyman, 1999, p. 143).

Because utility (u) is measured in terms of wealth (first part in brackets below) and in terms of received care (second part in brackets), for the case of an issued insurance, it can be written as:

1. $u_{iM} = u_{iM}(w,iM) = u_{iM}[W-P,iM]$ (1) and

2. $u_{aM} = u_{aM}(w,aM) = u_{aM}[W-P,aM]$ (2).

If insurance is not contracted, utility can be calculated the following way:

3. $u_{iM} = u_{iM}(w,iM) = u_{iM}[W-C_M,iM]$ (3) and

4. $u_{aM} = u_{aM}(w,aM) = u_{aM}[W-C_M,aM]$ (4).

From these functions, expected utility (EU) can be modeled depending on the individual's insurance status:

1. $EU = \pi_u u_{iM}[W-C_M,iM]+(1-\pi_u) u_{aM}[W-C_M,aM]$, without insurance (5) and

2. $EU = \pi_i u_{iM}[W-P,iM]+(1-\pi_i) u_{aM}[W-P,aM]$, with insurance (6).

In this model, expected utility (EU) is influenced by (1) the risk of losing money, that is spent for medical care ($W-C_M$), or by (2) the character of medical care itself (M). For simplicity, it is firstly assumed that the costs for medical care (C_M) do not exceed gross wealth (W) of the individual ($C_M<W$). For a purchaser of health insurance (equation (6)) utility therefore increases, if appropriate medical care (aM) increases and inappropriate care (iM) decreases. His personal wealth (W-P) is, on an individual basis, not affected by his decision to seek or not seek medical care (M).[14] The individual might instead be aware that his wealth decreases, if a large number of people increase consumption (Pauly, 1968). For a person without health insurance, the same is true concerning his utility derived from medical care. Concerning his personal wealth ($W-C_M$), utility is maximized when health care consumption is kept low.

---

[14] The reader might at this point rightly wonder, if an insured person will endlessly consume appropriate care. This is not the case due to two reasons: 1. Appropriate care is not endlessly available, as it is appropriate only in relation to the individuals situation. The service that was appropriate at t_0 might, after consumption, be inappropriate in t_1. 2. The consumption of health care is not only restricted by monetary, but also by timely means (Zweifel and Manning, 2000, pp. 411–412). The investment in health is therefore costly in terms of opportunity costs, even if there are no financial constrains for health care consumption (Grossman, 1972). Maximizing personal utility is therefore unequal with maximizing (appropriate) health care consumption.

Comparing the two insurance states, it can be concluded that participants of neither group have an incentive to increase the consumption of inappropriate medical care (iM). Incentives for appropriate medical care (aM) consumption are, for insured individuals, neutral in financial terms and positive in medical terms. For uninsured individuals, incentives are negative in financial and positive in medical terms. From a consumer point of view, the model therefore implies increased health care usage only due to the consumption of diagnosis related medical reasons.

Box 1: Maximizing the individual's expected utility (EU):

To maximize the purchaser's utility (EU), equations (5) and (6) have to fulfill the first ($EU'=0$) and second ($EU''<0$) order conditions. This is possible by either assuming inappropriate (iM) or appropriate medical care (aM) being fixed. For the first case, first order conditions ($EU'=0$) can be denoted as:

1. $EU'(u_{aM}) = (1-\pi_u)\, u_{aM}'[W-C_M, aM] = 0$, without insurance ($5_{a'}$) and
2. $EU'(u_{aM}) = (1-\pi_i)\, u_{aM}'[W-P, aM] = 0$, with insurance ($6_{a'}$).

The second order condition ($EU''<0$):

1. $EU''(u_{aM}) = (1-\pi_u)\, u_{aM}''[W-C_M, aM] < 0$, without insurance ($5_{a''}$) and
2. $EU''(u_{aM}) = (1-\pi_i)\, u_{aM}''[W-P, aM] < 0$, with insurance ($6_{a''}$).

Respectively, if fixing aM, first order conditions ($EU'=0$) can be denoted as:

1. $EU'(u_{iM}) = \pi_u\, u_{iM}'[W-C_M, iM] = 0$, without insurance ($5_{i'}$) and
2. $EU'(u_{iM}) = \pi_i\, u_{iM}'[W-P, iM] = 0$, with insurance ($6_{i'}$).

And the second order condition ($EU''<0$):

1. $EU''(u_{iM}) = \pi_u\, u_{iM}''[W-C_M, iM] < 0$, without insurance ($5_{i''}$) and
2. $EU''(u_{iM}) = \pi_i\, u_{iM}''[W-P, iM] < 0$, with insurance ($6_{i''}$).

This shows that maximizing EU ($EU'=0 \wedge EU''<0$) is either possible by maximizing u_{aM} ($EU'(u_{aM})=0 \wedge EU''(u_{aM})<0$) or u_{iM} ($EU'(u_{iM})<0 \wedge EU''(u_{iM})<0$).

2.2.1.3 Implications

Remodeling the value of health insurance in the above way merges the theories of Arrow, Pauly/deMeza and Nyman. It also assures that health and welfare effects are measured according to the appropriateness of delivered care.

Arrow's finding, that the value of health insurance arises from the protection against financial risks (Arrow, 1963, p. 959), is reflected in equations (5) and (6). The insured individual's utility (EU) is, in terms of personal wealth, only limited by the insurance premium (W-P), but not by the direct cost of health care (equation (6)). Without insurance, in contrast, the person's expected utility (EU) is, concerning the financial aspect, reduced in proportion to the medical care consumption (W-C_M) (equation (5)).

The finding that moral hazard increases health consumption through issuing insurance (Pauly, 1968) is also observable and can be tested through comparing equations (5) and (6). If the consumed medical care (M) stays the same between these two equations, moral hazard can be regarded as absent; if it varies, moral hazard does exist. In this context, it is interesting to see that insured individuals are not incentivized to increase the consumption of inappropriate (iM) but only of appropriate (aM) medical care. An increase of inappropriate care (iM) consumption must consequently stem from external factors, like for example lack of information or physician induced demand (McGuire, 2000b).

Nyman's finding, that the increase in service consumption stems from the facilitated access to health services, becomes visible if the assumptions from equations (5) and (6) are altered so that medical care (M) exceeds gross wealth (W). In that case (C_M>W), expected utility can be measured as:

1. EU = π_u u_{iM}[W,0]+(1- π_u) u_{aM}[W,0], without insurance (7) and
2. EU = π_i u_{iM}[W-P,iM]+(1- π_i) u_{aM}[W-P,aM], with insurance (8).

Comparing formulas (6) and (8), no differences can be found as medical treatment (M) is paid by the insurance (W-P). However, comparing equations (5) and (7), the low gross wealth (W) and high cost of medical care (C_M) constrain the individual to buy health care (M=0). The consumption of health care (M) is zero, because it is unaffordable for the care seeker to get access to services. Granting access to health care is in that case the contribution of health insurance.

In addition, by measuring utility depending on the appropriateness of care, the above presented model adds a new view on the moral hazard and the access theory.[15] Moral hazard, understood as increased health service usage due to lower marginal costs of care (Pauly, 1968, p. 535), does not only show a tendency towards welfare loss, but also towards welfare gain. It may be termed welfare gain, if appropriate medical care is increased more than inappropriate medical care (aM>iM) and expected utility (EU) is shifted upwards. It must be termed welfare loss, if it is the other way around (iM>aM).

The access motive, on the other hand, does not only include welfare gain, but also welfare loss tendencies. Again, the evaluation depends on the proportion between appropriate (aM) and inappropriate medical care (iM). If insurance provides access to health care that mainly consists of inappropriate medical care (iM), EU will be negative and insurance will produce welfare loss. If access to primarily appropriate medical care (aM) is insured, EU will be positive and the effects will count as welfare gain.

Last but not least, by not measuring utility (u) depending on the individual's state of health (sick-healthy polarity), but on appropriateness of delivered care, the new model is able to include preventive care actions. In former models, healthy people cannot gain utility from health care (Arrow, 1963; Nyman, 1999; Pauly, 1968) and are therefore implicitly believed to not take preventive actions. On the contrary, these views even suggest that they rather increase their risk for illness (Zweifel and Manning, 2000, pp. 413–420). In the appropriateness approach however, healthy people increase their utility, if provided care is appropriate (e.g. consultancy, vaccination, screening). Using appropriateness and inappropriateness to differentiate therefore allows the evaluation of preventive actions within the health insurance model.

The appropriateness approach in total might lead to focusing more on the character of services that are financed through our health care systems and thereby increase people's health status and create welfare gain for society.

---

[15] The utility derived from financial protection (Arrow's contribution) is not influenced by the appropriateness approach, as health costs from appropriate care can be as threatening as those from inappropriate care.

2.2.2 Practical approaches concerning services in health insurance systems

As shown above, the assumption that health insurance produces a positive social value through reducing user fees and granting increasing access and financial protection, is strongly depending on the appropriateness of the services offered. This new insight goes beyond what is meant when quality of services is stressed (WHO, 2014a, p. viii; WHO and Lerberghe, 2008, p. 25). Appropriateness does further point towards the issue that, in some cases, health services are delivered which do not serve the patients' health interest. This issue has not been shown in economic theory before and shall therefore be analyzed within the Chinese context.

As mentioned before, the depth dimension is concerned with the questions "Which benefits are covered?" (Figure 3) and "Which services to expand first?"(Table 1). To fully understand the concrete requirements of this topic, it should firstly be mentioned that UHC goes beyond a minimum package of services. UHC should go beyond treatment and curative services and include public health and population measures, promotive, preventive rehabilitative and palliative services as well as services targeting non-communicable diseases – including both, individual- and population-based interventions (Kieny and Evans, 2013, p. 305; UN, 2012a; WHO, 2014a, pp. 3, 11, 12). As the above section indicates, this large selection of important health services calls for a method on how to choose appropriate services that ensure the health of a country's people (WHO, 2014a, p. 11). The World Health Report of 2008 gives the following advice:

- "The exercise should not be limited to a set of predefined priorities: it should look at demand as well as at the full range of health needs.
- It should specify what should be provided at primary and secondary levels.
- The implementation of the package should be costed so that political decision-makers are aware of what will not be included if health care remains under-funded.
- There have to be institutionalized mechanisms for evidence-based review of the package of benefits.

- People need to be informed about the benefits they can claim, with mechanisms of mediation when claims are being denied." (WHO and Lerberghe, 2008, p. 27)

Following these points will help to overcome the problem that can arise from following an extreme strategy of either scaling up too many or too few health interventions. If only a limited number of interventions are included, a country might be able to rapidly cover the entire population, however, they will also encounter problems deriving from increased usage of services that are not appropriate for some health problems observable within the population. This again might give rise to medical services providers with inadequate medical education and dubious practices (WHO and Lerberghe, 2008, p. 28). On the other hand, including a large number of interventions might lead to problems concerning the speed of reform and the quality of services provided and thereby the acceptance of the population.

Another, maybe more practical approach to overcome the problem of choosing the right services and the right amount is given in the Final Report of the WHO Consultative Group on Equity and Universal Health Coverage (WHO, 2014a). It proposes a method on how to choose and prioritize services. The basic idea is to rank services into brought classes such as high priority, medium-priority, and low-priority services. It is suggested that high priority classes are extended first, until all people are covered (compare breadth dimension), before services of middle or low priority are included into the scope of services (WHO, 2014a, p. 11).

Concerning the criteria that are used to classify services as high, middle or low ranking, cost-effectiveness, priority to the worse off, financial risk protection, severity of disease (present and future health gap), realization of potential, past health loss, socioeconomic status, area of living, gender, race, ethnicity, religion, sexual orientation, economic productivity, care for others and catastrophic health expenditures were discussed (WHO, 2014a, pp. 13–20). Among them, cost-effectiveness, priority to the worse off and financial risk protection were worked out as the core indicators (WHO, 2014a, p. 20). According to the countries that work with priority setting and according to scholars, a special position is furthermore assigned to the cost-effectiveness criterion[16] (Bobadilla et al., 1994; WHO, 2014a, p. 12). Cost-effectiveness has furthermore been suggested to serve as the main measure by many national and international initiatives, such as the 2001 Commission on Macroeconomics and Health and the 2009 Taskforce on Innovative International Financing for Health Systems (WHO, 2014a, p. 14). Consequently, it is proposed by the WHO to start off with the cost-effectiveness criteria in order to roughly sort services into three groups of high, middle and low importance. This will lead to firstly favor those services that produce the greatest value in terms of health for a certain amount of money. Only after this step is completed, should the other two categories be used to adjust the former decisions (WHO, 2014a, pp. 20, 21, 23).

To answer the question posed above, "Which services to expand first?", in a general way, it can be said: The higher a service is ranked, the more important it is to expand its coverage to the whole population (WHO, 2014a, p. 37).

2.3 Breadth: "Who is insured?"

The answer to "Who is insured?" (Figure 3) is closely related to the answer to "Whom to include first?" (Table 1) and can be found in WHO's recommendations of a three way strategy for countries seeking a fair progressive realization of UHC. Within this strategy, it is suggested to insure everyone (breadth dimension) from the beginning providing a certain set of high-priority services[17] (see depth dimension) (WHO, 2014a, p. 37). A special focus must once again be laid on disadvantaged groups, as otherwise insurance participation would follow a socio-economic gradient. This can be demonstrated by looking at the coverage rate of vaccines and skilled birth attendance, two key services that should be covered for the whole population. In below Figure 8, it is shown how different countries manage to include their population more or less equally. In all three

---

[16] Cost-effectiveness is mostly measured in lives saved, life years saved, QALYs and DALYs (WHO, 2014a, p. 13).
[17] The complete three-part strategy suggested by WHO includes the following: "(a) Categorize services into priority classes. Relevant criteria include those related to cost-effectiveness, priority to the worse off, and financial risk protection; (b) First expand coverage for high-priority services to everyone. This includes eliminating out-of-pocket payments while increasing mandatory, progressive prepayment with pooling of funds; (c) While doing so, ensure that disadvantaged groups are not left behind. These will often include low-income groups and rural populations." (WHO, 2014a, p. 37)

countries, the different income quintiles show different coverage rates that follow the income gradient. A diverse situation exists in Columbia, where only the coverage rate for skilled birth attendance follows the income gradient. Coverage rates for vaccines are concentrating on the middle income quintile suggesting that special attention has been given to lower income groups. In Ethiopia, most of the beneficiaries of health services are from the upper quintile while the other quintiles are not significantly covered. In India, the coverage rates for service provision seem to be nearly linearly correlated with the income level of the population. Here, the belonging to an income quintile is hence a good predictor for the individual coverage rate of service utilization – at least for vaccines and skilled birth attendance (WHO, 2014a, p. 25).

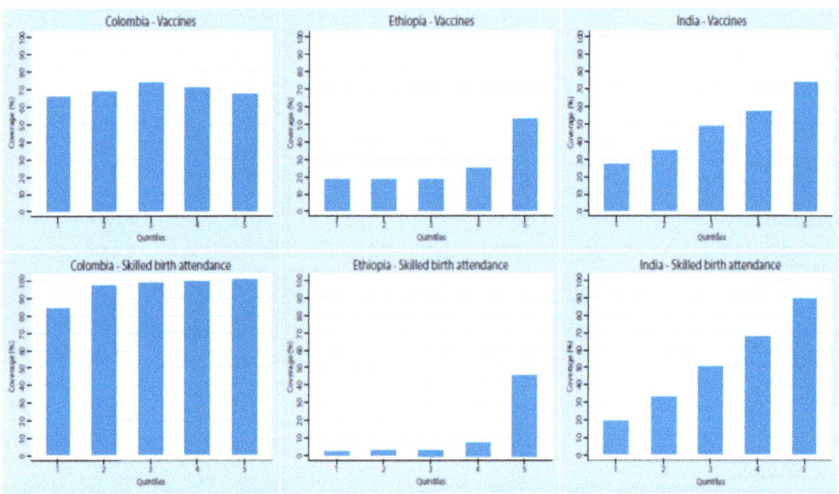

Figure 8: "Socioeconomic inequalities in coverage rates in three countries", data for Ethiopia from 2011, for India and Columbia from 2014 (WHO, 2014, p. 25).

In addition to the finding that lower income quintiles are mostly worse-off in terms of service access than the upper income quintile, the lower income quintiles are often also disadvantaged with regard to having lower health levels and – tautological but worth mentioning – lower income. It can therefore be summarized that those groups of the population with the biggest need – low financial power and low health status – are in general less protected in terms of access to services (WHO, 2014a, p. 28). This finding

34

is well known in the literature as the "inverse care law", which states that "the availability of good medical care tends to vary inversely with the need of the population served" (Tudor Hart, 1971, p. 412). Although the inverse care law was demonstrated using income as a social determinant, the above example is true for other determinants as well. According to the Final Report of the Commission on Social Determinants of Health, these other determinants include income, ethnicity, gender and rural/urban residency (WHO, 2008a, p. 94).

In order to overcome the inverse care law, vulnerable groups should be particularly targeted by giving more weight to respective policies. Such attempts can either directly focus on vulnerable groups or indirectly on the area where underprivileged people live. Another possibility for policy action is not to focus on groups but to target those services that are mostly consumed by the underprivileged. As already mentioned before, targeting vulnerable groups should not become a mean to itself but shall always be weighed against other social determinants in order not to lose the support of the majority (WHO, 2014a, pp. 28–30).

The final answer to the initial question "Whom to include first?"(Table 1) is therefore that it is very important to include disadvantaged groups from the very beginning and make sure that they are not left behind (WHO, 2014a, p. 37).

2.4 Overall findings

To summarize what was worked out as the methodological concept, the three central dimensions of UHC are essential: (1) The degree to which services are reimbursed, (2) the amount and type of benefits covered and (3) the amount of people insured. These three dimensions have graphically been formalized as a cube which was introduced in Figure 3. With regard to these three dimensions, a set of questions was posed: (1) "Whom to include first?", (2) "Which services to expand first?" and (3) "How to shift from out-of-pocket payment toward pre-payment?" (Table 1).

The question "How to shift from out-of-pocket payment toward prepayment?" (height dimension of UHC, part 2.1) is supported by health economic theory which suggests that low OOP helps to financially protect the insured and grant them access to health services. The WHO recommendations additionally pointed out two basic aspects related to the height dimension: Firstly, it is important to share the risks among society through pooling and install pre-payment mechanisms instead of OOP (WHO, 2014a, p. 34, 2005, p. 139). The resulting effect of separating the *use* of services from *payment* for services was found to be most important and shall further serve as the leading structure for analyzing the issue of equitable distribution, especially with focusing on vulnerable groups (WHO, 2014a, p. 36).

Investigating the question "Which services to expand first?" (depth dimension of UHC, part 2.2), a detailed analysis of the health economic theory was undertaken to point out that modern health economic theory requires to deliver appropriate health services to those in need. Apart from this theoretical request, the depth chapter brought to light multiple concrete factors that can be used to classify services into high, middle and low ranking categories. The initial list of factors – cost-effectiveness, priority to the worse off, financial risk protection, severity of disease (present and future health gap), realization of potential, past health loss, socioeconomic status, area of living, gender, race, ethnicity, religion, sexual orientation, economic productivity, care for others and catastrophic health expenditures (WHO, 2014a, pp. 13–20) – was found to include three main indicators: cost-effectiveness, priority to the worse off and financial risk protection (WHO, 2014a, p. 20). Among them, cost-effectiveness is judged to be most important and can be used to make a first classification of the services in question (WHO, 2014a, p. 12). The answer to "Which services to expand first?" is hence: those that are appropriate and classified as high priority services. The initial and most important classification can be achieved by classifying a service according to its cost-efficiency (2.2).

Investigating "Whom to include first?" (breadth dimension of UHC, part 2.3) has shown that health insurance systems are prone to first insure the rich quintiles of society as gains can be achieved easiest in this area. Unfortunately, this might lead to neglecting poor quintiles in later years and as a result put the greatest pressure on those who need the most support. The answer to "Whom to include first?" is therefore to include everyone from the very beginning, but especially focus on the poor and deprived part of the population in order to achieve protection for the whole society (2.3).

In addition to summarizing the findings of the section before, the WHO publication, "Making fair choices on the path to universal health coverage", gives answers to the three questions posed above which are very close to the findings of this thesis:

1. "First expand coverage for high-priority services to everyone. This includes eliminating out-of-pocket payments while increasing mandatory, progressive prepayment with pooling of funds;
2. Categorize services into priority classes. Relevant criteria include those related to cost-effectiveness, priority to the worse off, and financial risk protection;
3. While doing so, ensure that disadvantaged groups are not left behind. These will often include low-income groups and rural populations." (WHO, 2014a, p. 37)

Against the background of above findings, the following section 3 will analyze the tree dimensions of UHC (height, depth and breadth) within the Chinese context by applying what was discussed above.

3 The situation in the People's Republic of China

It has already been mentioned in chapter 1.3 that China is a partner in many international treaties of the WHO and the UN which recognize health as a fundamental goal that should be achieved by every people (UN, 2012a, 2012b; WHO, 2014a, 2011a, 2005).

Therefore, UHC has been an important target of health reform in China. This can for example be seen by the 2009 "Implementation Plan for the Recent Priorities of the Health Care System Reform (2009-2011)" (PRC, 2009). It sets the goal to insure more than 90% of the people (breadth), establish a national essential medicines system (depth) and increase the reimbursement rates to six times of the per-capita net income (height) until 2011 (PRC, 2009). Additionally, universal coverage is aspired until 2020 (Guo et al., 2010; PRC, 2009).

In 2011, the achievement of those goals was prolonged until 2015, through issuing the 12th Five-Year Plan, a document of guidelines for the 2011-2015 development strategy of China. It thereby gained further political importance as achieving the goals of the

Five-Year Plan is an important precondition for the career of provincial politicians (PRC, 2011; Shih, 2011). The 12th Five-Year Plan has therefore been labeled to increase and optimize the allocation of human resources, control costs, increase government investment and reduce health spending of the citizens (Marten et al., 2014, p. 4).

These two documents prove the strong push of the Chinese government towards UHC. The situation in China will therefore be analyzed in more detail in the following sections by taking into account these two and other official documents. For structuring purposes, the three dimensions that are explained above: height, depth and breadth. Due to the complex subject and the goal not to be superficial, the following analysis will focus only on central issues of these three dimensions and examine those focuses in best possible depth.

The structure of the following analysis is hence:

4. The height dimension in China (3.1)
   a. The value of health insurance with respect to user fees and OOP (3.1.1)
   b. The situation of benefits and financial protection in China (3.1.2 - 3.1.3)
5. The depth dimension in China (3.2)
   c. Appropriateness of health services in the Chinese catalogue of benefits (3.2.1)
   d. Potential of including NCD interventions into the Chinese catalogue of benefits (3.2.2 - 3.2.5)
6. The breadth dimension in China (3.3)
   e. Overview of literature: Does marginalization of migrant workers matter in the context of health? (3.3.1)
   f. Health Insurance Coverage in China – *status quo* and future projection (3.3.2 - 3.3.5)

3.1 The height dimension in China

According to the chapter "Definition and Concept" (chapter 2), there are two reasons why the height dimension is important to achieve: Firstly, improved access to health care and secondly, reduced financial risk for individuals and families (2.1.1). As shown above, achieving these social gains is possible through (1) low user fees and OOP and (2) the separation of benefits and payments, especially focusing on equity and vulnerable groups (2.1 and 2.4). The following sections will hence discuss these points with regard to the situation in China.

3.1.1 Low user fees and OOP

In order to examine if China is working towards low user fees and OOP, section 2.1.2 has defined the level at which financial catastrophes and impoverishment reaches an acceptable level that lies at least below 15-20% of total health expenditures (WHO, 2014a, p. 33, 2010a, p. xiv). Some scholars have even argued to aim for a 10% threshold as OOP and catastrophic expenditures show an exponential relationship (compare Figure 4) and because households are forced to sacrifice basic needs, sell assets, indebt themselves and are impoverished as long as OOP is above 10% of total household expenditure (Doorslaer and O'Donnell, 2008, p. 6).

Table 4 below shows that neither of these two targets have been met by China which only recently (2012) managed to reduce its OOP expenditure to less than 35% of total health expenditure. Furthermore, some scholars even find higher values of OOP than stated by World Bank. For example, van Doorslaer and O'Donnell find that roughly 60% of all health expenditure is still covered by OOP in 2008 and 60-70% in 2010 (Doorslaer and O'Donnell, 2008, p. 4).

Country Name	2003	2004	2005	2006	2007	2008	2009	2010	2011	2012
China	55.87%	53.64%	52.21%	49.31%	44.05%	40.42%	37.46%	35.29%	34.77%	34.34%

Table 4: "Out-of-pocket health expenditure (% of total expenditure on health) in China" (World Bank, 2014).

However, as even the most favorable target of 20% is not easy to reach for most low- and middle-income countries, the Member States of the WHO Western Pacific Region have set a target of 30-40% for themselves (WHO, 2010a, p. xiv). According to World Bank data, China has managed to achieve this target between 2008 and 2009 (Table 4). It is furthermore remarkable that China has shown a steady progress towards the goal of reducing OOP. From a share higher than 50% until 2005, it reduced OOP to a 40% level in 2008 and to less than 35% until recently (2012) (Figure 9 and Table 4).

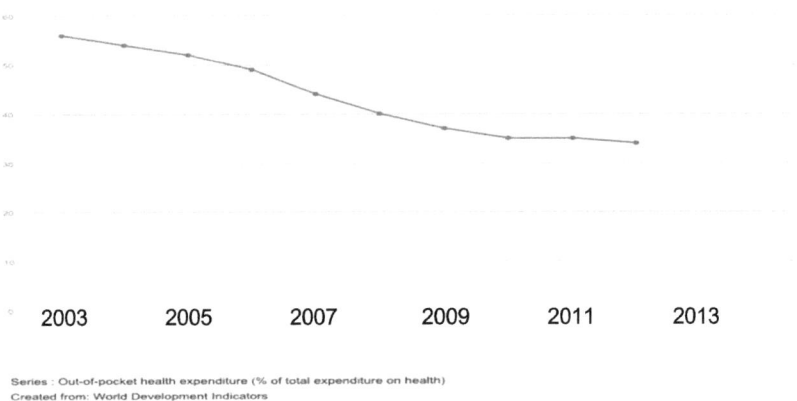

Series : Out-of-pocket health expenditure (% of total expenditure on health)
Created from: World Development Indicators
Created on: 12/20/2014

Figure 9: "Out-of-pocket health expenditure (% of total expenditure on health) in China" (World Bank, 2014).

Although China has reached its self-set goal of 30-40% (WHO, 2010a, p. xiv), caveats still remain due to the warning that only after OOP falls at least below 15-20% of total health expenditures, the incidence rate of financial catastrophe and impoverishment will reach an acceptable level (Doorslaer and O'Donnell, 2008, p. 6; WHO, 2014a, p. 33, 2010a, p. xiv).

Looking at the development of OOP, it can be observed that its share has been increasing until 2001 and decreasing after 2003 (Alcorn and Bao, 2011, p. 1557). Despite the final improvement, a persistently missing protection against catastrophic health payments could be observed which affected roughly 13% of Chinese households (Chen and Jin, 2012, p. 782; Meng et al., 2012a, pp. 809, 812). In 2003, 12.2% of all registered Chinese households have experienced catastrophic health expenses, in

40

2008 14.0% and in 2011 12.9% (Meng et al., 2012b, p. 809). This finding needs further explanation and interpretation as it seems to be in contrast with the above finding that the amount of total OOP steadily decreased after 2003 (Figure 9 and Table 4) and the observation that the rate of health insurance (from 29.7% in 2003 to 87.9% in 2008 and 95.7% in 2011) and the inpatient reimbursement rates (14·4% in 2003, 35.2% in 2008 and 46.9% in 2011) steadily increased (Meng et al., 2012b, p. 809). At least partially, this phenomenon can be explained by health economic theory. As Nyman states that low reimbursement rates tend to inhibit people's access to health services (Nyman, 1999, pp. 143–145), it is natural to assume that the consumption of health services rises when it becomes affordable for the consumer. The unchanged percentage of households that experience catastrophic health expenditures might therefore be a consequence of the granted access to health care through increasing rates of health insurance and increasing inpatient reimbursement rates. Although the stagnant rate of catastrophic health expenditure in China loses some of its negative touch through this interpretation, the phenomenon itself also shows that a substantial part of the population that has formerly been excluded from access to health services. Subsidizing formerly exclusion and potential health problems with financial hardship must still be judged as a social problem that needs to be solved, e.g. through sufficiently high reimbursement rates for all necessary in- and outpatient health services.

A less masked indicator of the effects of OOP is the rate of self-discharge. Taking the group of patients who discharged themselves from inpatient health care as the denominator, the rate of those patients who did so for financial reasons decreased by more than 50%, with the largest decrease between 2003 and 2008 from 63.6% to 35.0% and a final drop to 28.0% in 2011 (Meng et al., 2012b, p. 809). Taking the total inpatient population as the denominator, the rate of patients who discharged themselves for financial reasons dropped from 27.5% to 8.9% between 2003 and 2011 (Meng et al., 2012b, p. 810). Despite this positive development, it still can be observed that nearly one third (28%) of all self-discharges happens due to financial reasons which equals nearly a tenth (8.9%) of all care seeking inpatients (Meng et al., 2012b, pp. 809–810).

It can hence be followed that the major theoretic goals set in part 2.1.1 – that is to protect against financial losses that arise from (1) the costs of medical care and (2) the

41

limited or entire loss of personal income (Arrow, 1963, p. 959) and to assure access to health services (Nyman, 1999) – have neither been met in current China.

3.1.2 Benefit distribution according to the need

Within this section, a special focus will be laid on vulnerable groups in order to investigate the underlying reasons for the problems sketched above.

In general, social health insurance ensures pooling of large groups and can hence be expected to balance between healthy and ill (through different levels of use), the employed and the unemployed (through different levels of contribution), and between the young and the old (through different levels of use and contribution). If family members are insured for free, redistribution from singles to families (through different levels of contribution) can be observed (Fischer et al., 2003, pp. 27–28; WHO, 2014a, p. 36, 2010a, pp. xiv, xv). Following what has been discussed in chapter 2.1.2.2, inequalities like those mentioned above can only be labeled inequitable if they are inequalities in chances (Fleurbaey and Schokkaert, 2011, p. 3). In turn, equalities in chances (and hence equity) exist if differences only arise due to different needs (Doorslaer and O'Donnell, 2008, p. 5; Gravelle et al., 2006, p. 193). This can be claimed to be the case for the general structure described above. In order to understand if the differences within the Chinese health system are equitable, the following paragraphs will look at the differences *between* and *within* different categories.

As the three schemes NCMS, UEBMI, and URBMI (compare section 1.4) are separated from each other, no distributional effects can be observed *between* them. In this respect, the Chinese health insurance system cannot be labeled equitable as it does not distribute according to the peoples' needs. However, *within* the three schemes some of the re-distributions can appear, because the three schemes insure the whole group accounted to them. As NCMS insures all rural citizens, the distributional effects are possible *within* all of the four distribution groups except for the singles-to-families group (Fischer et al., 2003, pp. 27–28). Looking at UEBMI and URBMI, re-distributional effects can only potentially be found between the young and the old and between the healthy and ill. It is however unfortunately impossible to make explicit statements as relevant data is missing.

Investigating the explicit rate of reimbursement that is received by the patients, it becomes obvious that their magnitude is one of the reasons for the still high OOP rates and the negative consequences described in the last section (3.1.1). The reimbursement rates differ depending on the care category (inpatient care or outpatient care) and the insurance scheme that a person is inscribed in (NCMS, UEBMI and URBMI). The percentage rate that is reimbursed for inpatient care is 43.9% in the NCMS scheme, 47.9% in the URBMI scheme and 68.2% in the UEBMI scheme (numbers from 2010) (Yip et al., 2012, p. 835). The reimbursement rate for outpatient care is 30-40% in NCMS and URBMI (numbers from 2010). Numbers for outpatient care are missing for the UEBMI scheme (Yip et al., 2012, p. 836).

Concerning inpatient care and its differences *between* the schemes, it has been found that the NCMS scheme had the lowest, the URBMI scheme a middle and the UEBMI scheme the highest reimbursement rate (Yip et al., 2012, pp. 835, 836). As the rural population is in general less well-off than the urban population, and jobless urban dwellers are less fortunate than those with work, it can be stated that the average participant of the NCMS scheme is the least fortunate, that of the URBMI scheme lies in the middle and that of the UEBMI scheme is the most advantaged one (Meng et al., 2012b, p. 810). The differences in the reimbursement rates that were mentioned above consequently show that benefits are supplied according to the economic strength instead of need indicators and hence do not resemble an equitable distribution.

Although those classifications are very brought, the finding regarding inequity is supported by other sources describing the differences within the schemes. They show existing inequalities according to income and degree of urbanization and also partly to region. Referring to the income level, the reimbursement rates of inpatient care make patients in the richest quintile spend 11% of their monthly per capita income, but account 84% for patients in the poorest quintile. With regard to the degree of urbanization, reimbursement rates of inpatient care averaged only 32.9% for rural but 41.6% for urban citizens (numbers from 2008). An exception of these clearly inequitable distributions is found with regard to the regions. In that case, it is impossible to label the distribution as equitable or inequitable per se. While participants in the poorer western and central provinces benefitted from an inpatient reimbursed rate of 37.4% and 32.1% respectively, a middle value of 35.3% was found in the richer eastern provinces (Meng et al., 2012b, p. 809). Outpatient care, as already mentioned above, is said to have a reimbursement rate of 30-40% for NCMS and URBMI. However, it is impossible to distinguish the differences between the two schemes, and numbers for the UEBMI scheme are absent (Yip et al., 2012, p. 836). Differences for outpatient care *within* the schemes can still be observed. The share of outpatient care only accounts for 10% of annual per capita income in the richest quintile but for 140% in the poorest quintile (Brixi et al., 2011, p. 5). Consequently, it can be stated that, with one exception, all these inequalities are found to be inequitable as they redistribute "inappropriately" differently concerning income, region and the degree of urbanization.

These findings can partly be attenuated because of the mostly positive development over time. The evaluation differs, however, depending on the focus. While it is relatively clear for the differences *between* the insurance schemes (see Table 5 below), contradicting results can be found for the differences *within* the insurance schemes.

	Inpatient reimbursement rates in the three social health insurance programs			difference ("between") as ratio of disadvantaged/advantaged		
	UEBMI	URBMI	NCMS	URBMI/ UEBMI	NCMS/ UEBMI	NCMS/ URBMI
2008	67.0%	43.8%	37.8%	0.65	0.56	0.86
2010	68.2%	47.9%	43.9%	0.70	0.64	0.92
Difference (2010-2008)	1.2	4.1	6.1	0.05	0.08	0.06

Table 5: "Inpatient reimbursement in the three social health insurance programs, 2008 and 2010", numbers from Yip et al., 2012, p. 835, author's investigation.

Regarding the differences *between* the insurance schemes, the UEBMI scheme increased its inpatient reimbursement rates from 67.0% in 2008 to 68.2% in 2010, the URBMI scheme from 43.8% to 47.9% and the NCMS scheme from 37.8% to 43.9%. That is equal to an increase of 1.2 percentage points in the UEBMI scheme, 4.1 percentage points in the URBMI scheme and 6.1 percentage points in the NCMS scheme. This can be judged as an improvement of the inequitable situation described above (Table 5). In accordance with this finding, the ratio between the reimbursement rates of the disadvantaged programs and the more advantaged programs shows a positive tendency over time. While in all cases and both years the ratio has been lower than one[18], these numbers increase by 0.05 for the URBMI/UEBMI ratio, 0.08 points for the NCMS/UEBMI ratio and 0.06 for the NCMS/URBMI ratio (Table 5). With regard to the increasing ratio, these findings as well can be interpreted as inequity-reducing.

The differences *within* each insurance scheme's reimbursement rates show less clear effects. In one of the paragraphs above, inequitable differences have been found according to income, degree of urbanization and partly to region. Among the inequitable differences that increased from 2008 to 2011 were those related to some regional comparisons and to the degree of urbanization. Concerning the regions, the differences between the relatively rich eastern provinces and the relatively poor central provinces have risen from 3.2 percentage points to 5.6 percentage points (Table 6). Regarding the degree of urbanization, the inequitable differences within rural and urban reimbursement rates rose from 8.7 percentage points in 2008 to 10.9 percentage points in 2011[19]. Positive tendencies can be found in the regional comparisons between the relatively rich eastern and the relatively poor western provinces. These differences have already before been in favor of the disadvantaged and have further risen from 2.1 percentage points in 2008 to 4.4 percentage points in 2011 (Table 6).

---

[18] This means that people who were enrolled in the disadvantaged programs received relatively less benefits than those enrolled in the advantaged programs.
[19] Inpatient reimbursement rates 2008: rural-urban = 32.9% - 41.6% = -8.7%; Inpatient reimbursement rates 2011: rural-urban = 43.7% - 54.6% = -10.9% (2011) (Meng et al., 2012b, p. 809).

	Inpatient reimbursement rates in the three social health insurance programs			difference ("between")	
	West	Central	East	East-West	East-Central
2008	37.4%	32.1%	35.3%	-2.1	3.2
2011	51.2%	41.2%	46.8%	-4.4	5.6
Difference (2011-2008)	13.8	9.1	11.5	-2.3	2.4

Table 6: "Inpatient reimbursement in the three regions, 2008 and 2011", numbers from Meng et al. 2012b: 809, author's investigation.

Looking at ratios between less advantaged and more advantaged comparison groups between 2008 and 2011, the somewhat indifferent picture which was presented above is strengthened. Comparing the inpatient reimbursement rates of the poorest quartile with the richest, an increase from 0.85 to 0.97 can be observed. (The ratio being smaller than one shows that the less advantaged group (the numerator) receives less reimbursement than the more advantaged group (the denominator). The increase

	Ratios of inpatient reimbursement rates			
	Rural/ Urban	Quartile1/ Quartile4	Central/ East	West/ East
2008	0.79	0.85	0.91	1.06
2011	0.80	0.97	0.88	1.09
Difference (2011-2008)	0.01	0.12	-0.03	0.03

Table 7: "Ratios of inpatient reimbursement rates between less advantaged and more advantaged comparison groups, 2008 and 2011", numbers from Meng et al. 2012b, p. 810, author's investigation.

of this ratio shows an improvement of the situation.) The same tendency, however contradicting with the result from the same author's presented above, can be found between rural and urban citizens where the ratio increased slightly from 0.79 to 0.80. Between the poorer western and the richer eastern provinces the ratio has already been in favor of the less advantaged group. This positive ratio has further increased from 1.06 to 1.09. Also this calculation method shows that the only ratio suggesting a worsening of the equity situation is that between the poorer central and the richer eastern regions where a decrease from 0.91 to 0.88 can be observed (Table 7).

Summarizing the findings of the benefit section, it was stated that, firstly, no benefit transfer can be observed *between* the three insurance schemes as they are structurally separated from each other. A benefit transfer is only potentially possible *within* each of the schemes. Secondly, concerning the different benefit distribution for inpatient care *between* the schemes, it has been found that the more advantaged group is always favored compared to the less advantaged group. This also holds true for the differences *within* the three schemes regarding to the levels of income, regions and the degree of urbanization. (One exception is the difference between the western and eastern provinces where more benefits are received by the disadvantaged western provinces.) Analyzing the development over time, above investigation was able to show that the inequitable differences which were found *between* the three insurance schemes have improved. However, the investigation of the differences *within* did not lead to a clear picture.

3.1.3 Payments according to the ability to pay

Looking at fundraising according to the ability to pay, the two main financing mechanisms – taxes and social health insurance – can be analyzed.

Regarding the fundraising through the tax system, there are mainly three levels that are of interest: 1. The distribution between political governing levels (national vs. local). 2. The distribution between provinces (rich vs. poor). 3. The distribution between regions (urban vs. rural).

Concerning the first level, the distribution between political governing levels (national vs. local), one of the major observations is the high fragmentation of the institutional structure of Chinese politics. Concerning the tax system, especially the five vertical levels of state council, provincial government, city government, county government and township government (Figure 10) are important[20] (Liu and Yi, 2004, p. 14; Word Bank, 2013, p. xxiii). In the Chinese system, health financing is decentralized and resources are mainly collected at the two lowest of the five vertical levels – county and township government (Brixi et al., 2011, p. 3). Two sides of the tax system should receive attention: Firstly, the process of levying taxes and secondly the process of distributing tax revenues.

---

[20] A graphical depiction of the financing of health insurance can be found in Yip et al. (Yip et al., 2012, p. 835).

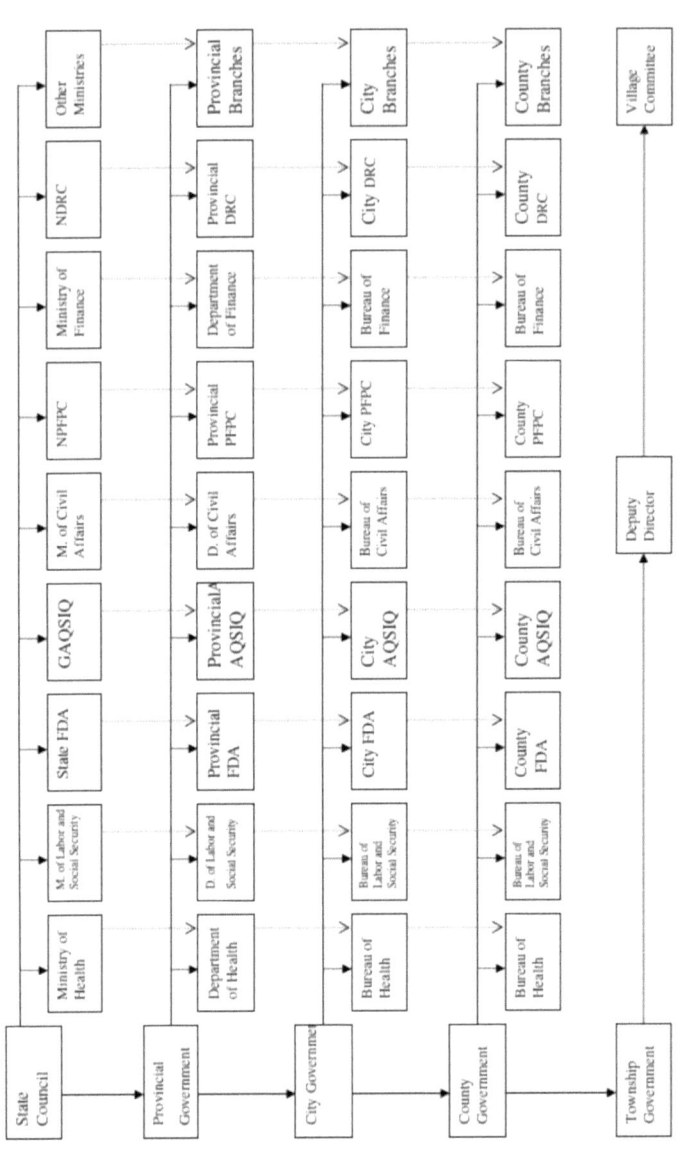

Figure 10: "Overall administrative structure of health sector" (Liu and Yi, 2004, p. 14; also compare Yip et al., 2012, p. 835).

48

Due to statutory orders that ascribe the right to levy taxes to the central government, local governments are left with a limited autonomy to raise their income through taxes (such as user charges and property tax). Empirical evidences show that the disparity of fiscal capacity between local governments, and therefore fiscal inequity, has increased. The rise of fiscal inequity can be observed before and after 1994, when the tax system was reformed[21]. The situation might even have worsened further since 2004, when important local governmental tax laws were abolished[22] without adequate compensation. Consequences of this underdeveloped tax base are insufficient fiscal capacities on the local level and difficulties in providing the demanded health care services. Differences in fiscal capacity between provinces do mainly arise from different economic levels, but also from policies, such as tax reductions that often favor rich provinces instead of supporting the poor (Hong, 2010, pp. 11–14). The observed inequality in the tax levying process therefore exists due to "inappropriate" inequalities and can be labeled inequitable.

Regarding the second level, the distribution between provinces (rich vs. poor), the central government has implemented a formula-based adjustment mechanism with the aim to equalize transfers and the different fiscal capacities across China's provinces. According to measures of expenditure needs and fiscal capacity central government's grants are distributed to different localities (Brixi et al., 2011, p. 3). Enrolment subsidies for example do exist for western and central regions but not for eastern provinces. In this case, the division between central, provincial, and municipal funding for Ningxia, a relatively poor northwestern province, is ¥124, ¥68, ¥8. For Shandong, a relatively rich eastern province it is ¥0, ¥55, ¥75 and, on the county level, ¥70 (Yip et al., 2012, p. 834). These grants can be labeled equitable because they (re)distribute taxes according to different needs of the regions. This finding holds true despite the fact that the distribution mechanisms have been valued "non-predictable" and "non-transparent"

---

[21] The tax-sharing reform of 1994 established a national and a local tax bureau that were acting independently from each other. The central government has thereby strengthened the role of the national agency's tax levy rights and weakened the local ones (Hong, 2010, p. 72).
[22] The shift of the right to levy taxes from local to central governmental levels is viewed as sense making as it reduces the competition between localities for the lowest tax rates (Hong, 2010, p. 34). The negative impact of this reform does not primarily originate from the shift of rights, but more from the insufficient compensation.

(Hong, 2010, pp. 11–14) and redistribution is seen to insufficiently follow the needs and payment abilities of the regions and provinces (Yip et al., 2012, p. 839).

Concerning the third level, the distribution between regions (urban vs. rural), rural and urban residents who are not covered receive additional financial support of ¥200 (a tenfold increase since 2003) to enroll in NCMS or URBMI. In addition, the Civil Affairs Ministry pays an individual contribution for 68.76 million poor people through the MFA program (Marten et al., 2014, p. 4; Yip et al., 3, p. 834). In recent years, total public spending on health has risen considerably. For the period 2009-2011, an additional spending of ¥850 billion (2.8% of 2008 GDP) was granted by Premier Wen Jiabao at the 11th National People's Congress. This decision led to an increase of government funding from 0.7-0.9% to 1.4% of GDP. With this increase, China still spends less than the average of 2% of other middle income countries but gets closer to the necessary 1.5-2.0% estimated by the WHO (Brixi et al., 2011, p. 2). As all these financing mechanisms support those in need, the general tendency can again be labeled equitable, even if their amount might not yet be sufficient.

The second financing mechanism (besides the tax system) is social health insurance (SHI). Again, it is important to differentiate the mechanisms that concern the different ability to pay *between* and *within* the three main insurance schemes – UEBMI, URBMI and NCMS. The further analysis of the costs that individuals have to contribute to SHI will be drawn from Table 8.

	UEMI		URBMI		NCMS	
	2008	2010	2008	2010	2008	2010
Target population	Formal sector urban workers	Formal sector urban workers	Children, students, elderly people without previous employment and migrants (in some cities)	Children, students, elderly people without previous employment and migrants (in some cities)	Rural residents	Rural residents
Risk-pooling unit	City	City	City	City	County	County
Enrollment, %	80·7%	92·4%	63·8%	92·9%	90·0%	96·6%
Total premium per person (¥)*	1443	1559	131	138	96	157
Government subsidy per person	0	0	80	120 (200 in 2011)	80	120 (200 in 2011)
Central government contribution	0	0	40	60 (100 in 2011)	40	60 (100 in 2011)
Individual contribution†	2-3% of salary (about ¥494-741)‡	2-3% of salary (about ¥454-741)‡	20-170 in central and western provinces; 40-250 in eastern provinces‡	20-170 in central and western provinces; 40-250 in eastern provinces‡	20-30 in western and central provinces; 30-50 in eastern provinces‡	20-30 in western and central provinces; 30-50 in eastern provinces‡
Employer contribution†	6-8% of salary (about ¥1483-1977)‡	6-8% of salary (about ¥1483-1977)‡	0	0	0	0
Benefit design						
Inpatient reimbursement rate (%)§	67·0%	68·2%	43·8%	47·9%	37·8%	43·9%
% of counties or cities covering general outpatient care	Savings accounts	Savings accounts	12·5%	57·5%	29·1%	78·8%
% of counties or cities covering outpatient care for major and chronic disease	Savings accounts	Savings accounts	61·6%	82·7%¶	63·0%	89·4%¶
Total reimbursement ceiling	NA	Six-times average wage of employee in the city	NA	Six-times disposable income of local residents	NA	Six-times income of local farmers

¥6·5 is about US$1. UEBMI=Urban Employee Basic Medical Insurance. URBMI=Urban Resident Basic Medical Insurance. NCMS=New Cooperative Medical Scheme. NA=data not available. *For UEBMI and NCMS, total premium can be greater than the sum of government subsidies and individual contribution because local governments can contribute more than the minimally required amount. †Variations exist in western, central, and eastern provinces because individuals in richer provinces contribute more than the minimum required amount. ‡2009 data. §% total inpatient expenditure reimbursed by insurance taking into account deductible, copayment, and ceiling. ¶Rates as of end of March, 2011.

Table 8: "Summary of three social health insurance programs" (Yip et al. 2012, p. 835).

Regarding the difference *between* the insurance schemes, Table 8 shows that the less privileged part of the population is favored at all occasions. To make this clearer, the difference between the economically underprivileged and the more privileged insurance scheme has been calculated in Table 9. In both localities under investigation – central and western, as well as eastern provinces – the results show a lower individual contribution in insurance schemes that target the economically underprivileged. Furthermore, it can be seen that the difference *between* the two schemes that insure not-working people (URBMI and NCMS)[23] is the lowest and both of these schemes show high differences towards the scheme which is only for workers (UEBMI). Out of these two (URBMI and NCMS), the least privileged (NCMS) shows the highest differences towards the scheme solely insuring working people (UEBMI). Health insurance is therefore issued by taking into account income and wealth. Due to these findings, it can be followed that inequality in the individual contribution rate is equitable.

individual contribution (in ¥)	social health insurance programs			difference ("between")		
	UEBMI (from-to)	URBMI (from-to)	NCMS (from-to)	URBMI-UEBMI (from-to)	NCMS-UEBMI (from-to)	NCMS-URBMI (from-to)
cities	494 741					
central&western provinces		20 170	20 30	-474 -571	-474 -711	0 -140
eastern provinces		40 250	30 50	-454 -491	-464 -691	-10 -200
difference ("within")	247	20 80	10 20	20 80	10 20	-10 -60

Table 9: "Individual contribution in the three social health insurance programs, 2010", numbers from Yip et al. 2012 p. 835, author's investigation.

---

[23] "Children, students, elderly people without previous employment and migrants (in some cities)" in the URBMI scheme and "Rural residents" in the NCMS scheme (Yip et al., 2012, p. 835).

52

The differences that can be observed *within* the health insurance schemes favors people living in western and central provinces compared to those in eastern provinces. The amount of this difference varies between ¥20-80 for URBMI and ¥10-20 for NCMS (for UEBMI the relevant numbers are missing) (Table 9). Again, both schemes raise the individual contribution according to the financial capability of the insured. It is therefore labeled equitable. Furthermore, within each scheme differences are visible that stem from lower contributions of individuals in relatively poor provinces and higher contributions from individuals in richer provinces. In UEBMI, people pay ¥494-741, in URBMI ¥20-250, and in NCMS ¥20-50 (Yip et al., 2012, p. 835). Again, it can be stated that health insurance is financed according to personal income and wealth and the individual financial situations are, at least partly, balanced.

3.1.4 Intermediate findings and interpretation

To finally understand how benefits are distributed in China and if the system puts a special emphasis on vulnerable groups, a study by van Doorslaer and O'Donnell is central, where the impact and interrelation of direct payments, pre-payments and benefits in China are analyzed (Doorslaer and O'Donnell, 2008, p. 3). Using the Concentration and Kakwani index, the authors furthermore find that high-income households contribute more financial resources to the health system than low-income households but also consume a higher amount of health care services[24] (Doorslaer and O'Donnell, 2008, pp. 4–5). If pre-payments (3.1.3) are interpreted as contributions and direct payments (e.g. through OOP) (3.1.1 and 3.1.2) as cost, then the examination undertaken above supports the findings that the better-off contribute more (labeled equitable) but at the same time receive more (labeled inequitable). The financing system of the PRC is therefore regarded as following the inequality increasing benefit principle (Doorslaer and O'Donnell, 2008, pp. 4–5).

Measuring the incidence of public spending on health care (pre-payment) in relation to the distribution of income, van Doorslaer and O'Donnell find that China's public

---

[24] Similar results, a higher contribution to (Brixi et al., 2011, p. 5) and use of medical care (Xie, 2011) by the rich, are also found in more recent studies.

spending is pro-rich. Paradoxically, public spending is also found to be inequality-reducing (Doorslaer and O'Donnell, 2008, p. 15). The conflicting finding that health spending in China is pro-rich but inequality-reducing at the same time can be explained by the crowding out effect. Government spending might reduce the payments on health for the rich (crowding out) but less so for the poor. It is pro-rich in this spirit. As however, the poor are only able to consume health care because of this small additional government spending, their demand and access to health services might rise. The demand of the rich on the other hand might stay unchanged or only rise slightly as they have already been able to access health services before. In this spirit, the pro-rich government spending can at the same time be inequality-reducing (Doorslaer and O'Donnell, 2008, p. 16). Despite this positive connotation, it has to be concluded that a higher inequality-reducing effect could be achieved if government spending would support those in need. Currently, the inequality increasing benefit principle is still prevalent; hence the situation is still judged as inequitable and should be targeted in further policy reforms.

As the findings of this and earlier sections do not draw from the same sources, it is remarkable that both approaches detect the same tendency. In short, two characteristics can be found regarding the re-distribution mechanisms within the Chinese health insurance system: (1) Re-distribution mechanisms follow the benefit-principle, because although contributions to the system do not show inequities (that is the rich pay more than the poor), health services are consumed inequitable (that is the rich consume more than the poor). (2) Public health spending is pro-rich (inequity), however, at the same time granting access to the poor (inequality reducing)[25]. In addition, it might be added that these negative tendencies have shown to have improved over time. Hence, it may also be concluded that China is in many aspects, despite its existing inequities, moving towards a more equitable situation.

---

[25] In other words, while China is currently supporting a pro-rich growth strategy in absolute terms, it is at the same time achieving a relative pro-poor growth (Slaymaker et al., 2007, p. 7).

3.2 The depth dimension in China

In the "depth-part" of the "Definition and Concept" chapter (2.2), health economic theory has pointed towards the need of health services being appropriate in the sense that they increase people's health. A further, more practical approach by the WHO has pointed towards the possibility of ranking medical services according to their efficiency in generating health. The approach which was found most useful concerning this question is the classification of potential services into three categories: high, middle and low. The criteria for a service to be ranked as a high-priority service includes a high cost-effectiveness ratio, the support of vulnerable parts of the population and a high impact on financial risk protection. Out of these three criteria, the results of cost-effectiveness analyses (CEA) were ranked most important. The following analysis will therefore start with an investigation of the Chinese health system and institutions and their capability to assure the delivery of appropriate health care to their people (3.2.1). Furthermore, below analysis will go beyond the situation of China in 2011 and will investigate which services should be prioritized when health care is expended. In order to be able to undertake an in-depth analysis, the second part (3.2.2) will focus on investigating the cost and effectiveness – and additionally the benefits – of NCDs in China.

3.2.1 The situation of appropriate health care in China

As suggested above, this section will be concerned with the question in how far the Chinese health insurance system is able to assure access to "appropriate" care and exclude "inappropriate" care from insurance through a need oriented catalog of benefits. One of the major problems concerning the implementation of a need oriented catalog of benefits is the institutional fragmentation of the Chinese health system (compare section 3.1.3). [26] A horizontal (multiple institutions at the same governmental level) diversification as well as a vertical (different levels of the government) can be found (Liu and Yi, 2004, p. 13; Yip et al., 3, p. 835).

---

[26] A positive aspect of this multi-ministry system is the large number of financial sources and the administrative support it can draw from (UN, 2005, p. 29).

On the horizontal level, the following ministries are involved in the policy making process: "the National Development and Reform Commission, the ministries of Agriculture, Construction, Finance, Health, Labor and Social Security, Science and Technology, the State Food and Drug Administration, the State Administration of Traditional Chinese Medicine, Ministry of Civil Affairs and the National Population and Family Planning Commission and several others" (UN, 2005, p. 29). One of the main problems arising from this administrative structure is the missing clarification of each ministry's role, leading to over- as well as under-provision (UN, 2005, p. 33[27]).

In addition, the Chinese administrative system is spread over five vertical governmental levels: central, provincial, prefectural, county, and township (Liu and Yi, 2004, p. 13; Word Bank, 2013, p. xxiii). As already described in the above section on payments (3.1.3), China went through a massive shift of health care responsibilities towards lower governmental levels (Meng et al., 2012b, p. 805). As the central government also reduced its spending on health (Meng et al., 2012b, p. 812), today, a substantial share of the medical costs is shouldered by lower governmental levels (Meng et al., 2012b, p. 812). The volume of a package of benefits does therefore largely depend on the financial situation of the relevant local subdivisions (Meng et al., 2012b, p. 812). Redistributions between regions and provinces do furthermore not sufficiently follow the needs and the payment abilities of citizens (Yip et al., 2012, p. 839), leaving remote and rural areas unable to provide sufficient specialized care – including emergency obstetric services and trauma, adequate facilities, and trained health professionals (WHO, 2008b, pp. 10–11). As a consequence, underutilization of health services by the poor, as well as underinvestment in public health goods can be observed (WHO, 2008b, pp. 10–11).

Concentrating on the benefit package of the Chinese health system, the vertical fragmentation is identified as the source of mismanagement. In China, the first vertical level, the central government, defines the benefit packages for three medical fields: drugs, services and equipment[28] (Stuecker, 2008, p. 6). The national essential drug list

---

[27] Similar to the comment above, also these statements can be regarded as valid despite the early publication date, due to the phenomenon of path dependency (Page, 2006).
[28] The third list that is concerned with equipment, and therefore the structural quality of health care institutions (Stuecker, 2008, p. 6), will not be examined in detail. Firstly, because it is only indirectly referring medical treatment and, secondly, information from the literature is insufficient.

includes 21 categories of western drugs, eight categories of traditional Chinese medicines and one category of prepared Chinese herbal medicines (Liu and Yi, 2004, p. 39)[29]. The national essential services list is compiled by three characteristics:

> "1) the items are clinically necessary, safe and effective, expenditure appropriate; 2) their prices have been set by Pricing Bureaus; 3) they are various diagnosis and treatment items provided by designated health facilities within the scope of designated medical services" (Liu and Yi, 2004, p. 39).

This framework allows three conclusions concerning the Chinese system: 1. clinically unnecessary services with uncertain efficacies or belonging to special medical service categories (e.g. having an operation earlier than scheduled, naming a higher ranked doctor to carry out the operation) are not financed by insurance. 2. Clinically necessary items with proven efficacy that may however be easily abused or expensive, will only partly be covered by the basic health insurance. 3. Within the living facilities at hospitals, only hospital bed fees are covered (Liu and Yi, 2004, pp. 39–40; Yip et al., 2012, p. 838). Leaving out the medical discussion of the question which drugs and services are "appropriate" and which are "inappropriate",[30] the Chinese package of benefits seems, at least mainly and de jure, to follow the requests of UHC as laid out above: cost sharing tools are not used to reduce health care use in general (compare economic theory in 2.2.1). Instead, the differentiation between "appropriate" and "inappropriate" services is leading the decision about coverage. Merely the issue of "appropriate expenditure" (Liu and Yi, 2004, p. 39; Yip et al., 2012, p. 838), which has been mentioned above, might lead to decisions where copayment measures are introduced due to economic (easiness of abuse and price level) instead of medical arguments (clinical necessity and efficiency) (Liu and Yi, 2004, pp. 39–40; Yip et al., 2012, p. 838). This is contrary to the theory theoretical findings (2.2.1), where copayment tools are assumed to have the best effect if adapted to "inappropriate" services (Newhouse, 2004, p. 111). Too many financial restrains might be the consequence of this regulation and might overshadow decisions that should be made according to "appropriateness" and "inappropriateness". In other words, the result may be a "limited benefit package and large scope of uncovered services" (Liu and Yi, 2004, p. 41).

---

[29] Also compare Yip et al. (Yip et al., 2012, p. 838).
[30] The quality of the national and local lists is indeed a matter of discussion (Yip et al., 2012, p. 838).

In addition to the competencies that the central government holds, also the second vertical level, the local government, is involved in the constitution of the content of the benefit package in form of the essential drug list. The 21 categories of western drugs and 8 categories of traditional Chinese medicines, that are included in the national essential drug list, include A and B types of drugs. Local governments are allowed to add 15% of B-type-drugs (Liu and Yi, 2004, p. 39) to that list. To reach a low price and ensure the quality of drugs, a province-based competitive-bidding system has been set up. [31] While the National Development and Reform Commission tracks the price and supply of essential medicines on the market and sets price ceilings for drugs on the essential list, pharmaceutical manufacturers are bidding for the price via internet. Due to unclear selection criteria on the local provincial level however, corruption is reducing the system's efficiency. [32] The above mentioned possibility of local governments to add 15% of B-type drugs has led to corruptive influence and the inclusion of formerly excluded "inappropriate" medicine. For example cimetidine and diethylstilbestrol had been excluded from the national drugs list because of their negative side-effects or low effectiveness, but have been restored to the provincial supplementary list again (Yip et al., 2012, p. 837). This procedure is highly against theoretical requests as "inappropriate" services can be financed by social health insurance that might serve financial interests of the pharmaceutical industry, but neither the health of the patients nor the efficiency interests of the financiers.

A second problem emerges from the horizontal fragmentation of the health system's institutions. The national essential drug list only binds public primary health-care institutions to stock and sell solely the defined drugs (Yip et al., 2012, p. 834). The second and third tire, out of the three tiers of the health network[33], heavily rely on "encourag[ing] doctors to prescribe more and costlier drugs to earn mark-ups" (Liu and

---

[31] As an adequate quality control of medicine is still missing in China, competitive bidding on prices has not only resulted in a reduction of price, but also in a quality reduction of drugs. Furthermore, manufacturers sometimes fail to deliver the drugs for which they have signed contracts and thereby create shortages (Yip et al., 2012, p. 834).

[32] It is reported that corruption is allowing providers to receive kickbacks despite the control attempt of the national governmental level (Yip et al., 2012, p. 837).

[33] The three tires are primary health care, secondary care and tertiary care. In the rural sector they consist of 1. village clinics, 2. township hospitals, 3. county hospitals; In the urban sector they are 1. street health stations, 2. community health centers, 3. district hospitals (Liu and Yi, 2004, p. 50).

Yi, 2004, p. 11; see also Sun et al., 2008, p. 1047). Although primary health-care institutions are *de jure* required to sell their drugs with zero-profit[34], this regulation does not apply to second and third tire hospitals (Liu and Yi, 2004, p. 11; Yip et al., 2012, pp. 834, 838). The *de facto* implementation within the first tier is equally far from successful in preventing misuse. As the financial resources are limited, local governments have not been able to introduce payment mechanisms that would compensate physicians for the loss of income that a zero-price policy on drugs effectively means (drug revenues in the primary sector account for more than 50% of revenue and bonuses for staff are tied to these profits) (Yip et al., 2012, p. 840). The magnitude of these incomes in second and third tire hospitals is comparably high. Total hospital income generated from the selling of drugs was accounted for about 45%-58% in 2008 (Stuecker, 2008, p. 5). Looking at the remaining roughly 50% of income, it becomes obvious that also in this case economic reasons overrule medical needs. In 2010, government operated general hospitals only received 7.2% of their income through government subsidies and generated 92.6% by selling services and medicines[35] [36] (Meng et al., 2012b, p. 813). A further aspect that visualizes the power of economic reasoning over medical concerns is that roughly 50% of the total income of senior physicians is earned through corruption involving pharmaceutical companies and individuals and hence only about 2% of all prescribed drugs are compliant with best practice according to the medical needs of the patients (Liu and Yi, 2004, p. 42; Sun et al., 2008, p. 1047). It can therefore be stated that all three tires are massively relying on revenues generated by selling medicines and diagnostic services and are heavily steered by corruption (Liu and Yi, 2004, pp. 11, 42; Meng et al., 2012b, p. 813; Sun et al., 2008, p. 1047; Yip et al., 3, p. 840).

Hence, it has to be stated that the lack of the *de facto* implementation of the essential service and medical lists neutralizes the positive judgments made for the *de jure* generation of these lists. It seems that medical care which is given by Chinese health service providers is not primarily motivated by the differentiation between "appropriate"

---

[34] Health insurance programs additionally have to provide higher reimbursement for these drugs (Yip et al., 2012, p. 834).
[35] A similar financing structure can be found in for-profit-hospitals (Stuecker, 2008, p. 4).
[36] This dependency has its roots in the reform of the 1990s when the central government withdrew from financing health care. Back then, the physicians' and hospitals' income became dependent on fees for services and the selling of drugs (Alcorn and Bao, 2011, p. 1558; Liu and Yi, 2004, p. 11).

and "inappropriate" care or the needs of patients. Instead profit maximization seems to be the main motivation of health service provision.

Not having managed to *de facto* implement a need oriented catalog of benefits that builds on "appropriate" care, the access to health care cannot be regarded as health increasing. The positive effects of rising reimbursement rates (Meng et al., 2012b, p. 810), the increasing hospital admission rates and the decreasing rates of inpatient self-discharge (Meng et al., 2012b, p. 809) are (at least partly) offset by the "inappropriateness" of volumes of services supplied and of medicines prescribed (Meng et al., 2012b, p. 813).

As there are strong evidences for misleading payment incentives [37] and severe corruption (Liu and Yi, 2004, pp. 11, 42; Meng et al., 2012b, p. 813; Sun et al., 2008, p. 1047; Yip et al., 3, p. 840), upcoming reforms have to include provider payment systems and not only the insurance system. Health insurance could however play a crucial role in the strengthening of the primary care system. So far, financial incentives are favoring hospital outpatient departments over primary care facilities. Only in a few municipalities, financial incentives have been initiated to promote primary care use, including higher levels of reimbursement and outpatient coverage for primary care services. Overall, the reimbursement rate for inpatient care remains higher than for outpatient care (Meng et al., 2012b, p. 813) and people are increasingly using more of it while the use of outpatient care stagnates (Meng et al., 2012b, p. 809). The role of a gate keeper is therefore nearly absent in the Chinese health system and people use specialized hospitals for the treatment of minor illnesses (Yip et al., 2012, p. 836). "Inappropriate" hospital admission rates could be lowered if reimbursement policies would focus more on strengthening outpatient and primary care (Meng et al., 2012b, p. 813).

One of the fields where outpatient and primary health care could play a more central role is the field of NCDs. This topic will be discussed in the next chapter (3.2.2).

---

[37] The underlying reason is mainly seen in the fee-for-service payment method and the extra profits that can be gained through the selling of drugs (Alcorn and Bao, 2011, p. 1558).

3.2.2 Relevance of the NCD-topic

The relevance of the topic of NCD becomes obvious through at least three different aspects. Firstly, the largest part of deaths in lower-middle income countries can be attributed to NCDs. Secondly, the "deadly quartet" (see below) is directly linked to a large share of these deaths. Thirdly, in China the monetary burden resulting from these risk factors is already huge and mostly still growing. These three observations will be explained in more detail below.

Among the "Top 10 causes of death in lower-middle income countries", NCDs play a large role (Figure 12). Ischemic heart disease, stroke, COPD, diabetes mellitus and cirrhosis of the liver make up 62.15%[38] and consequently the majority of deaths. Comparing the situation of "lower-middle income countries" to "high income countries", the importance of NCDs becomes even more obvious. In "high income countries", NCDs contribute 94%[39] (Figure 11) to the deaths of the top-ten group and 87% to the total (WHO, 2014b, 2014c). Looking at the historical development, the share of NCDs in these countries shows a large increase from roughly 20% 100 years ago (Kolenda and Ratje, 2013, p. 9) to today's 94%. It is therefore not unrealistic to assume a similar development in lower and middle income countries such as China (FAO, 2006; Herd et al., 2010; Mayer-Foulkes and Pescetto-Villouta, 2012, p. 15).

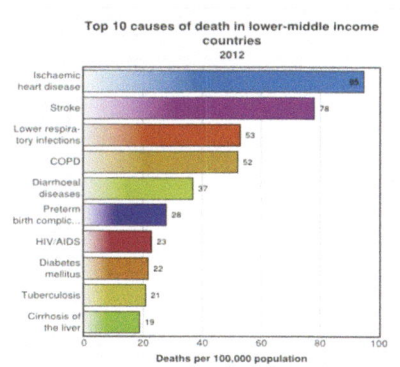
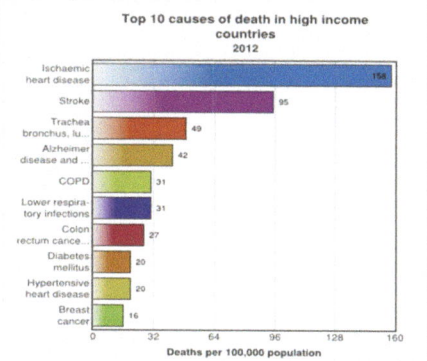

Figure 12: "Top 10 causes of death in lower-middle income countries, 2012" (WHO 2014a).

Figure 11: "Top 10 causes of death in high income countries, 2012" (WHO 2014a).

[38] %NCD = total deaths by NCDs / total deaths = 266/428 = 0,6215.
[39] %NCD = 1 - (deaths by „lower respiratory infections" / total deaths) = 1 - (31/489) = 0,94.

61

Secondly, the most important risk factors and physiological risk markers for the above mentioned NCDs, the so called "deadly quartet" makes up a large share of the observable disease burden. It consists of tobacco use [40], dietary risks, physical inactivity and alcohol abuse (Chisholm et al., 2011; Kolenda and Ratje, 2013; WHO, 2011b, p. 14). According to the Global Burden of Disease study of WHO, the first of these four factors, tobacco use, is responsible for 2.6 million deaths in middle

	Risk Factor	Deaths (millions)	Total (percentage)
1	High blood pressure	4.2	17.2
2	Tobacco use	2.6	10.8
3	Overweight and obesity	1.6	6.7
4	Physical inactivity	1.6	6.6
5	Alcohol use	1.6	6.4
6	High blood glucose level	1.5	6.3
7	High cholesterol level	1.3	5.2
8	Low fruit and vegetable intake	0.9	3.9
9	Indoor smoke from solid fuels	0.7	2.8
10	Urban outdoor air pollution	0.7	2.8

Table 10: "The 10 leading risk factors for death in middle income countries", 2004 data (Narayan et al. 2010, p. 1197).

income countries like China. This makes up 17.2% of the total death rate in these countries. Low fruit and vegetable intake, one aspect of the dietary risk factor, leads to 0.9 million deaths (3.9% of all deaths). Physical inactivity, factor number three, accounts for about 1.6 million deaths, which is 6.6% of the total (Table 10). Additionally, dietary habits and low physical activity are closely linked to physiological risk markers which are very dominant within the 10 most important factors: High blood pressure (4.2 million deaths, 17.2%), overweight and obesity (1.6 million deaths, 6.7%), high blood glucose level (1.5 million deaths, 6.3%) and high cholesterol level (1.3 million deaths, 5.2%). The combined effects of diet and physical activity are therefore much more significant than those attributable to each of them individually[41]. The fourth of the above mentioned risk factors, alcohol consumption, is responsible for 1.6 million deaths, a total of 6.4% of all deaths in middle income countries (Narayan et al., 2010, p. 1197; WHO, 2009).

---

[40] A detailed description of the "smoking epidemic" can be found in "Improving China's Health Care System" (Herd et al., 2010, pp. 9–10).
[41] It is impossible to tell the amount that these risk factors account for in combination, because of their interdependence and overlapping. Simply summing up the numbers would therefore most probably overestimate their effect.
It may additionally be added, that a shift from meat intensive to mainly vegetable based eating habits would also contribute to the reduction of air pollution (Amann et al., 2014, pp. 8–12) and hence a further reduction of the death rate. Including the indirect effects of a healthy diet has therefore a larger effect than is claimed above.

Using numbers from the IHME's burden of disease study, it is possible to draw a more precise picture for China. The first category, tobacco use, is responsible for 1.4 million deaths in this country. The second one, dietary risks, accounts for 2.5 million deaths. Looking at the two sub categories of dietary risks which were mentioned in Table 10, it is found that 1.4 million people die from low fruit and 0.2 million from low vegetable intake. Physical inactivity accounts for 0.5 and alcohol use for 0.4 million deaths. The associated physiological risk markers account for 2.0 million deaths regarding high blood pressure, 0.4 million due to

Risk factor	Deaths (millions)
Tobacco use	1.4
Dietary risks	2.5
Physical inactivity	0.5
Alcohol use	0.4

Table 11: "The 'deadly quartet' in China", 2010 data (IHME 2014a), author's contribution.

a high body mass index, 0.6 million due to high fasting plasma glucoses and 0.3 million due to high total cholesterol (Table 11).

The third aspect that makes the NCD topic a relevant research area is its high monetary burden[42]. In order to derive data concerning the economic burden, this analysis uses an approach from OECD that builds on the country-specific value of a statistical life (VSL) (OECD, 2014a, 2012, pp. 13–15). More details of this approach can be found in section 3.2.3.2 and Annex 4. Adapting this calculation, it is possible to take a look at the specific situation of China. The graphics and numbers below are showing results per 100.000 Inhabitants in order to be able to make a comparison between the different population sizes in each of the three years. Regarding the earliest and latest measured data, it can be observed that the three risk factors tobacco use, unhealthy diet and physical inactivity are increasing – alcohol use shows a slight decreasing tendency (Table 12, Figure 13).

---

[42] This section refrains from providing a comparative analysis between different countries because it is not vitally important for the later analysis and is furthermore prone to equity issues that would need further discussions (Annex 5). However, taking into account the basic equity concerns, a comparison between the status quo of China, Europe and the USA is presented in Annex 6.

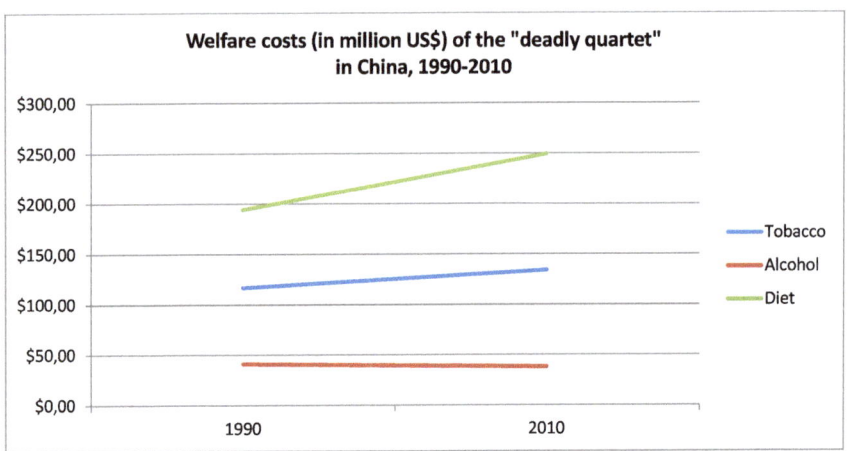

Figure 13: "Welfare costs (in million USD) of the 'deadly quartet' in China", per 100,000 inhabitants, 1990-2010 data, health data from IHME (IHME, 2014a), author's calculations.

In recent years (data from 2005 and 2010), the upward trend is not as clear as for the 20 year period from 1990 till 2010. However, in these years, additional data is available for the risk factor physical inactivity which clearly shows a growing tendency (Table 12, Figure 14).

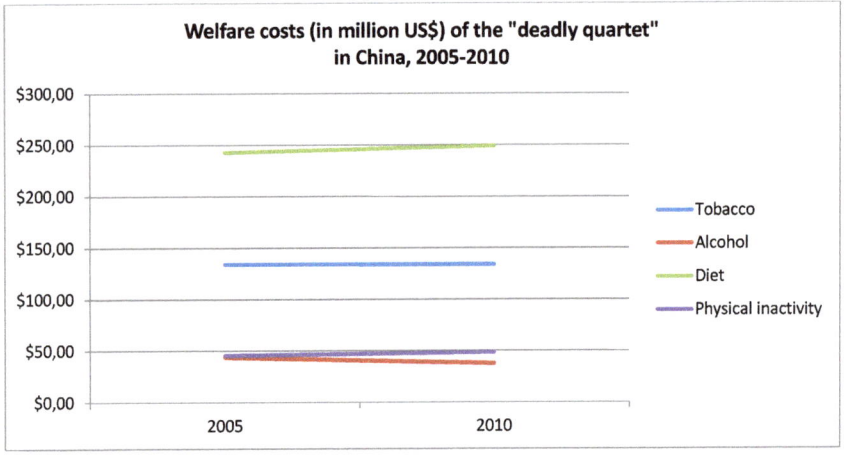

Figure 14: "Welfare costs (in million USD) of the 'deadly quartet' in China", per 100,000 inhabitants, 2005-2010 data, health data from IHME (IHME, 2014a), author's calculations.

The three reasons that consolidate the relevance of the NCD topic are summed up in Table 12 below. It builds on data from the IHME database for the years 1990, 2005 and 2010 (IHME, 2014b) and shows death numbers, DALYs and monetary losses from mortality and morbidity.

	Tobacco				Alcohol			
	Deaths (mortality per 100.000)	DALY (mortality & morbidity	Mio. US$ (mortality)	Mio. US$ (mortality & morbidity	Deaths (mortality per 100.000)	DALY (mortality & morbidity	Mio. US$ (mortality)	Mio. US$ (mortality & morbidity
1990	87.57	2,430.18	$105.98	$116.58	30.50	1,117.43	$36.91	$40.60
2005	100.60	2,296.36	$121.75	$133.93	32.65	1,169.82	$39.52	$43.47
2010	100.45	2,206.51	$121.58	$133.74	28.20	1,013.35	$34.13	$37.54

	Diet				Physical inactivity			
	Deaths (mortality per 100.000)	DALY (mortality & morbidity	Mio. US$ (mortality)	Mio. US$ (mortality & morbidity	Deaths (mortality per 100.000)	DALY (mortality & morbidity	Mio. US$ (mortality)	Mio. US$ (mortality & morbidity
1990	145.60	3,199.08	$176.23	$193.85				
2005	182.25	3,806.96	$220.58	$242.64	34.02	805.97	$41.17	$45.29
2010	186.97	3,801.99	$226.29	$248.91	36.42	841.18	$44.08	$48.49

Table 12: "Welfare costs of the "deadly quartet" in China (per 100,000 inhabitants)", 1990-2010 data, in 2010 million USD, health data from IHME (IHME 2014a), author's calculations.

These results are already showing the large burden from unhealthy diets (with roughly USD 250 million), a five times higher financial burden than for physical inactivity and alcohol (with roughly USD 50 million). Even compared to the burden arising from tobacco use (around USD 130 million), dietary issues account for nearly double the burden (Table 12).

As mentioned above, welfare costs were calculated per 100.000 inhabitants in order to compare different years. Looking at the total population (and only at the year 2010), the burden in China equals 30 thousand DALYs or USD 1.8 trillion for tobacco related diseases, nearly 14 thousand DALYs or USD half a trillion for alcohol, 52 thousand DALYs or USD 3.4 trillion for diet and 11 thousand DALYs or USD 2 trillion for physical inactivity related diseases (Table 13). Naturally, within the context of the total population, the burden resulting from dietary risks is also around five times higher than the one from alcohol and physical inactivity, and nearly double as high as the burden from tobacco related risks (Table 13).

Welfare costs of the "deadly quartet" in China, 2010			
Deaths (mortality)	DALY (mortality & morbidity)	Mio. US$ (mortality)	Mio. US$ (mortality & morbidity)
Tobacco	1,365,980	30,004,600	$1,653,245.81	$1,818,570.39
Alcohol	383,479	13,779,800	$464,124.70	$510,537.16
Diet	2,542,410	51,700,300	$3,077,079.23	$3,384,787.15
Physical inactivity	495,305	11,438,600	$1,801,101.35	$1,981,211.49

Table 13: "Welfare costs of the 'deadly quartet' in China", 2010 data, total population, in 2010 million USD, health data from IHME (IHME 2014a), author's calculations.

Doing these calculations for the physiological risk markers, one can see that the burden equals nearly 40 thousand DALYs or USD 2.5 trillion for high blood pressure, more than 12 thousand DALYs or USD 0.5 trillion for high BMI, 16 thousand DALYs or USD 0.7 trillion for high fasting plasma glucose and close to 6 thousand DALYs or USD 0.4 trillion for physical inactivity related diseases (Table 14).

Welfare costs of the "deadly quartet" in China, 2010			
Deaths (mortality)	DALY (mortality & morbidity)	Mio. US$ (mortality)	Mio. US$ (mortality & morbidity)
Tobacco	1,365,980	30,004,600	$1,653,245.81	$1,818,570.39
Alcohol	383,479	13,779,800	$464,124.70	$510,537.16
High blood presure	2,042,690	37,939,900	$2,472,268.03	$2,719,494.84
High BMI	362,707	12,256,300	$438,984.34	$482,882.77
High fasting plasma glucose	562,195	16,102,600	$680,424.70	$748,467.17
High total cholesterol	280,574	5,911,580	$339,578.76	$373,536.63

Table 14: "Welfare costs of the "deadly quartet" and the physiological risk markers in China", 2010 data, total population, in 2010 million USD, health data from IHME (IHME 2014a), author's calculations.

3.2.3 What are possible health interventions to reduce this burden?

Health interventions proposed for the reduction of the burden linked to the "deadly quartet" and the physiological risk markers are numerous and this analysis will not be able to address all of them. Although, this work will contribute an important analysis complementing what the WHO identified as "best buy" interventions. They are defined as being most important for the "current and projected burden of diseases (or their underlying risk factors, such as tobacco use), the cost effectiveness[43], fairness and feasibility of implementing interventions and political considerations" (Chisholm et al., 2011, p. 11). These criteria are identified by the WHO to guarantee a well-founded basis for policy makers' decision processes (Chisholm et al., 2011, p. 11). Table 15 gives a short overview about the interventions that were declared best buy interventions in the WHO paper:

Core intervention set: best buys

Population-based interventions addressing NCD risk factors	Tobacco use: Tax increases; smoke-free indoor workplaces and public places; health information and warnings about tobacco; bans on advertising and promotion Harmful alcohol use: Tax increases on alcoholic beverages; comprehensive restrictions and bans on alcohol marketing; restrictions on the availability of retailed alcohol Unhealthy diet and physical inactivity: Salt reduction through mass media campaigns and reduced salt content in processed foods; replacement of trans-fats with polyunsaturated fats; public awareness program about diet and physical activity
Individual-based interventions addressing NCDs in primary care	Cancer: Prevention of liver cancer through hepatitis B immunization; prevention of cervical cancer through screening (visual inspection with acetic acid [VIA]) and treatment of pre-cancerous lesions CVD and diabetes: Multi-drug therapy (including glycemic control for diabetes mellitus) to individuals who have had a heart attack or stroke, and to persons with a high risk (> 30%) of a CVD event in the next 10 years; providing aspirin to people having an acute heart attack

Table 15: "Summary of interventions included in the core scaling-up costing scenario" (Chisholm et al., 2011, p. 12).

---

[43] "Cost-effectiveness summarizes the efficiency with which an intervention produces health outcomes. A 'highly cost-effective' intervention is defined as one that generates an extra year of healthy life (equivalent to averting one disability-adjusted life year) for a cost that falls below the average annual income or gross domestic product (GDP) per person in the country or region in question." (Chisholm et al., 2011, p. 11).

Looking at Table 15, two things can be observed: Firstly, the table divides between population-based interventions and individual-based interventions. Secondly, the "deadly quartet" is only taken into consideration for population-based interventions, while individual-based interventions focus on – admittedly closely linked – specific diseases instead of the original risk factors. As the medical success of individual-based interventions concerning the four risk factors has been proven by many other studies (Aalto, 2001; Kolenda and Ratje, 2013) and also theory demands to include individual-based preventive actions (WHO, 2014a, p. 12), this analysis will focus on the research gap of determining effects of individual-based interventions on NCDs.

In order to give this study a strong scientific basis, a literature research on health effects resulting from individual based interventions has been carried out. Its results will be presented in four different sections: The core intervention on the four risk factors is presented as an "Overarching step for all four risk factors". This section is followed by a section on smoking, one on diet and physical inactivity and a last one on alcohol consumption.

3.2.3.1   Overarching step for all four risk factors

As this analysis is concerned with risk factors arising from behavior, one of the most crucial questions is whether the patient at risk is motivated enough to change his or her behavior which he she has cultivated for many years, sometimes decades. The initial answer to this question is mostly negative, even of primary doctors (Hoch et al., 2004; Kolenda and Ratje, 2013, p. 38). In order to not be driven by initial responses, it is however important to analyze the scientific evidence existing on this issue.

One model that explains how human behavior is built and how it can be changed is the "Trans theoretical model of behavioral change" by Prochaska et al. (Kolenda and Ratje, 2013, p. 112; Prochaska et al., 1992). It states that behavioral change basically goes through five stages: pre-contemplation, contemplation, preparation, action and maintenance. It is important to understand that patients within the first three stages are not yet ready to take action and primary physicians should not overburden those patients, but lead them with patience. Furthermore, observations were made that people are going back and forth within these stages several times before finally establishing the new behavior (Kolenda and Ratje, 2013, p. 112; Prochaska et al., 1992). It is likely that this aspect is the main reason for the generally negative perception of behavioral interventions (Hoch et al., 2004; Kolenda and Ratje, 2013, p. 38).

In the process of the first two stages of this model, several communication strategies can be applied helping the primary physicians to smoothly lead the patients to stages three and four, such as: the "five basic principles" (John et al., 2001), the "4A-interventions" (Batra, 2011; Bundesärztekammer, 2001) or the "5R-interventions" (Kolenda and Ratje, 2013, p. 40). During the first two stages, the "only" input need by the doctor is background information about the risk factor, in order to help the patient to understand the pros and cons of a behavioral change. To ensure the quality of the primary physician's intervention and to offer helpful structures to them, advanced training opportunities are available, such as the German 20 hour course "Qualifikation Tabakentwöhnung" (Batra et al., 2013). Furthermore, it is important to implement financial incentives for the doctor, in order to support and ensure his professional contribution (Hoch et al., 2004; Kolenda and Ratje, 2013, p. 38).

Having reached stage three, the intervention of the primary physician is minor in many cases. Taking an example from the change of smoking habits, it has been shown that 10% of smokers quit by themselves after having only a single talk, 13% after several short talks of less than 3 minutes. The remaining patients can be supported by special programs like the "LebensCompetenzTraining" and "Für immer rauchfrei!" (Kolenda and Ratje, 2013, pp. 46, 115). These programs offer structural guidance easing the task of care givers to lead patients through the process. Consequently, little additional work, in terms of organizing, must be done by the general practitioner. Surely, the content of these programs will have to be adapted to the Chinese cultural context. But the basic structure already exists and once adapted, these programs promise remarkable results. In the field of smoking for example, patients attending such programs are found to quit in more than 50% of the cases (DGNTF, 2014; Kolenda and Ratje, 2013, p. 49).

However, as these results depend on the patient's readiness to change his/her behavior (preparation stage), it cannot be assumed that all patients will profit from the mentioned programs. Unfortunately, data about the willingness to change does not yet exist for the Chinese context in general and only for the risk factor smoking in the German context. But nonetheless, two arguments support the use of available data from Germany: Firstly, the "Trans theoretical model of behavioral change" by Prochaska et al. is explicitly not bound to a cultural context. Secondly, the percentage of people that are ready for an intervention can be influenced by the physicians' ability to lead through stage one and two (pre-contemplation and contemplation) (Kolenda and Ratje, 2013, p. 112; Prochaska et al., 1992). The study that analyzed the willingness to change of smokers in Germany (SNICAS study) finds that 2/3 of the smokers see their smoking behavior as problematic and are ready to stop, if they get assistance by their primary physician (Hoch et al., 2004). Combined with the finding that more than 50% of participants of such programs finally achieve to change their behavior, it can be found that more than 1/3 potential changers exist in the population at risk (1/2 *2/3 = 1/3). This rate of 1/3 is also congruent with the findings of other programs that show a 20% to more than 40% quitting rate (Haustein et al., 2004; Mühlig and Nowak, 2004; Nowak and Hoch, 2005; Schön and Nowak, 2002).

3.2.3.2   Smoking

Positive health effects of stopping smoking are numerous. Besides lowering the risk of COPD, heart diseases, stroke and many other morbidities (Kolenda and Ratje, 2013), stopping smoking will also lead to a reduction in mortality. Although stopping to smoke before the age of 45 will at most slightly reduce the risk of early death, it is also found that

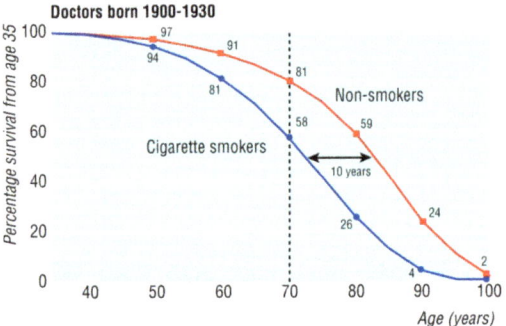

Figure 15: "Survival from age 35 for continuing cigarette smokers and lifelong non-smokers among UK male doctors born 1900-1930, with percentages alive at each decade of age" (Doll 2004).

keeping up smoking after that age will on average reduce life expectancy by 10 life

70

years. Comparing the group of 70 year old smokers to non-smokers, it is found that only about 60% of smokers but 80% of non-smokers survived. For the group of 90 year olds, about 5% of smokers and 25% of non-smokers are found to survive up to this age (Figure 15) (Doll, 2004). In total, an age-standardized mortality rate per 1000 men/year of 19.38 of non-smokers, 24.15 for former smokers and 35.40 for current smokers was found (Doll, 2004). This means that smoking compared to not smoking increases the amount of deaths by 16.02 lives per 1000 men[44] in this study group. Or, expressed in relative terms, 29.24%[45]. That means that nearly 30% of all deaths in this study group can be attributed to smoking. Out of these attributable deaths, 11.25 per 1000 men[46] could on average be avoided by quitting smoking. In relative terms this means that quitting smoking reduces the attributable (not total) number of deaths by 70.22%[47].

As the above intervention (3.2.3.1) was described as being able to reduce the rate of smokers by more than 1/3, it is assumed at this point that more than 23.41%[48], or roughly 25%, of deaths can be avoided by behavioral change interventions[49].

3.2.3.3   Diet & physical activity

The risk factors diet and physical inactivity will be considered together, as resulting effects are similar and Influence each other. Both risk factors are furthermore considered to be the main drivers of obesity, which develops through an imbalance between energy input (diet related) and energy output (physical inactivity dependent).

While the metabolism of human beings is adapted to a lifestyle with a high share of movement and restricted food consumption, the opposite situation is prevalent since a few decades – also in China. In order to make modern lifestyles once again congruent with physiological needs, one part of the strategy is to reduce the general energy intake

---

[44] $35.40 - 19.38 = 16.02$
[45] $16.02/(35.40+19.38)=29.24\%$
[46] $35.40 - 24.15 = 11.25$
[47] $11.25/16.02 = 70.22\%$
[48] $1/3*70.22\%=23.41\%$
[49] Although, as this study has concentrated on male doctors from the UK, it might be farfetched to regard this percentage to be the same for male and female citizens. As the morbidity and mortality risk of women is found to be more severely influenced by smoking, the above value can be regarded as conservative. Additionally, as this study is a prospective study conducted over 50 years, there is no other study yet which delivers comparable results. The above percentage rate of 25% will therefore be used in this study.

through diet and another is to increase the energy usage through increased amounts of sport and general movement. In order to achieve the first part, successful diets have been developed which allow the participants to have three full meals a day and at the same time reduce their energy intake by eating food with low energy density (meaning less fatty food and many fruits and vegetables) (Schusdziarra and Hausmann, 2007). If, in addition, food high in fiber (e.g. whole grain products) (Tuomilehto et al., 2001) and low in salt (using less salt for cooking and reducing convenience foods) (Middeke, 1998) is favored, and 30 minutes of physical activity are included in the daily schedule, the following health effects can be observed:

1. Reduction of weight by circa 10 kg per year (measured over two years) (Erdmann et al., 2008)
2. Diabetes prevented in 58% (3 year follow up) to 46% (7 year follow up) of people at risk (Tuomilehto et al., 2001)
3. Normalization of high blood pressure (mean value) (Ornish, 1998) by the effects of various factors and for nearly 100% of the patients (Kolenda, 2012; Kolenda and Ratje, 2013, p. 81)
4. Normalization of high total cholesterol levels (Ornish, 1998)
5. Per 10 kg weight reduction, 40% reduction of the 30% cancer deaths attributable to diet (Williamson et al., 1995)
6. Reduction of mortality of heart infarct patients by 20% (O'Connor et al., 1989)
7. Reduction of mortality of patients suffering from coronary heart disease by 31% (Jolliffe et al., 2001; Taylor et al., 2004)
8. Reduction of mortality of patients with chronic heart deficiency by 35% (Kolenda and Ratje, 2013)
9. Reduction of total mortality risk by 30-40% (Hambrecht, 2004) and even 47% if physical exercises are done regularly for two years (Kolenda and Ratje, 2013)

As this study does not aim to give a complete overview but to showcase effective medical interventions for specific risk factors, this section only focusses on the results made for excessive weight, diabetes, high blood pressure and high total cholesterol levels. Concerning the weight issue, according to the WHO numbers from 2010, 25.4% of the Chinese population are overweight (25-30kg/m^2) (WHO, 2011b, p. 144) and 5.7% are obese (>30kg/m^2) (WHO, 2011b, p. 145). An earlier sample from 2000[50] found that 23.8% of Chinese are either overweight or obese (Gu, 2006, p. 778). A reduction of body weight by 10 kg of overweight and obese Chinese (compare first point above) would lead to a reduction of overweight and obese citizens to only 3.3% (Table 16[51]).

No. of participants	17,998.00	20,742.00	17,128.00	17,429.00	16,658.00	14,745.00	13,233.00	18,466.00	13,227.00	5,110.00
Body weight, mean, kg	42.80	49.00	52.60	55.30	58.10	61.00	63.60	67.60	72.70	80.30
BMI, mean	17.20	19.30	20.50	21.50	22.50	23.50	**24.50**	25.90	28.20	32.30
Body height, mean, cm	157.75	159.34	160.18	160.38	160.69	161.11	161.12	161.56	160.56	157.67
Percentage of total	11.63%	13.40%	11.07%	11.26%	10.77%	9.53%	8.55%	11.93%	8.55%	3.30%
Body weight, mean, 10kg reduction, kg	32.80	39.00	42.60	45.30	48.10	51.00	53.60	57.60	62.70	70.30
BMI, mean, 10kg reduction	13.18	15.36	16.60	17.61	18.63	19.65	20.65	22.07	**24.32**	28.28
Percetage not overweight (BMI<25) before and after 10kg reduction							76.22%		96.70%	

Table 16: "Distribution of body mass index (BMI) in China", 2000 data, adapted to a 10 kg reduction scenario, data of the first three rows from Erdmann et al. (Erdmann et al. 2008), further data entries are author's calculations.

Building on the results from 2000, it can therefore be stated that roughly 4/5 of the Chinese overweight and obese population can be brought to a normal weight status (<25kg/m^2) if weight reduction up to 10 kg is achieved.

Taking into account that above results cannot be reached for all patients but for only 2/3 (see 3.2.3.1), the effects are calculated to be the following:

1. overweight: 2/3*4/5=8/15 (ca. 1/2)
2. diabetes: 50%*2/3=1/3
3. blood pressure: 90%[52]*2/3=60%
4. total cholesterol: 90%*2/3=60%

---

[50] As the BMI is consider to rise with adopting a western lifestyle and increased development (Herd et al., 2010, p. 2 as well as Table 45, Figure 26–Figure 29 in Annex 6) above numbers from 2000 will lead to rather conservative results.
[51] The table also shows that weight reducing interventions should only aim at overweight and obese people. Otherwise underweight might be the consequence (Table 16).
[52] The 90% value is used as a conservative figure to describe the finding of a normalization of high total cholesterol levels (Ornish 1998) and a normalization of high blood pressure (Ornish 1998) for nearly 100% of the patients (Kolenda 2012; Kolenda and Ratje 2013: 81)

3.2.3.4   Alcohol

Concerning the risk factor alcohol, it is important to know that only abusive, not moderate alcohol consumption is regarded to have negative effects on health. Within the data used in this analysis, positive health effects on heart diseases, strokes and diabetes, which arise from restrained drinking, are already factored in (IHME, 2014a; WHO, 2014d).

Due to the low total number of studies on primary interventions regarding alcohol consumption (Aalto, 2001; Bertholet, 2005; Muckle et al., 2012), the number of high quality analyses of excessive drinking behavior and possible interventions to reduce these levels to moderate drinking amounts is even more limited. One of the few studies that analyzed the clinically significant reduction of drinking was undertaken by Aalto and colleagues. They found that a one-time advice of a general practitioner (Group C in Figure 16) already reduced the drinking of patients to medically acceptable levels in 25-37% of the cases[53] (Figure 16). These results can be regarded as long-term results as the final examination was taken three years after the first contact. Within the same time span two other groups where examined. One group received three additional brief interventions of 10-20 minutes (Group B in Figure 16) and the other one received six of

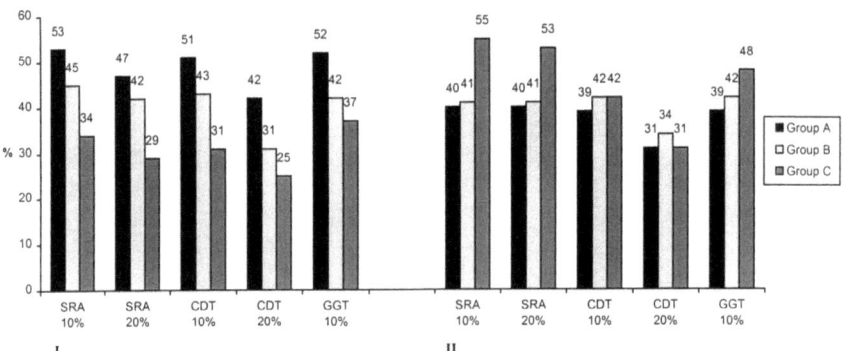

Figure 16: "Proportion of patients with decreased (I) and increased (II) values. Variable percentage refers to minimum decrease (I) or increase (II) from baseline to 3 years. There was no statistically significant difference between the study groups. SRA, self-reported alcohol consumption; CDT, carbohydrate-deficient transferrin; GGT, gamma-glutamyltransferase" (Aalto 2001).

---

[53] The variation results from the different endpoint measurement taken (e.g. self-reported alcohol consumption, carbohydrate-deficiency transferrin, gamma-glutamyltransferase).

these interventions (Group A in Figure 16). In order to reflect a real life situation, these interventions were not standardized. Within the first group, 31-45% of the participants were able to reduce their drinking levels to medically acceptable behaviors, and in the second group 42-53% (Aalto, 2001).

Taking into account that out of the total vulnerable population only 2/3 might be willing to change their risky behavior (3.2.3.1), this study will work with the conservative assumption that 30%[54] of all persons at risk will be able to reduce their drinking behavior to medically normal levels, if they are given six brief interventions of 10-20 minutes over the course of three years.

3.2.4 Making health effects comparable: cost-effectiveness and cost-benefit

In order to derive comparable results concerning the health interventions described above, two approaches can be followed. The first one, a cost-effectiveness analysis (CEA), can give information about the costs that each specific intervention will produce in comparison to an equalized unit of health effects – in this analysis disability adjusted life years (DALYs). The second approach is called a cost-benefit analysis (CBA) in which costs and benefits are expressed in monetary terms so that they can directly be expressed as a benefit-to-cost ratio.

It is obvious that for both approaches the same measurement of the costs is necessary, while benefits will have to be measured with the help of different methods. As benefits will be measured by the reduction of the health burden, one further chapter is necessary in which reduction values for both benefit approaches will be calculated. Therefore, the following chapters will begin with the calculation of the costs for the three health interventions described above (3.2.4.1). A further part will concern with the reduction values (3.2.4.2). The subsequent sections will provide an introduction to the CEA (3.2.4.3) and the CBA (3.2.4.4) including one sub-part presenting the results from each approach.

---

[54] 45% * 2/3 = 30%

75

3.2.4.1 Costs for CEA and CBA

In 2011, the WHO published a document that presents a measurement approach for the costs of the four risk factors mentioned above: the unhealthy consumption of tobacco, alcohol, diet and physical inactivity (Chisholm et al., 2011, p. 10).It is stated that the cost of scaling up an intervention can be determined by using the following parameters:

- population (in this case China)
- prevalence and incidence (of the four risk factors and four physiological risk markers)
- coverage (the proportion of population in need that is exposed to or receiving the intervention)
- resource quantities per case (which are needed to implement the intervention)
- unit costs (for each resource unit needed for the intervention) (Chisholm et al., 2011, p. 9).

The product of the first two parameters (population and prevalence) is used to define the coverage (population in need). In this study, data from the WHO Global Burden of Disease (GBD) studies, the "Global status report on non-communicable diseases 2010" (WHO, 2011b) and the "WHO Global Health Observatory Data Repository" (WHO, 2010b, 2010c) is used. The multiplication of the final two parameters (resource quantity and unit costs) provides the cost per case treated. These results (coverage and cost per case) can be multiplied to make up the final cost. To put it in formulas:

$$coverage \: / \: population \: in \: need = population * prevalence$$

$$cost \: per \: case = resource \: quantity * unit \: costs$$

$$cost = population \: in \: need * cost \: per \: case$$

76

Using the above way of calculating the final cost, furthermore requires three analytical steps. They will serve as the structure of the following chapters:

- definition of the intervention package
- estimation of the current intervention versus levels of need and coverage of the population
- calculation of the resource costs required to reach the desired coverage (Chisholm et al., 2011, p. 10)

3.2.4.1.1 Definition of the intervention package (step 1)

Chapter 3.2.3 already summarized the main health results of the interventions in question. This part will furthermore list the elements of the intervention package which is necessary to reach the results described above. However, it will only include the structural requirements (such as the amount of courses needed), but not the interventions in detail (for example the content of a course). The latter can be looked up in the original papers mentioned in chapter 3.2.3.

The intervention package which is needed for the four risk factors can be classified into three different topics. At first, the health care giver has to receive additional training that enables him or her to apply a certain intervention. Second, a questionnaire has to be used in order to screen the patients for those who are at risk. Third, the actual intervention has to be performed. All of these three topics have been described in chapter 3.2.3. Table 17 summarizes them and includes relevant details that have not been mentioned before.

Task	Tobacco	Diet & Physical activity	Alcohol
Skill enhancement	"Qualifikation Tabakentwöhnung" (20 hours) o	education for non-doctors (8 modules, 60 hours)[55] o	training in "brief intervention", for GPs and nurses (8 hours) (Aalto, 2001, p. 225)
Screening	nicotine dependency Fagerstroem test (Heatherton et al., 2014)	Findrisk (DiabetesStiftung DDS, 2007)	CAGE questionnaire (Nationales Programm Alkohol, 2014) and/or self-reported alcohol consumption (>280g of absolute ethanol per week) (Aalto, 2001, p. 225)
Intervention	short intervention (3min) plus individual training (5*30min) or group training (4-6 pers., 8*60min) plus relapse prevention (5*15min) and training in case of relapse (3*30min) plus medication (nicotine patch and nicotine gum)	short intervention (3min) plus group training (6-10 pers., 12*60min = 8 core interventions + 4 stabilization sessions) plus monthly contact by email, phone, mail etc. (Hermanns and Gorges, 2009, p. 2) doctor only for short intervention, else prevention manager	initial individual advise (10-20min) plus brief interventions (6*10-20min) doctor for 50% of the brief interventions, else nurse

Table 17: "Summary of health results of medical interventions to reduce the impact of the 'deadly quartet' in China", author's investigation.

3.2.4.1.2 Estimation of the need and coverage in the population (step 2)

As already mentioned in the introduction of this section (3.2.4.1), this paragraph will use data from the Global Burden of Disease (GBD) studies, explicitly the WHO Global status report on non-communicable diseases 2010 and the WHO Global Health Observatory Data Repository. Data of these two reports are used to calculate the population at risk through the product of population size and prevalence of risk factor. According to these data bases, the following can be found: 26.3% of the Chinese population is consuming tobacco products (WHO, 2011b, p. 108), 44.1% consumed alcohol during the last 12

---

[55] This training module focuses on Diabetes 2 (Kronsbein et al., 2011). Its aims are however equivalent to those laid out for the risk factors diet and physical inactivity (Kolenda, 2012). Although the content might have to be slightly adapted, the structure of this program can be used as a role model and show the amount of resources necessary.

months, 7.6% have had an episode of heavy drinking[56] within the past 30 days before the interview (WHO, 2010b), 30.6% lack physical activity (WHO, 2011b, p. 116,117), 38.2% suffer from raised blood pressure (WHO, 2011b, p. 128), 31.2% are overweight or obese (overweight 25.4% (WHO, 2011b, p. 144), obese 5.7% (WHO, 2011b, p. 145)), 9.4% suffer from raised blood glucose levels (WHO, 2011b, p. 136) and 33.5% from raised total cholesterol (WHO, 2011b, p. 152). In real numbers, these values range from approximately 100 million people to 450 million people, as indicated in Table 19 below.

In order to test these numbers, a comparison to the death cases attributed to the "deadly quartet" and the physiological risk markers has been done. It shows that the former outnumbers the latter by far – meaning, that more people are calculated to be at risk than those who actually die due to the risk factor. For tobacco use for example, roughly 360 million people are identified as being at risk, while "only" little more than one million deaths are attributable to this risk factor. The ratio between the people at risk and the attributable death cases is hence around 260 – meaning, that this analysis recommends checking about 260 people at risk for every one person actually dying of a certain risk factor. (Due to a lack of data, the morbidity ratio can unfortunately not be calculated.) For the remaining risk factors and physiological risk markers these ratios are: nearly 270 for alcohol use, more than 160 for physical Inactivity, more than 1,000 for diet, more than 250 for high blood pressure, nearly 1,200 for high BMI, nearly 230 for high fasting plasma glucose and more than 1,600 for high total cholesterol (Table 18).

---

[56] The WHO definition of Heavy Episodic Drinking (HED) is as follows: "HED is defined as consumption of 60 or more grams of pure alcohol (6+ standard drinks in most countries) on at least one single occasion at least monthly." (WHO, 2014e, p. 4)

Need for interventions compared to the actual death rate			
people at risk as percentage of total population	people at risk in real numbers	Deaths (mortality) in real numbers	risk/death ratio
Tobacco	26.30%	357,633,045	1,365,980	261.81
Alcohol	7.60%	103,346,431	383,479	269.50
Physical inactivity	30.60%	416,105,368	2,542,410	163.67
Diet	38.20%	519,451,800	495,305	1,048.75
High blood presure	38.20%	519,451,800	2,042,690	254.30
High BMI	31.20%	424,264,297	362,707	1,169.72
High fasting plasma glucose	9.40%	127,823,218	562,195	227.36
High total cholesterol	33.50%	455,540,191	280,574	1,623.60

Table 18: "Need for interventions and actual death rate of the 'deadly quartet' and the physiological risk markers in China", 2010 data, author's investigation.

Out of the people at risk, 1/3 has been shown to be resistant to behavioral change but 2/3 are open for doctors' advice and the programs explained above (3.2.31). This means that the screening as well as the first short intervention with the general practitioner has to be applied to all people at risk. The whole program however only has to be applied to the 2/3 of the population in need that is generally open for changing their behavior. These values have been inserted in the calculations underlying Table 19 (detailed description at the beginning of this section).

Need for interventions				
people at risk as percentage of total population	people at risk in real numbers (in million)	people at risk who are willing to change as percentage of total population	people at risk who are willing to change in real numbers (in million)
Tobacco	26.30%	357.63	17.53%	238.42
Alcohol	7.60%	103.35	5.07%	68.90
Physical inactivity	30.60%	416.11	20.40%	277.40
Diet	38.20%	519.45	25.47%	346.30
High blood presure	38.20%	519.45	25.47%	346.30
High BMI	31.20%	424.26	20.80%	282.84
High fasting plasma glucose	9.40%	127.82	6.27%	85.22
High total cholesterol	33.50%	455.54	22.33%	303.69

Table 19: "Need for interventions (total and willing to change group) to manage the 'deadly quartet' and the physiological risk markers in China", 2010 data, author's investigation.

80

Table 18 and Table 19 unfortunately originally lacked the value for the incidence of unhealthy diets. As the risk factor diet is considered together with physical inactivity, it could be argued that the coverage of physical inactivity could be used for dietary risks as well. However, as some of the related physiological risk factors show higher coverage rates than physical inactivity, consciousness calls for the adaption of one of these values. In order to be most cautious, it is hence assumed, that interventions laid out in step 1 must at least cover 38.2% of the Chinese population – the highest number of people at risk within the diet and physical activity related risk factors.

3.2.4.1.3 Calculation of resource costs required for the desired coverage (step 3)

The calculation of the resource costs required to reach the desired coverage also follows the three topics described in step 1: skill enhancement, screening and intervention. If not mentioned otherwise, the values for all three topics are based on the findings of the "WHO-CHOICE unit cost estimates for service delivery" (WHO, 2011c). For reasons of comparability, all currency values used were converted to 2010 USD values and health data was used from 2010 if possible.

The first task, skill enhancement, includes the finding that a Chinese doctor in a public hospital treats on average 9.52 patients per day. Each of these visits costs between 4.43 USD in rural hospitals and 6.29 USD in urban hospitals. The average amount is 5.36 USD. An hour is therefore on average worth 6.20 USD[57]. The payment for enhancing the skills of medical staff resembles the usual hospital payment. The number of doctor's that shall be educated is taken from a 2011 announcement of the Chinese government which declared that China will have one general practitioner (GP) per 10,000 inhabitants in 2020 (Xiong, 2011). This makes 135,982 GPs needed in China in 2020. Knowing that Chinese classes normally host 40-60 students (MKL, 2011), the conservative assumption is made that each class includes 35 GP students, and hence 3885 courses have to be run in order to educate all (future) GPs in China. Due to the large number of people that can be taught through such courses and the large amount of people treated by the GPs, the costs per person are less than one cent (see Table 20).

---

[57] 9.25 * 5.36/8= 6.20

As screening is used to find those citizens with the highest risk, questionnaires are handed out to every person who is supposed to be at risks (for the total amount of people at risk see Table 19). The questionnaires are easy to handle for the patients as well as for the medical care giver. They shall be filled in and be evaluated within a few minutes. The costs for evaluating the questionnaires and communicating the results are counted equal to a short appointment with the doctor.

The values for the interventions are only partly taken from the "WHO-CHOICE unit cost estimates for service delivery" (WHO, 2011c). Prices for medical products were taken from Chinese online selling websites as only prices for over the counter medicine were needed, and those are not listed in the "International Drug Price Indicator guide" (ERC, 2013).

An overview of the results of these calculations is given in below Table 20.

Task	Tobacco	Diet & Physical activity	Alcohol
Skill enhancement	less than 0.01 USD/pers.	less than 0.01 USD/pers.	less than 0.01 USD/pers.
Screening	4.73 USD/pers.	4.73 USD/pers.	4.73 USD/pers.
Intervention	short intervention (3min) =4.73 USD/pers. *plus* group training (5 pers., 8*60min) =8.55 USD/pers. *plus* relapse prevention (5*15min) =25.27 USD/pers. *and* training in case of relapse (3*30min) =15.62 USD/pers. **=54.17 USD/pers.** *plus* medication (nicotine patch and nicotine gum) =128.38 USD/pers. **=182.55 USD/pers.**	short intervention (3min) =4.73 USD/pers. *plus* group training (8 pers., 12*60min) =8.02 USD/pers. *plus* monthly contact by email =0.03 USD/pers.[58] **=12.78 USD/pers.**	initial individual advise (15 min) =5.05 USD/pers. *plus* brief interventions (6*15min) =30.32 USD/pers. **=35.37 USD/pers.**

Table 20: "Costs per person for the medical interventions to reduce the impact of the 'deadly quartet' in China", in 2010 USD, author's investigation.

[58] Email contact is calculated as two visits of one hour each (one "visit" to write the email and one "visit" to answer eventual questions) for all 350 people in the original study of Aalto and colleges (Aalto, 2001).

In order to calculate the total amount of the needed money, the results of Table 20 are combined with the values of the population in need shown in Table 18 and Table 19 of the last sub-section. While every person who potentially belongs to one of the risk groups ("total amount of people at risk" in Table 19) shall be screened and treated with the initial short intervention or individual advice, only those who show a willingness to change ("amount of people willing to change" in Table 19) will be included in the core intervention programs. Consequently the total costs of the above interventions are (Table 21):

Task	Tobacco (in million USD)	Diet & Physical activity (in million USD)	Alcohol (in million USD)
Skill enhancement	$0.43	$1.29	$0.17
Screening	$1,691.60	$2,457.01	$488.83
Intervention	$1,691.60	$2,457.01	$521.90
	$2,038.51	$2,777.34	$2,088.98
	$6,024.92	$10.39	
	$3,724.15		
	$30,608.62		
Total	$45,779.85	$7,703.03	$3,099.88

Table 21: "Total costs for the medical interventions to reduce the impact of the 'deadly quartet' in China", in 2010 USD, author's investigation.

3.2.4.2 The benefits of reducing the (health) burden

Measuring benefits in the context of health economics can sometimes be confusing. This is due to the fact that welfare costs, as presented in chapter 3.2.2, Table 12, are at the same time the source underlying the measuring of benefits. Although labeled "costs", it is wrong to think about it as actual money spent; it rather represents a burden borne by society which is expressed in DALYs or monetary terms in this study. A reduction of this burden (or "welfare cost") is a relief to society from former disutility and therefore labeled benefit.

In order to make the reduction of the burden ("cost") measurable, it has to be deducted by how many percent the values of Table 13 and Table 14 of chapter 3.2.2 can be reduced if the health interventions in chapter 3.2.3 are applied. Unfortunately, values for diet and physical inactivity could not be presented in 3.2.3 but the values for risks from tobacco and alcohol consumption as well as the related physiological risk markers: high blood pressure, high BMI, high fasting plasma glucose and high total cholesterol. For these the reduction values are as follows: for tobacco related risk 25%, for alcohol 30%, for high blood pressure 60%, for high BMI 50%, for high fasting plasma glucose 33% and for total cholesterol 60% (see chapter 2).

To get to derive the values for diet and physical inactivity, their related physiological risk markers were used to calculate the average reduction, taking into account their specific contribution to the death cases. The resulting weighted average value is 56% for diet and physical inactivity. (It is unfortunately not possible to diversify these values further, as the health interventions always build preventive actions in both fields.)

3.2.4.3 Cost effectiveness of individual NCD interventions

In order to choose cost-effective services for the catalogue of benefits of a health insurance system, WHO developed a CEA approach designed for practical use (WHO, 2014a). The basic idea is to rank services into broad classes such as high priority (green), medium-priority (yellow), and low-priority (red) services (Figure 17). High priority classes are suggested to stand for basic services which should be provided to the total population. Only after every person is covered with these high priority services, shall services of middle or low priority be included in the scope of insurance services (WHO, 2014a, p. 11).

To classify services as high, middle or low ranking, several criteria are used: cost-effectiveness, priority to the worse off, financial risk protection, severity of disease (present and future health gap), realization of potential, past health loss, socioeconomic status, area of living, gender, race, ethnicity, religion, sexual orientation, economic productivity, care for others and catastrophic health expenditures (WHO, 2014a, pp. 13–20). Among them, cost-effectiveness, priority to the worse off, and financial risk protection were worked out as the core indicators (WHO, 2014a, p. 20). A special position is assigned to the cost-effectiveness criterion[59] by most countries working with priority setting, by many scholars (WHO, 2014a, p. 12) and by many national and international initiatives such as the 2001 Commission on Macroeconomics and Health and the 2009 Taskforce on Innovative International Financing for Health Systems (WHO, 2014a, p. 14). Consequently, it is proposed by the WHO to start off with the cost-effectiveness criteria in order to roughly sort services into the three groups. This will lead to favor those services that produce the greatest value in terms of health for a certain amount of money. Only after this step is done, the other categories should be used to adjust the former decisions (WHO, 2014a, pp. 20, 21, 23).

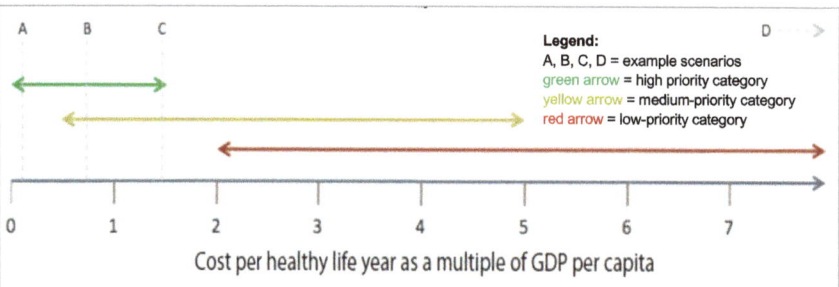

Figure 17: "Framework for integrating cost-effectiveness with other criteria when selecting services", Cost per healthy life year as a multiple of GDP per capita, (WHO 2014c, p. 21).

---

[59] Cost-effectiveness is mostly measured in lives saved, life years saved, QALYs and DALYs (WHO, 2014a, p. 13).

Figure 17 (see above) shows that cost-effectiveness studies do not necessarily lead to unequivocal results. This can be observed at the point where interventions are assigned to sections in which two colors overlap (examples B and C in Figure 17). As this tool furthermore uses a continuum (and no dichotomous variable) to classify the intervention in question, it should also be taken into account how far away a service is from the unequivocal area. A service closer to the non-overlapping area (example B) might be less likely to change to the lower category than a service located further away (example C). This is different for interventions that are classified in the non-overlapping area (examples A and D). They can directly be placed in the corresponding category.

Adopting the above three categories – high, middle and low – to the GDP per capita of China in 2010 (USD 4,515), it is found that the high category could include any service costing less than USD 6,772 per life year saved (1.5 times the per capita GDP, Figure 17). The middle category could include services using between USD 2,257 and USD 22,575 per life year saved (0.5-5 times the per capita GDP) and the low category above USD 9,030 (2 times the per capita GDP). A policy maker spending USD 1,000 for an intervention would hence require gaining at least an extra 0.15 life years in order to categorize the intervention as high. This makes even the least effective interventions of Figure 18 (breast cancer and colposcopy) eligible for the high priority category, but not so services like dialysis which only saves 0.02 healthy life years (WHO, 2014a, p. 13).

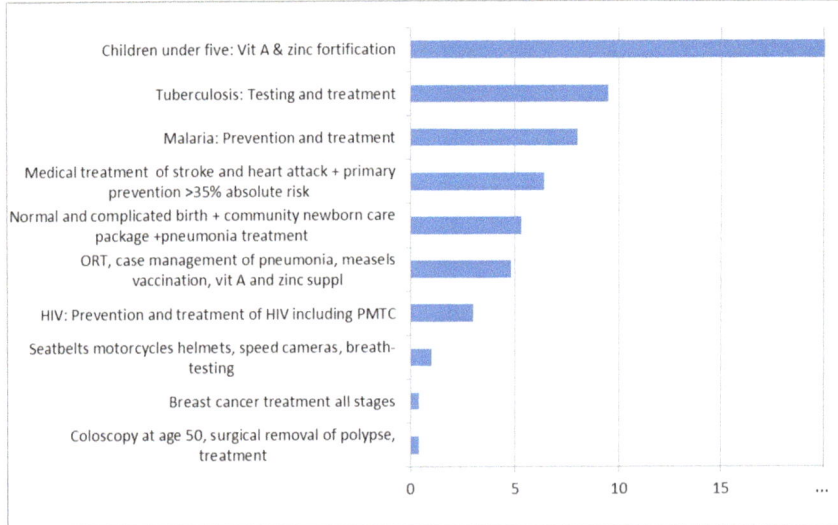

Figure 18: "Cost-effectiveness of services targeting high-burden conditions" (WHO 2014c, p. 14).

Results

Applying the reduction rates described in chapter 3.2.4.2, the following results can be found for the four risk factors smoking, diet, physical inactivity and alcohol use, as well as for the four physiological markers high blood pressure, high BMI, high fasting plasma glucose and high total cholesterol: Reducing the risks stemming from tobacco use will save 7.5 thousand DALYs, from diet more than 29 thousand DALYs, from physical inactivity nearly 6.5 thousand DALYs and from alcohol use more than 4 thousand DALYs (see Table 23a below). Reducing the physiological risks can reduce the DALY burden by nearly 23 thousand in the case of high blood pressure, 6.5 thousand in the case of high BMI, nearly 5.5 thousand in the case of high fasting plasma glucose and more than 3.5 thousand in the case of high total cholesterol (see Table 23b below).

Putting these results in relation to the costs derived in chapter 3.2.4.1, it can be stated that the cost of all risk factors and physiological markers are below the 1.5 times of GDP per capita that are needed to be eligible for the high priority category for a health insurance catalogue of benefits (WHO, 2014a, pp. 20, 21, 23). Furthermore, with the exception of interventions for smoking, all of the interventions deliver results that also cost below the 0.5 times of GDP per capita which marks the unequivocal area that is only assigned to the high priority category (High total cholesterol is close to this line with a value of 0.48.) (see Table 23a and Table 23b.) A graphical depiction can be found in Figure 19 (see below). The orange circles represent the four risk factors; the yellow rhombs the four physiological parameters. According to these results, it can

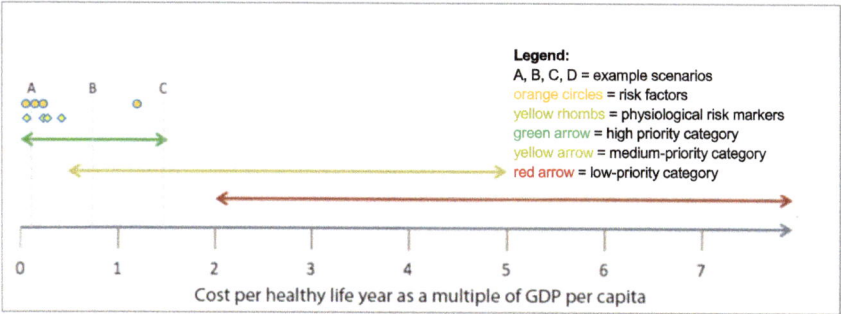

Figure 19: "Inclusion of the "deadly quartet" and associated physiological risk markers into the framework for integrating cost-effectiveness with other criteria when selecting services" (WHO 2014c, p. 21), author's adaptation.

hence be concluded that all of the associate NCD risk factors and markers are eligible to be included into the Chinese catalogue of benefits with the highest priority – for all interventions, except for individual tobacco interventions, this conclusion is without alternatives as they are located in the unequivocal area (position A) (see Figure 19). As individual interventions targeting tobacco smoking are found to be at location C, and therefore an equivocal area (Figure 19), they should additionally be discussed under other aspects like priority to the worse off, financial risk protection, severity of disease (present and future health gap), realization of potential, past health loss, socioeconomic status, area of living, gender, race, ethnicity, religion, sexual orientation, economic productivity, care for others and catastrophic health expenditures (WHO, 2014a, pp. 13–20).

Regarding above findings, it is obvious that these results are extremely conservative as they overestimate costs and underestimate benefits, at least for diet and pysical activity and the four physiological markers. This is due to the fact that they all share the same medical interventions. Hence, costs would in reality only be paid once in order to obtain all of the mentioned effects. However, the shown results include the same costs repeat-edly in each of the interventions. Unfortunately, the data at hand does not allow to either attribute a certain part of these costs to a certain outcome, as they are all interconnect-ed. It neither allows to sum up the benefits, as double counting of the positive effects would then be the case. In order to give the reader a somewhat realistic idea about the cost-effectiveness of these interventions, the following paragraphs will show the cost-effectiveness as minimum and maximum values. The minimum values will include the full health intervention costs for each intervention, but only the particular benefits of each of them. The maximum value will compare the full costs of the intervention with the agglomerated health benefits of diet and physical activity on the one hand and high blood pressure, high BMI, high fasting plasma glucose and high total cholesterol on the other hand.

The minimum benefits per 1,000 USD are hence: 0.16 DALYs for tobacco related interventions, 3.79 DALYs for diet related interventions, 0.84 DALYs for physical activity related interventions and 1.33 DALYs for alcohol related interventions (Table 23a). For interventions targeting high blood pressure 2.96 DALYs, regarding high BMI 0.85

DALYs, high fasting plasma glucose 0.70 DALYs and high total cholesterol 0.46 DALYs are gained per 1,000 USD (Table 23b). The maximum benefits of interventions regarding diet and physical inactivity amount to 6.81 DALYs, and of high blood pressure, high BMI, high fasting plasma glucose and high total cholesterol to 5.51 DALYs per 1,000 USD spend (not shown in Table 23a or Table 23b).

Figure 20 (see below) clearly shows the prominent position of unhealthy diet and high blood pressure among the single risk factors and physiological markers (second orange and yellow bars from the top). The combined effects of diet and physical activity as well as the combined effects of the four physiological makers also show good results compared to the other interventions (first orange and yellow bars from above). The results of the minimum and maximum values suggest that health interventions targeting diet and physical activity can be suspected to reduce the Chinese burden of disease by up to 6.81 DALYs per USD 1,000 spent and at least by 4.21 DALYs per USD 1,000 (diet alone). Interventions targeting the four physiological risk markers could be able to reduce the burden of disease in China by up to 5.51 DALYs per USD 1,000 and at least by 3.28 DALYs per USD 1,000 spent (high blood preassure alone). Even if the minimum values are taken into account, interventions targeting these risk factors would be ranked among the top ten efficient reduction methods for "high-burden conditions" (WHO, 2014a, p. 14).

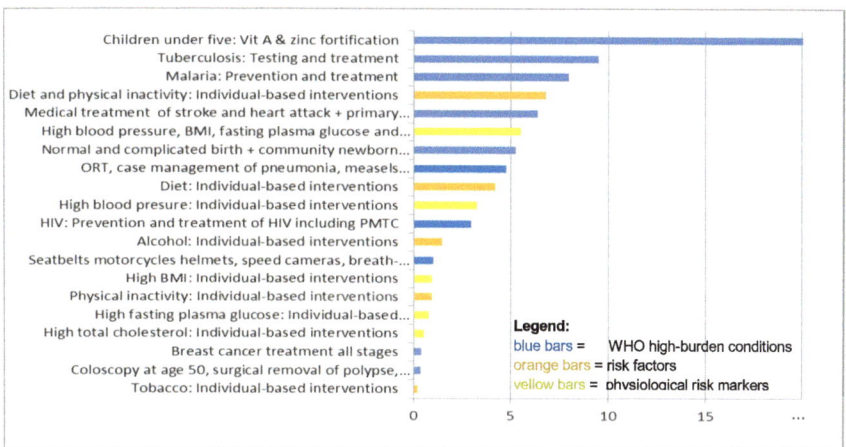

Figure 20: "Inclusion of the 'deadly quartet' and associated physiological risk markers into the ranking of cost-effectiveness of services targeting high-burden conditions" (WHO 2014c, p. 14), author's adaptations.

The results described above are sumarized in Table 23a and Table 23b (see below).

Measurement	Costs (in million USD)	DALYs	DALYs per 1,000 USD	Cost per DALY as multiple of GDP per capita
Individual based interventions for tobacco related risks	$45,779.85	7,501,150	0.16	1.35
Individual based interventions for diet related risks	$7,703.03	29,188,789	3.79	0.06
Individual based interventions for physical inactivity related risks	$7,703.03	6,457,968	0.84	0.26
Individual based interventions for alcohol related risks	$3,099.88	4,133,940	1.33	0.17

Table 23a: "Benefits in DALYs for reducing the risk from the 'deadly quartet' in China", total population, in 2010 USD, health data from IHME (IHME 2014a), author's calculations.

Measurement	Costs (in million USD)	DALYs	DALYs per 1,000 USD	Cost per DALY as multiple of GDP per capita
High blood presure	$7,703.03	22,763,940	2.96	0.07
High BMI	$7,703.03	6,536,693	0.85	0.26
High fasting plasma glucose	$7,703.03	5,367,533	0.70	0.32
High total cholesterol	$7,703.03	3,546,948	0.46	0.48

Table 23b: "Benefits in DALYs for reducing the risk from unhealthy diets, physical inactivity and associated physiological risk markers in China", total population, in 2010 USD, health data from IHME (IHME 2014a), author's calculations.

3.2.4.4 Cost-benefit analysis of individual NCD interventions

It is stated that cost-benefit analyses can also be called social cost-benefit analyses if they include impacts on the whole society instead of specific entities (for example individuals, enterprises or the state government) (Boardman et al., 2011, p. 2). Although it could be argued that this is the case for the study at hand, the term CBA is used further on due to its higher publicity.

Apart from the inclusion of all actors of a society, CBAs can also measure benefits and costs of different areas. Without doubt, the focus of this study is only on costs and benefits arising within the health field, where the most holistic way of measuring benefits probably is the „total economic value" (TEV). The benefits measured by TEV basically consist of three different types of reduced burden/welfare costs (Holland et al., 2014a, 2014b): medical, productivity and welfare. (For more details of this kind of calculation see Annex 4.)

Some authors argue that approaches measuring welfare, in particular the value of a statistical life approach, are those rooted best in the theory of economics (OECD, 2014a). Although approaches measuring productivity and medical expenses are well rooted in other theoretical contexts, the following analysis will exclusively focus on the welfare cost, because firstly, the data necessary to calculate the medical expenses (COI analysis, see Figure 25 in Annex 4) and productivity impacts are incomplete. And, secondly, focusing on welfare costs (that is "costs borne by the victim", see Figure 25 of Annex 4) will make it possible to show the impact that the "deadly quartet" and its accompanying physiological risk markers have on the quality of life of individuals.

The calculation of the welfare impact will be undertaken with the help of the following formula (OECD, 2014a, pp. 54–55; WHO and OECD, 2015, p. 18):

$$VSL\ China\ 2010 = VSL\ OECD\ 2005 * (Y\ China\ /Y\ OECD)^{\beta} * (1\ + \ \%\Delta P\ + \ \%\Delta Y)^{\beta}$$

The parameters used in the equation above are explained in Table 24 (see below):

Abbreviation	Explanation
VSL OECD 2005	The base value for the calculation of the VSL for the OECD group of countries as a whole. The value is USD 3 million.
Y China/ Y OECD	Gross Domestic Product (GDP) per capita at the purchasing power parity (PPP), in 2011. The GDP is converted to international dollars using the PPP rates.
% Δ P	The percentage increase in consumer price from year 2005 to 2010. This is measured by consumer price index (CPI) that reflects the inflation or changes in the cost to the average consumer of acquiring a basket of goods and services.
% Δ Y	The percentage change in real GDP per capita growth from year 2005 to 2010. This is derived from real GDP per capita annual growth.
ß	Income elasticity of VSL. It measures the percentage increase in VSL for a percentage increase in income. The value used here is 0.8.

Table 24: "Country-specific VSLs: Explanation of adjustment factors", content from (OECD, 2014a, pp. 54–55), slightly modified by the author.

For classification reasons, it might furthermore be important to mention the different types of CBA studies that can be undertaken. Firstly, an ex-ante CBA can be carried out which aims to inform policy makers about the benefits they can expect to gain. Secondly, an in-medias-res CBA would be carried out in order to understand the actual performance of a running project and thirdly, an ex-post CBA aims to evaluate the gains of a closed project (Boardman et al., 2011, p. 3). In the case of this study, an ex-ante CBA is carried out as the aim is to inform about the expectable results of including NCD interventions related to the "deadly quartet" in the Chinese catalogue of benefits.

Results

Results of a CBA are generally provided in two ways: Firstly, as the ratio between the costs necessary to finance the interventions and the benefits that arise from these interventions. The ratio is calculated by dividing benefits by costs (R=B/C), hence the resulting number will inform about the amount of USD gained for every USD invested. Secondly, results can be presented as net benefits. The net benefit results from the calculation of the difference of benefits and costs (NB=B-C) and informs about the net value that certain interventions produce in monetary terms (Boardman et al., 2011, p. 31).

It is obvious that both calculations, for R and for NB, need costs as well as benefits as input. The costs necessary to finance the interventions have been discussed in chapter 3.2.4.1. Benefits, as mentioned in chapter 3.2.4.2, are measured by the reduction of the health burden (welfare costs), which in turn arises from the medical interventions described in chapter 3.2.3. The calculation of the benefits from the reduction of the four risk factors builds on Table 13 and Table 14 in section 3.2.2. They amount to USD 0.5 trillion for tobacco related diseases, roughly USD 0.2 trillion for alcohol, USD 2 trillion for diet and more than USD 1.1 trillion for physical inactivity related diseases (Table 25).

	Benefits from reducing the welfare costs of the "deadly quartet" in China, 2010			
	Deaths (mortality)	DALY (mortality & morbidity)	Mio. US$ (mortality)	Mio. US$ (mortality & morbidity)
Tobacco	341,495	7,501,150	$413,311.45	$454,642.60
Alcohol	115,044	4,133,940	$139,237.41	$153,161.15
Diet	1,435,386	29,188,789	$1,737,247.50	$1,910,972.25
Physical inactivity	279,638	6,457,968	$1,016,860.01	$1,118,546.01

Table 25: "Benefits from reducing the welfare costs of the 'deadly quartet' in China", total population, in 2010 million USD, health data from IHME (IHME 2014a), author's calculations.

The reduction of the physiological risk markers amounts to benefits of USD 1.6 trillion for high blood pressure, USD 0.3 trillion for high BMI, USD 0.2 trillion for high fasting plasma glucose and USD 0.2 trillion for physical inactivity related diseases (Table 26).

Benefits from reducing the welfare costs of the "deadly quartet" in China, 2010			
	Deaths (mortality)	DALY (mortality & morbidity)	Mio. US$ (mortality)	Mio. US$ (mortality & morbidity)
Tobacco	341,495	7,501,150	$413,311.45	$454,642.60
Alcohol	115,044	4,133,940	$139,237.41	$153,161.15
High blood presure	1,225,614	22,763,940	$1,483,360.82	$1,631,696.90
High BMI	193,444	6,536,693	$234,124.98	$257,537.48
High fasting plasma glucose	187,398	5,367,533	$226,808.23	$249,489.06
High total cholesterol	168,344	3,546,948	$203,747.25	$224,121.98

Table 26: "Benefits from reducing the welfare costs of the 'deadly quartet' and associated physiological risk markers In China", total population, in 2010, million USD, health data from IHME (IHME 2014a), author's calculations.

It can be observed that these results are indeed high, especially in comparison with the costs calculated in chapter 3.2.4.1. As a consequence, the results derived from the benefit/cost ratio are also impressive. In the case of the risk factor tobacco, a ratio of nearly 10:1 is found, indicating that a benefit of roughly 10 USD is achieved by the investment of 1 USD.

Although already showing a very positive result, the other three risk factors are even many times the amount. Diet shows a ratio of nearly 250:1, physical inactivity of more than 145:1 and alcohol nearly 45:1. This means that investments in all four risk factors

Measurement	Effect	Costs (in million USD)	Benefits (in million USD)	Benefit:Cost ratio	Net Benefit (in million USD)
Individual based interventions for tobacco related risks	Reduction of 25% of the burden	$45,779.85	$454,642.60	9.93	$408,862.75
Individual based interventions for diet related risks	Reduction of 56% of the burden	$7,703.03	$1,910,972.25	248.08	$1,903,269.22
Individual based interventions for physical inactivity related risks	Reduction of 56% of the burden	$7,703.03	$1,118,546.01	145.21	$1,110,842.98
Individual based interventions for alcohol related risks	Reduction of 30% of the burden	$3,099.88	$139,237.41	44.92	$136,137.53

Table 27: "CBA results for reducing the risk from the 'deadly quartet' in China", total population, in 2010 USD, health data from IHME (IHME 2014a), author's calculations.

deliver high returns of social value, ranging from USD 10 to USD 250 for every USD invested. Looking at the net value, the results of the benefit-to-cost ratio are supported. For tobacco related risk reductions more than USD 0.4 trillion are achieved, for diet more than USD 1.9 trillion, for physical inactivity more than USD 1.1 trillion and for alcohol more than USD 0.1 trillion (see Table 27).

Not only the four risk factors, but also the four physiological risk markers show high benefits/cost ratios from the interventions described in chapter 3.2.3. The reduction of high blood pressure shows a ratio of more than 210:1, and also high BMI, high fasting plasma glucose and high total cholesterol deliver a result around 30:1. Also, this means that interventions reducing the four physiological risk markers deliver high returns of social value, this time ranging from roughly USD 30 to USD 210 for every USD invested. Looking at the net value, the results for a reduction of high blood pressure are more than USD 1.6 trillion and for high BMI, high fasting plasma glucose and high total cholesterol each more than USD 0.2 trillion (see Table 28).

Measurement	Effect	Costs (in million USD)	Benefits (in million USD)	Benefit:Cost ratio	Net Benefit (in million USD)
High blood pressure	Reduction of 60% of the burden	$7,703.03	$1,631,696.90	211.83	$1,623,993.87
High BMI	Reduction of 53% of the burden	$7,703.03	$257,537.48	33.43	$249,834.45
High fasting plasma glucose	Reduction of 33% of the burden	$7,703.03	$249,489.06	32.39	$241,786.02
High total cholesterol	Reduction of 60% of the burden	$7,703.03	$224,121.98	29.10	$216,418.95

Table 28: "CBA results for reducing the risk from physiological risk markers in China", total population, in 2010 USD, health data from IHME (IHME 2014a), author's calculations.

Although already achieving a high benefit-to-cost ratio, it should be reminded that diet and physical inactivity (see Table 27), as well as physiological risk markers (see Table 28) are reduced by the same interventions. In the two tables above, the ratio and net benefit was however calculated by taking into account the full cost for each of the risk factors without accounting for synergy effects. If only a partial fraction of the costs is accounted for, a higher ratio and net benefit will logically be the result (compare 3.2.4.2).

3.2.5 Conclusion

This study was able to show that NCDs make up most of the death incidents in low- and middle-income countries and identified four risk factors (tobacco use, unhealthy diet, physical inactivity and high alcohol consumption), the so called "deadly quartet", and four closely linked physiological risk markers (high blood pressure, high BMI, high blood glucose and high cholesterol) as the major drivers of bad health effects. Part 3.2.2 of this analysis showed the high relevance of NCDs by referring to the death rate associated with specific non-communicable diseases but also with the "deadly quartet" and its accompanying physiological risk markers. On the basis of an OECD/WHO approach, this chapter has also shown how the health burden resulting from NCDs can be translated into comparable health indicators (DALYs) and economic values. Looking at the health burden per 100,000 inhabitants, it was shown that the general trend of the NCD burden in China is going upwards comparing the years 1990, 2005 and 2010. Looking at the health burden of the total population in the year 2010, this section was able to show the total effect from the health as well as the economic perspective for the whole of China.

In chapter 3.2.3 of this analysis, it was made clear that the situation described in chapter 3.2.2 can be changed. A literature review described in detail some health interventions on the individual level that are able to reduce the NCD burden. This was done separately for the risk factors smoking and alcohol abuse, while diet and physical inactivity were analyzed together. Within the last group, health effects could only be expressed in relation to the four physiological risk markers (high blood pressure, high BMI, high fasting plasma glucose and high total cholesterol). The results from all of these groups were furthermore adapted by overall findings describing the people's general willingness to change.

Building on the results of the literature review, chapter 3.2.4 calculated the costs, summarized the reduction rates of the health burden and calculated the effectiveness (DALYs) and benefits (monetary values). The results of this section were positive to the extent that all risk factors and all physiological risk markers were classified as services that should be included in the Chinese catalogue of benefits with the highest priority. Comparing the cost efficiency rates of interventions targeting the four risk factors and the four physiological markers to that of other diseases, it shows that, even under the worst assumptions, the interventions concerning the risk factors diet and alcohol as well as the physiological marker high blood pressure are ranked within the top ten cost-effective interventions. Under more optimistic assumptions, interventions targeting physical inactivity and the other physiological risk markers are also included in the top ten group. Solely interventions to stop smoking habits show less positive results. This might foremost be the case due to high costs arising from pharmaceutical support demanded in the course of stopping smoking.

Looking at the benefits in monetary terms compared to the costs needed for these interventions, impressive results were obtained. The value that society attaches to the possible relief of the burden of disease due to NCDs outweighs the costs for interventions by far. This can be shown by the high benefit/cost ratio and the high net benefit that was calculated in chapter 3.2.4.4.

As a résumé, this analysis hence concludes that it is highly recommendable to include individual focused health interventions targeting the four major risk factors underlying NCDs (and/or the accompanied physiological risk markers) in the Chinese catalogue of benefits. The main reasons for this conclusion are the potential of these interventions to reduce mortality and morbidity of the Chinese population and thereby reduce the health burden and social costs currently borne by society. Structured as an ex-ante analysis (compare 3.2.4.4), it is hoped that this study will help to inform about the large potential of individual based health interventions targeting the "deadly quartet". Its translation into policy interventions is believed to be highly profitable to the Chinese society.

3.3 The breadth dimension in China

The "Definition and Concept" chapter (chapter 2), and in particular the breadth chapter (2.3), showcased that policy interventions have to focus on vulnerable groups as they are otherwise easily marginalized. In order to investigate this issue in depth, the following chapters will concentrate on migrant workers as one of the big vulnerable groups in China. Firstly, the investigation will review some literature in order to answer the question if migrant workers are indeed marginalized concerning their health status (3.3.1). Secondly, the health insurance coverage in China will be investigated concerning the breadth dimension, with modeling the special situation of migrant workers with regard to the state of 2011 and future situation of 2020 (3.3.2).

3.3.1 Overview of literature: Does marginalization of migrant workers matter in the context of health?

A literature review about the marginalization of migrant workers in China has to verify two aspects: firstly, the question if migrant workers are at all marginalized and secondly, if the potential marginalization matters to the health outcomes. This differentiation is not trivial – at least not in the field of health. While migrant workers, especially rural-to-urban migrants, are generally seen as being more at risk (Chen et al., 2013; Zheng and Lian, 2005, p. 8) and less well protected by health insurance (Giles et al., 2013, p. 35), some health outcomes are not significantly worse compared to Chinese citizens that always lived in rural or urban areas (Hesketh et al., 2008a, p. 193). Hence, the research question that shall be answered is if there exist differences in health risks and health access and if so, do they translate to different health outcomes?

In order to achieve the aim sketched above, the following chapters will firstly investigate the situation of health risks of migrant workers (3.3.1.1), then analyze the situation of health access (3.3.1.2) and finally investigate the observable health situation (3.3.1.3).

3.3.1.1   Health risks

It is well understood that, and partly how, Chinas impressive economic growth has negatively influenced the environment. Holdaway's introduction to the links between environment and health in China (Holdaway, 2010) serves as a good overview on this topic. Building on these findings, Chen and colleagues point at air and water pollution as the most important sources of environmental hazards and health risks (Chen et al., 2013). (Other more minor topics that are mentioned are noise, poor ventilation and dust (Zheng and Lian, 2005, p. 8).) According to a World Bank study using the value of a statistical life (VSL) approach, health effects attributable to outdoor air pollution amount to 519.9 billion Yuan and to more than 66 billion Yuan for health effects associated with water pollution (World Bank, 2007, pp. 74–75). Chen et al. point at the problem of migrant workers being exposed to these environmental risks as lower economic status is generally associated with living closer to environmentally hazardous sites and industrial facilities. Furthermore, their economic situation will not allow them to quit jobs with high health risks such as in the fields of mining, construction and chemical industries (Chen et al., 2013). Looking at three environmental hazards – air pollution, water pollution and industrial waste –, Chen et al. conclude:

> "The results indicate that when compared to urban residents, rural-to-urban migrants perceive significantly higher levels of environmental hazards: in the model of perceived water pollution, the coefficient for migrants is 0.79 (odds ratio = 2.19, p < 0.01), and in the model of perceived industrial waste, it is 0.69 (odds ratio = 1.99, p < 0.05). The coefficients on migrants in the models where the factor index measures the perccived overall environmental hazard as the dependent variable are also statistically significant (coefficients = 0.36 and 0.38, p < 0.01)." (Chen et al., 2013, p. 90)

However, not only the natural, but also the working environment exposes migrant workers to higher risks than their urban counterparts. Township enterprises for example[60], where most of the workers are rural migrants, were found to offer unsafe workplaces in 83% of the cases. Furthermore, 60% of them have not installed any protective measures against these risks (Zheng and Lian, 2005, p. 8).

Besides higher health risks through air quality, water quality, industrial waste (Chen et al., 2013) and the working environment (Li, 2013, p. 1466; Zheng and Lian, 2005, p. 8), the bad housing situation is an additional environmental health risk that migrant workers are exposed to more than others. The reason for this additional risk is twofold. On the

---

[60] Although township enterprises have a declining role in the Chinese economy, the problem described above is still a large concern for occupational health and safety issues (Wang et al., 2011). Comparably dangerous settings exist also in other enterprises were migrants work (Li, 2013, p. 1466).

one hand, social housing is only offered to urban residents (defined by their local residence permit *hukou*) (Wang and Murie, 2011; Wu, 2002, p. 93). On the other hand, migrant workers value housing quality less than urban residents, as they normally only stay for a fixed period of time (Wu, 2002, p. 94). Consequently, they do not own their living places, but rather rent them (>50%) or live in dormitories (>30%)[61] (Wu, 2002, p. 101). Furthermore, 75% of the rental housings of working migrants is either in areas that used to be or still is on the outskirts of the metropolis, or it takes place in rooms built without proper permits or for other than living purposes (Wu, 2002, pp. 100–102)[62].

Without surprise, it has therefore been found that the housing quality of migrants is by far lower than that of urban residents:

"Housing conditions for temporary migrants do not compare favorably to those of urban residents and permanent migrants[63]. In both cities, temporary migrants occupy far less space and endure poorer conditions. Overcrowding seems to be a feature of migrant housing, with each person using only about a third of the space occupied by a typical urban resident. These migrants also tend to live in dwellings that are less equipped with kitchen/bathroom facilities[64], are used for working or other purposes in addition to serving as residences, and have less stable structural features (such as temporary dorms on construction sites). It is not unusual to see a family of three sharing a single rental room with no facilities and using a corner to set up a small cooking area with either a kerosene burner or propane stove. A small portion of temporary migrants (about 3%-4% in both cities) encounters the worst housing conditions for prolonged periods of time, ranging from sleeping on hospital benches to resting by vendor stalls sheltered by only plastic sheets to sleeping under staircases in multistory apartments."[65] (Wu, 2002, p. 105)[66]

It is obvious that a life under these conditions is associated with a higher risk of falling ill, firstly, due to the low hygienic standard and secondly, due to the crowding which brings along a higher risk of infectious diseases (Li, 2013, p. 1462; Zheng and Lian, 2005, p. 71).

---

[61] Studies in other regions, e.g. Zhejiang province, support these results by finding that 52% of migrant workers live in dormitories and only 32% rent accommodations (Hesketh et al., 2008a, p. 191).
[62] As these references are rather old, it might be that the percentage values differ by now. The general tendency is however supported by later sources as well (Wang and Murie, 2011).
[63] See Annex 2.
[64] Compare Annex 1.
[65] Also compare Li et al. (Li et al., 2006, p. 4) and Li (Li, 2013, p. 1462).
[66] Also here, housing conditions might not be as severe as described in this text as the source is rather old and the development in China might have improved. The general tendency is however described by other scholars as well (Wang and Murie, 2011).

The latter point, infectious diseases, affects especially migrant workers through two further pathways: Firstly, migrants are less likely to be vaccinated against basic infectious diseases (Biao, 2003, p. 11; Fu et al., 2010; Mou et al., 2013, p. 22; Zheng and Lian, 2005, p. 5; Mou et al., 2010; Vail, 2009). Secondly, migrant workers – also called floating population – are moving through the entire country (Annex 3) and thereby are connecting previously isolated locations. This fact has played an important role in the spread of communicable infectious diseases (Gong et al., 2012a, p. 844; Mou et al., 2013) (e.g. SARS (Zheng and Lian, 2005, p. 7)).

The increase of infectious diseases since the 1990s is however mainly driven by sexually-transmittable diseases and AIDS (Herd et al., 2010, p. 5). Also here, migrant workers carry a large part of the disease burden. The freedom of traveling, and therefore living outside of the normal boundaries of society, is seen as one of the explanations for the higher rate of sexual partners that is found within the migrant workers community (Zhang et al., 2013, p. 136; Zheng and Lian, 2005, p. 4). Together with their comparatively young age – associated with being less aware, having less knowledge and low information – migrant workers are less likely to use health services and protective measures such as condoms. They are consequently found to be more at risk for sexually transmittable infections such as HIV/AIDS (LI et al., 2007; Mou et al., 2013; Zheng and Lian, 2005) [67]. In addition to the reasons mentioned above, misconceptions about sexual-transmittable diseases that have been reported to be prevalent in China ten years ago, might still shape social behavior in traditional settings. It has for example been believed that loyal spouses are immune against the HIV virus of their returning partner (Zheng and Lian, 2005, p. 4). This hypothesis is supported by the finding of a newer study undertaken in a migrant worker community in Beijing. It showed that migrant workers possess a low understanding about infectious diseases and limited access to health information (Li, 2013).

As a consequence, it can be concluded that migrant workers are prone to higher health risks than their urban residential counterparts through numerous measures. Among them are: environmental health risks (due to air quality, water quality and industrial

---

[67] A study by Sun et al., for example, found that 59.8% out of 393 female migratory workers in the service sector had multiple sex partners and only 34.4% of them used condoms (Zheng and Lian, 2005, p. 4).

waste), more dangerous working environments, bad housing situations, high infection risks and low immunization rates, as well as risky sexual behavior and a higher risk for sexually transmittable diseases.

The following chapter will give an overview about the migrant workers' possibilities to compensate these higher health risks with good access to health services.

3.3.1.2   Health service access

Analyzing migrant workers' access to health services, the different levels of protection and degree of fund pooling (Giles et al., 2013, p. 3) make it difficult to come up with statements which are valid for each province and city of China. The analysis in this study therefore only describes the average situation which might differ in specific areas. It is however evident that coverage of migrant workers lags far behind that of local residents due to two reasons. Firstly, until recently, insurance schemes have set insti-tutional barriers for migrant workers: Urban health insurance schemes (UEBMI and URBMI) explicitly excluded those migrant workers who were not able to register at the local authorities and hold a local residence permit (*hukou*) and rural health insurance schemes (NCMS) rarely accept bills from health institutions of other parts of the country (Giles et al., 2013, p. 10; Mou et al., 2013, pp. 30–33)[68]. New insurance systems such as the Medical Assistance Program (MAP) for the poor and the Urban Resident Scheme (URS) are in most cases also depending on a locally valid *hukou* and do therefore exclude most of the migrants (Mou et al., 2013, p. 31). Secondly, the fragmentation of the health insurance system is a disincentive for migrating populations as it lacks the option of portability (Giles et al., 2013, pp. 3, 12–14). It is consequently not surprising to find a negative correlation between urban insurance status and rural origin defined by *hukou* (Giles et al., 2013, p. 35).

---

[68] Several exceptions to this structure exist but they are in general locally or structurally limited and can-not be regarded as a negation of the statement above. For example, some policy directives aim to extend coverage. However, they exclude work injury insurance and remain voluntary in practice (Giles et al., 2013, pp. 7, 29). Furthermore, some provinces and cities, such as Shanghai and Chengdu, started pilot social insurance programs that target migrants in order to solve apparent labor shortages (Giles et al., 2013, p. 10).

As a consequence, only a fraction of migrants are inscribed in health insurance schemes. Due to the fragmentation of the system described above and due to the different calculation methods used, the insured amount of migrant workers varies. Hesketh et al. find evidence that 19% of migrants working in Zhejiang, China's richest province, are enjoying health insurance coverage (Hesketh et al., 2008a, p. 194; Mou et al., 2013, p. 30), but Peng et al. give a lower number of only 6% for those working in Beijing (Mou et al., 2013, p. 30; Peng et al., 2010, p. 4). On the contrary, Giles et al. calculate a higher number of 30% using data from the Chinese Ministry of Human Resources and Social Security (MOHRSS)[69] (Giles et al., 2013, p. 11).

As health insurance coverage among migrant workers is low, seeking health care is very costly in terms of money and/or time: If care is sought in a local hospital, bills are mostly paid out of pocket; if care is sought in origin hospitals, travelling time (and money) have to be taken into account as well and if bills from urban hospitals are to be reimbursed, a time consuming administrative process with the respective insurance scheme is obligatory. It is hence with no surprise that the willingness and ability of migrant workers to use health services is very low (Liang and Guo, 2014). Peng et al. found that out of 309 migrant workers (with 324 incidents), 36.4% had seen a doctor, 33.3% had taken self-medication and 30.3% hadn't taken any measures. The most common reasons for those who did not visit a doctor were the affordability of medical expenses (40.5%), neglecting the severity of the diseases (33.4%) and the lack of free time (26.1%). The group who did visit a doctor did so by mostly choosing the cheaper alternative of village health clinics or community health service stations (44.6%) and so-called private clinics (20.0%) which are not officially authorized and are conducted by unqualified practitioners. Out of the 114 respondents who had received hospital inpatient care within the past twelve months (4.6%), 42 (36.8%) selected local hospitals and 72 (63.2%) selected hospitals in their hometown. Among the reasons for selecting hometown hospitals were lower medical expenses (52.7%), inconvenience and inaccessibility to services (28.6%), and discrimination (4.8%) (Peng et al., 2010, pp. 4–5). Other studies, such as Hesketh et al.

---

[69] It has to be mentioned that Giles et al. use the number of rural-urban migrants and not of all migrants to calculate the coverage rate (Giles et al., 2013, p. 42). This might be seen as the reason for this relatively high result.

(Hesketh et al., 2008a) or Li (Li, 2013, pp. 1464–1465, 1467) show results that support these observations, although the specific numbers might differ.

It can therefore be concluded that migrant workers do not only face higher health risks, but are also less well insured and therefore use less health services than urban dwellers. The next section will analyze in how far this situation affects the actual state of health of migrant workers.

3.3.1.3   Health situation

Measuring health status is possible through subjective as well as objective measurements. On the subjective side, Hesketh et al. find that migrants generally report better health and less acute and/or chronic diseases after statistically adjusting for age and education (Hesketh et al., 2008a, p. 193). This might be due to two reasons: Firstly, migrant workers show low knowledge about about health in general (Li, 2013, p. 1465) and secondly a double-self-selection process, known as the "healthy migrant worker effect" (Hesketh et al., 2008a, p. 195; Razum, 2006; Razum et al., 2000), is described. The first self-selection phase of the "healthy migrant worker effect" happens as children and the elderly (and hence, the more vulnerable and less healthy) tend to stay at their hometowns while only the generations in their working ages migrate (Hesketh et al., 2008a, p. 195). The second selection-phase enlarges the differences by the fact that those migrant workers fallen ill tend to return home (Hesketh et al., 2008a, p. 195; Zheng and Lian, 2005, p. 8). It is therefore understandable that migrant workers are on average found to be healthier than their rural counterparts and also that their subjective health status is very high if estimated in comparison to their peers.

Looking at the objective health status of migrant workers, unfortunately not only the increase of future risks, but also the existence of a higher rate of health issues is observable. In accordance with the higher health risks concerning communicable infectious diseases (compare 3.3.1.1), it was found in a study in Guangdong province that migrants made up 53% of all rubella cases in 2001, despite only accounting for less than 20% of the total population (Biao, 2003, p. 11). Furthermore, diseases like malaria, hepatitis, typhoid fever, respiratory infections and measles infections are more commonly found within migrant than urban populations (Herd et al., 2010, p. 8; Mou et al., 2013; Vail, 2009; Zheng and Lian, 2005, p. 7). At the peak of its spreading, SARS, for example, was more prevalent in the migrant workers group, which played a crucial role in the containment of this disease (Zheng and Lian, 2005, p. 7).

Focusing on sexually transmittable diseases, similar observations can be made. A recent meta-study by Zhang et al. included 54 studies on HIV in rural-to-urban migrants. Compared to the official national HIV prevalence level of 0.057% (78,000 people), this meta-study found that rural-to-urban migrants already had a HIV prevalence of 0.15% (odds ratio of 2.63) before leaving their home towns, which increased to 0.38% (odds ratio of 6.70) when surveyed in their destination areas (Zhang et al., 2013, p. 137). Looking only at those migrants who returned to their hometowns, it was found that their HIV prevalence was 0.18% (odds ratio of 3.16) which was not found significantly different from the prevalence rate of those just leaving their rural home places (Zhang et al., 2013, p. 141). The difference between the HIV prevalence rates of currently working and of returning migrants can be explained by social stigmatization which happens because the transmission of HIV is not well understood by rural inhabitants (compare 3.3.1.1).

Mental diseases are a further group of illnesses that are found to be more prevalent within the migrant worker population. As already pointed out above, 4.8% of the migrant workers are seeking health care in a hospital out of fear of discrimination (Peng et al., 2010, pp. 4–5). However, discrimination is not the only stress factor that migrant workers are facing in their daily city lives. A literature review by Mou et al. found stigmatization, stress from economic pressure, high work load, separation from their families, discrepancy between expectations and existing possibilities and problems with cultural adaptation as main stress factors influencing migrant workers' mental health. The mental health level of migrant workers – for example in Chongqing and Shenzhen and during the economic crisis in 2008 – is therefore found to be significantly worse than that of the average Chinese person (Mou et al., 2013, p. 25). Li et al. find that 9% of the total Chinese population, but 25% of migrant workers are affected by mental health symptoms like depression, anxiety, hostility and social isolation (Li et al., 2006; compare also Li, 2013). At a final stage, these circumstances and symptoms can lead to an increased suicide rate (Lau et al., 2012) as it was prominently shown, also in western media, in the case of the Foxcon suicides (Chan and Pun, 2010).

Despite the severe and conclusive aspects of suicide, the mental health of migrant workers might play an even more important role in the long term. It is found that their mental health also strongly affects their families leading to symptoms like major depression, depressive symptoms and insomnia in the family members (Mou et al., 2013, p. 25). Concerning the children of migrant workers, studies found lower self-esteem and higher levels of depression and anxiety, a higher internet addiction rate, higher tendencies towards smoking and binge drinking, suicidal ideation, along with less potential coping possibilities such as social connections or the feeling of a bond with their home families (Mou et al., 2013, p. 26). The conclusion that existing health disparities between migrant workers and the average Chinese population might increase in the future is even shared by those authors who did not find a marginalization of migrant workers regarding their subjective health status. They concluded that migrant workers' apparent inattention to health and their reluctance to seek proper health-care (see above), will lead to a worsening of existing health conditions and to severe pathologies later on. As an example, the widespread use of over-the-counter analgesics for conditions like gastric ulcer is mentioned. (This therapy does not at all cure the reason of this condition and consequently does not prevent further deterioration.) (Hesketh et al., 2008a, p. 196) A similar example is tuberculosis, where the delayed diagnosis and a low case detection rate can result in severe health problems in later times (Tobe et al., 2013). The future risk within the migrating population is mainly due to the low utilization of services, the tendency to ignore symptoms, the habit to delay doctor visits and the decline of referral for medical treatment (Mou et al., 2013, p. 33).[70]

It is therefore possible to conclude that migrant workers, although showing good results concerning self-reported health, objectively are found to suffer from more illnesses than urban dwellers, which are in addition expected to increase in numbers in their later life years.

---

[70] In addition, major differences in health outcomes are also found if mortality is analyzed instead of morbidity. In 2003, for example, about 80% of the fatal accidents in mining, construction, and dangerous chemical industries occurred within the migrant worker population (Zheng and Lian, 2005, p. 8).

3.3.2 Health Insurance Coverage in China – 2011 and 2020

The literature review (3.3.1) has clearly shown that migrant workers are a marginalized part of the Chinese population regarding health risks (3.3.1.1), health access (3.3.1.2) and health status (3.3.1.3). The following chapters will build on these findings and further investigate the insurance situation in China with special focus on migrant workers.

Key to the following analysis is the recent announcement of the Chinese government to no longer distinguish between urban and rural *hukou* holders (新华, 2014) which points to the large social problems that migration in China poses to the social systems. Until lately, migrants[71] have mostly been excluded from urban social insurance systems by being excluded from local residential registration (*hukou*). This is despite the fact that they are playing a crucial role as the driving force of the economic rise of China in general and its cities in particular (Giles et al., 2013, p. 10). In order to address this problem, the Chinese government announced in 2014 to grant urban *hukou*s to 100 million additional migrants (新华, 2014, p. 13).

Apart from this rather new policy, the Chinese government has already undertaken large efforts to increase the coverage rate of social insurance schemes. For the field of health insurance, the 2009 "Implementation Plan for the Recent Priorities of the Health Care System Reform (2009-2011)" (PRC, 2009) and the 12th Five-Year Plan (2011-2015) (PRC, 2011) point out this attempt. The former document sets the goal of insuring more than 90% of the Chinese population until 2011 and of reaching universal coverage until 2020 (Guo et al., 2010; PRC, 2009). The latter document, the 12th Five-Year Plan, endorses the goals of the first document and at the same time adds stronger obligingness to them. As already stated earlier, the strong binding character of Five-Year Plans arises as achieving its goals is an important precondition for the career of provincial politicians (PRC, 2011; Shih, 2011). The goals to reach 90% of health insurance coverage in 2011 and universal coverage in 2020 are therefore high on the political agenda of the Chinese government.

---

[71] The term "migrants" includes rural-to-urban as well as urban-to-urban migrants (Giles et al., 2013).

Research questions that arise from the described policies are twofold: The first question is concerned with the situation in 2011 and asks if the Chinese government succeeded with insuring more than 90% of its population to health insurance plans until then. The second question focuses on the future, asking if universal health insurance coverage can be reached in 2020 with the policy targeting migrant workers' *hukous*.

With the help of existing literature, the first question can only partly be answered; the second question remains – due to its novelty – unanswered. But the general judgment is that the People's Republic of China (PRC) has made huge progress towards reaching universal health care. Sometimes, it is even stated that they have already reached or are close to reach universal coverage (Giles et al., 2013; Herd et al., 2010; Marten et al., 2014; Meng et al., 2012b; Tang et al., 2012; WHO, 2014a; Yip et al., 2012). Despite the wide consensus on this issue, many scholars are none the less aware of severe problems arising from marginalizing vulnerable sub groups like migrant workers (Giles et al., 2013; Marten et al., 2014; Meng et al., 2012b; Tang et al., 2012; Yip et al., 2012). However, an analysis of the percentage of population covered has not been undertaken with regard to migrant worker's special conditions. Consequently, both research questions above can be regarded as unanswered and are surveyed by this analysis.

In order to answer both of these questions, this study will apply three different scenarios – a best, lowe and high estimate scenario. All three scenarios will be used to analyze the present and the expected future situation.

The structure of this analysis therefore proceeds as follows: Firstly, it gives a short overview about the situation of migrant workers up to 2011 and, including the future plans of the Chinese Communist Party, of 2020 (3.3.2.1). Secondly, a chapter on data used in this study and the reason for the three scenarios is carried out (3.3.2.2). Thirdly, the methodology used to analyze the situation of 2011 and the future situation will be explained (3.3.2.3). Fourthly, the results derived are given for the total (3.3.2.4.1) as well as the urban part of the population (3.3.2.4.2). Potential weaknesses of this study will be discussed in the discussion-section (3.3.2.5). A concluding chapter will summarize the study and points towards policy implications that could be used to further address the gaps discovered beforehand (3.3.2.6).

3.3.2.1　Status quo and tendencies in the Chinese health insurance system

In 2009, the Chinese government issued a far reaching reform through its "Implementation Plan for the Recent Priorities of the Health Care System Reform". In this document, five reform targets are mentioned to ease access to medical services and reduce the financial burden for citizens. Concerning health insurance coverage, a high percentage of insured people (more than 90% of the population) is aspired for 2011 in each one of the three big insurance schemes: UEBMI, URBMI and NRCMS (compare 1.4). Furthermore, essential health-care is supposed to reach universal coverage by 2020 (Guo et al., 2010, p. 1056). In 2011, the objective of wide coverage has gained further political importance bye issuing the 12th Five-Year Plan, a document of guidelines for the 2011-2015 development strategy of China (PRC, 2011, pp. 39, 41). The additional weight does not only come from the repeated support of the outlined strategy, but also from the higher political importance of this document. Targets laid out in this document have a country wide impetus as achieving the goals of the Five-Year Plan is – once again – an essential precondition for the career of provincial politicians:

> "Meeting targets for a city, region or province, for example, is the path to advancement for officials in the Party. Those who do a superlative job get chosen for prime leadership positions. Those who fail to meet those targets get sidetracked" (Shih, 2011).

This political setting and the former positive development might be a part of the explanation why scholars today nearly unanimously stress the huge progress of the recent health insurance reform in China (Giles et al., 2013; Marten et al., 2014; Meng et al., 2012b; Tang et al., 2012; WHO, 2014a; Yip et al., 2012). Concerning the analysis of health insurance coverage rates, one of the most detailed analyses has been done by Meng and colleagues. They build on data from the "National Health Services Survey" (NHSS) that interviewed 57,023 households/193,689 individuals in 2003, 56,456/177,501 in 2008, and 18,822/59,835 in 2011. Out of these interviewed people, 29,7% where found to be insured in 2003, 87.9% in 2008 and 95.7% in 2011 (Meng et al., 2012b). These findings do however exclude the group of migrant workers. Two problems – one within the study design, one within the legal framework – are responsible for this shortcoming: Firstly, as Meng and colleagues state themselves, studies building on the NHSS data are doomed to under-represent the large number of migrant workers, because data is gathered through a household survey which by nature does barely include floating populations (Meng et al., 2012b, p. 813). Secondly, it is important to notice that a Chinese citizen could be inscribed in one insurance scheme (e.g. the rural NRCMS or an urban UEBMI) but work in a place belonging to another scheme (e.g. the UEBMI of a different town or city). As the belonging to a Chinese insurance scheme is determined by permanent residence, the place of birth determines where social benefits, such as health insurance, can be obtained[72] (Holdaway, 2008, p. 9; WHO, 2008b, p. 10). A person could therefore *de jure* own health insurance (e.g. a rural one), but *de facto* not be able to receive benefits in case of illness (because of working, for example, in an urban area) (Yip et al., 2012, p. 839).

Although reforms did not eliminate this restrictive system, exceptions to this rule do exist. First of all, the Chinese health insurance system offers opportunities to insure oneself privately, independent from *hukou* through commercial and non-commercial insurance schemes (Meng et al., 2012a, p. 3). As this option requires financial strength, it might be considered as a non-opportunity for migrant workers. Programs which migrant workers might be able to join exist in form of the so called "All-in-One Card", for example. This system was introduced to allow people to switch between the different insurance schemes. Although these programs are *de facto* able to assure the insurance status al-so for those who travel (人力资源和社会保障部 et al., 2009), their scope is not yet wide enough as they are not rolled out on a national scale, but only in single pilot projects (China.org.cn, 2012). Due to the still small range of these programs, existing exceptions are not interpreted as contradicting with the statement that migrant workers are largely left without *de facto* servable health insurance. Considerably influential programs on a national scale, such as the Medical Financial Assistance system (MFA) which insured 68.76 million poor people in 2012 (Marten et al., 2014, p. 4), are well documented – e.g. by the National Bureau of Statistics of China (NBSC, 2012, 2009) and several scholars

---

[72] As the above source is from 2008, it should be stressed that the stated fact still holds true after the 2009 reform. Firstly, the reform has not changed the general connection between the permanent residence and the assigned insurance scheme (PRC, 2009). Secondly, the individual insurance scheme still only offers access to health care in a certain location. Exceptions to these statements are discussed further below.

(Giles et al., 2013; Hesketh et al., 2008a; Marten et al., 2014; Mou et al., 2013; Peng et al., 2010) – and will therefore be included into the calculations of *de facto* insured people. It is hence possible to state that migrant workers are, as a general rule, *de facto* uninsured Aberrancies from this general rule are included into the calculation as far as they are documented in the literature.

As shown in chapter 3.3.1.2, using health services for the *de facto* uninsured is very costly in terms of money and time. Concerning monetary costs, migrant workers are additionally burdened by costs arising from OOP in hospitals at their working place, or travel expenses that have to be carried out. But not only in terms of monetary costs, also in terms of time costs do migrant workers face a higher barrier to health care than their sedentary counterparts. Those arise from the administrative requirements for submitting bills, as well as traveling to the home places might be very time intensive. In addition, bureaucratic barriers are often set artificially high in order to avoid the higher health costs that are generally paid in urban health facilities. As a result, the mentioned medical expenses, inconvenience, inaccessibility and discrimination - or simplified, time and money - are among the main reasons for the low willingness and ability of migrant workers to use high quality health services (Hesketh et al., 2008b; Liang and Guo, 2014; Peng et al., 2010).

As a consequence of the fragmentation of the insurance system into different, mainly insurmountable schemes and the lack of portability, health insurance coverage comprises lower value for migrant workers. Therefore, only a fraction of migrants is inscribed in health insurance schemes which are valid at both, their places of working and their places of living. Reviewing the literature does not give a clear picture on how high the fraction of *de facto* insured migrants is. On the one hand, the variation between numbers seems to be attributable to the disparity of the Chinese health insurance system – comparing rural and urban insurance schemes, but also comparing urban schemes in different locations. On the other hand, different calculation methods seem to further intensify these differences. Scholars therefore give different values for the health insurance rate of migrant workers in China: As also already mentioned in chapter 3.3.1.2, Peng et al. find that only 6% of migrant workers located in Beijing enjoy health insurance coverage (Mou et al., 2013, p. 30; Peng et al., 2010, p. 4). Hesketh et al. find

111

evidence that 19% of migrants who work in Zhejiang, China's richest province, are insured (Hesketh et al., 2008a, p. 194; Mou et al., 2013, p. 30). Using data from the Chinese Ministry of Human Resources and Social Security (MOHRSS), Giles et al. calculate a higher number of 30% insurance coverage[73] (Giles et al., 2013, p. 11). In this analysis, the differences given by different scholars will be used to calculate different scenarios of health insurance coverage. The concrete approach will be explained in detail in the following chapters.

3.3.2.2   Data and scenarios

In order to answer both research questions posed above, this study runs two approaches: Firstly, it sets up a scenario describing the health insurance coverage at present (2011). Secondly, it works out a scenario for the future (2020) which includes the goals advertised by the Chinese government in 2014.

3.3.2.2.1   Present scenario

For the present scenario, the data of the National Health Services Survey (NHSS) is of high value. It used a multistage stratified cluster sampling to select 94 out of China's 2859 counties within the 31 provinces and municipalities. In these locations, 57,023 households were interviewed in 2003, 56,456 in 2008 and 18,822 in 2011. The response rates for these years were 98.3%, 95.0% and 95.5%. That makes a total number of interviewed individuals of 193,689, 177,501 and 59,835, respectively (Meng et al., 2012b). As primary data is not available, this analysis builds on other scholars which find a coverage rate for health insurance of 29.7% in 2003, 87.9% in 2008 and 95.7% in 2011 (Meng et al., 2012b; 黄, 2012).

A weakness of the NHSS data is the fact that it does not sufficiently take into account the migrant workers population. As shown above, this is due to two reasons: Firstly, the design as a household study exempts most of the floating populations like migrant workers. Secondly, the juristic structure does barely cover health services used in areas

---

[73] It has to be mentioned that Giles et al. use the number of rural-urban migrants and not all migrants to calculate the coverage rate (Giles et al., 2013, p. 42). While they thereby use a different denominator than the study at hand, the numerator is similar (compare part 4, "Methodology"). This is most likely the reason for the relatively high percentage value.

outside of a citizen's *hukou* area. In order to include the numbers for the missing migrant workers, the NHSS data is combined with findings from studies that primarily focus on the situation of migrant workers (rural-to-urban and urban-to-urban). The literature review above (3.3.1) showed that the percentage of migrant worker *de facto* owning urban health insurance is unclear. As mentioned before, scholars propose values of 6% (Mou et al., 2013, p. 30; Peng et al., 2010, p. 4), 19% (Hesketh et al., 2008a, p. 194; Mou et al., 2013, p. 30) and 30% (Giles et al., 2013, p. 11) for migrant workers profiting from insurance coverage in Chinas cities.

Three reasons exist to assume that the 19% value describes most precisely the number of migrant workers who *de facto* own servable health insurance in cities. Firstly, the argument that roughly 20% of migrant workers are insured is further supported by the China Urban Labor Survey (CULS). CULS surveyed migrants (with a rural as well as an urban background) and local residents separately. It furthermore collected a high number of observations – 500 households of local residents and 500 households of migrants in each of the five surveyed cities, Shanghai, Wuhan, Shenyang, Fuzhou and Xian. A disadvantage of this survey is that migrants were sampled through neighborhood committees and unregistered migrants and those living in factory dormitories or construction sites may be underrepresented. Further weaknesses of this survey are that it only includes big capital cities with higher living standards and therefore more established migrants (Giles et al., 2013, pp. 18–19). Both "weaknesses" point towards the conclusion that the 19% value is rather an overestimation than an underestimation and will therefore lead to rather conservative results. Secondly, the 19% figure seems to get the most support within the literature (Giles et al., 2013, pp. 18–19; Hesketh et al., 2008a, p. 194; Mou et al., 2013, p. 30) and can therefore be regarded as the most probable value. Thirdly, the 19% value is supported by official data sources. Calculating the ratio of (re)insured migrants in urban areas (46.41 million) to the total migrant population (252.78 million) in the year 2011 using the data from the National Bureau of Statistics of China (NBSC, 2012), results in a ratio of 18.36%[74]. Consequently, this result is assumed to be the best estimate as indicated by the three points above.

---

[74] $\frac{\text{urban insured migrants}}{\text{total migrant population}} = \frac{46.41 \text{ million}}{252.78 \text{ million}} = 0.1836$

To gain additional credibility for the study at hand, the two outliers mentioned before will be included into the study in order to add a sensitivity analysis of the best estimate by also producing low and high estimate values. One of the two outliers derived from the literature is the case of Beijing, where only 6% of migrant workers were found to profit from health insurance coverage (Mou et al., 2013, p. 30; Peng et al., 2010, p. 4). It might be argued that this value is too low to be realistic, as the health insurance coverage rate increased after the study had taken place (Meng et al., 2012a). On the other hand, the studies that promoted the 19% value were judged to potentially overestimate. To assume a value between 6% and 19% is therefore not unrealistic at all. The analysis at hand will consequently calculate the low estimate value as a 50% reduction of the best estimate (18.36%) deriving 9.18% as the low estimate value. The high estimate is geared to the calculation of Giles and colleagues, who propose a 30% rate (Giles et al., 2013, p. 11). As already mentioned in footnote 73 (see above), Giles et al. use the number of rural-urban migrants instead of all migrants as their denominator (Giles et al., 2013, p. 42). Indirectly, this leads to the assumption that only those migrants moving from rural-to-urban areas (but not urban-to-urban migrants) will encounter problems with their de facto health insurance coverage. Such a view is not supported by the literature. Those authors rather state that the de facto insurance status will also be lost if people migrate from one urban area (potentially small cities as categorized in the "National New Urbanization Plan" (新华, 2014, p. 15)) to another urban area (WHO, 2008b, p. 10). Despite the fact that no evidence could be found for the underlying assumptions above, this analysis will include the proposed 30% value (Giles et al., 2013, p. 11) as a high estimate value for the calculation of the health insurance status of Chinese citizens. This will be done by adding 50% to the formerly described best estimate (18.36%) – resulting in a value of 27.54%. In the following chapters, the depicted three scenarios will consequently rely on a value of 18.36% for the best, 9.18% for the low and 27.54% for the high estimate scenario.[75]

---

[75] Additional data needed for the calculations, for example in the case of population and subgroup data, will be retrieved from official sources like the National Bureau of Statistics of China (NBSC, 2012).

3.3.2.2.2 Future scenario

As in the 2011 analysis, the calculations for 2020 will be performed based on the three scenarios – low, best and high estimates of insured migrant workers. As the same percentage values will be used – 9.18%, 18.36% and 27.54% – this point will not be discussed any further. Instead, the following passages will build on the former chapters' argumentation.

The values that need further explanation, as they vary from the former chapter, are the amount of newly insured migrant workers and of the growing urban population. This information can be retrieved from the "National New Urbanization Plan", published by the Chinese news agency Xinhua in 2014. This government policy plans to grant urban *hukou*s to approximately 100 million more migrant workers. Although these *hukou*s will mainly be issued in smaller cities than bigger[76] ones (新华, 2014, p. 15), this study only refers to the fact that health insurance access will be granted to 100 million further migrants in urban areas. The future scenario will analyze in how far these additional 100 million insured make a difference concerning the insurance coverage rate. The number of newly insured migrant workers shall however be put in relation to a growing urban population, as the Chinese government announced to further increase the rate of urban inhabitants to 60% (新华, 2014, p. 13). Compared to 2011, this is an increase of 8.73 percentage points[77].

In addition to the mentioned tendencies regarding reinsured migrant workers and urban population growth, the future scenario will furthermore include calculations that prognosticate a growing Chinese population. A population division of the United Nations prospects 1.433 billion[78] Chinese citizens in 2020 (UN, 2014), the World Bank 1.408 billion[79] (World Bank, 2014b). Despite being only slightly different, this difference might be important if the results come close to the 90% and universal coverage aims. In order to

---

[76] The exact size of cities and exact restrictions on each of them is laid out in the "National New Urbanization Plan" in more detail (新华, 2014, p. 15).

[77] Author's calculations based on the National Bureau of Statistics of China (NBSC, 2012): $0.6 - \frac{urban\ dwellers\ (2011)}{total\ population\ (2011)} = 0.6 - 0.5127 = 0.0873$. This calculation is also consistent with World Bank data that finds 50.57% of the Chinese population living in cities in 2011 (World Bank, 2014b).

[78] The exact number is 1,432,867,566 (UN, 2014).

[79] The exact number is 1,407,884,000 (World Bank, 2014b).

not to be prone to critique, this analysis will work with the more conservative estimates of the World Bank.

Further data needed will be retrieved from the National Bureau of Statistics of China (NBSC, 2012).

3.3.2.3 Methodology

The chapter above (3.3.2.2) has shown that the data from the NHSS, despite its high quality and value, do not properly reflect the health insurance coverage of the Chinese population including the special situation of migrant workers. In order to gain an understanding of China's health insurance coverage situation including migrant workers, the following part will merge the findings of the NHSS with those of other scholars and the modeled three scenarios described above.

3.3.2.3.1 Calculating the present amount of *de facto* health insured citizens

The need to combine the two data sources dealing with, firstly, the health insurance coverage rate of migrant workers (Giles et al., 2013, pp. 18–19; Hesketh et al., 2008a, p. 194; Mou et al., 2013, p. 30; NBSC, 2012; Peng et al., 2010) (chapter 3.1) and, secondly, the health insurance coverage rates of Chinese households (Meng et al., 2012b; 黄, 2012) arises from two observations: Firstly, the NHSS household survey under-represents migrating people (Meng et al., 2012b, p. 813). Secondly, being *de jure* inscribed in an insurance scheme is not equal to being *de facto* insured if the place of living is different from the reach of the insurance scheme and the issued *hukou* (Holdaway, 2008, p. 9; WHO, 2008b, p. 10) (compare 3.3.1.2).

The first observation leads to two assumptions that the following analysis will build on. Firstly, it is assumed that an inclusion of all migrant workers will not lead to a change of the relative insurance rates given by Meng and colleagues. As the former analysis has shown that migrant workers, due to institutional barriers and inverse incentives, are in general less well insured (3.3.1.2), this assumption can once again be regarded to be conservative and hence adds to the credibility of its findings. Secondly, it is assumed that migrant workers already included in the numbers of Meng and colleagues are distributed over the insured and uninsured groups with the same ratio as sedentary people are. This as well, due to the same reasons that were mentioned for the first assumption, can be regarded as a conservative hypothesis and hence also adds to the credibility. Building on the two assumptions described, this study will calculate the *de facto* insured part of the population by assuming that the NHSS data included the same proportional part of migrant workers in the *de jure* insured part of the population as their proportional representation in the total population and will not be altered by migrant workers that have not participated in the household survey. This issue is explained in more detail in the following paragraph and in Box 2.

In order to be able to calculate the specific numbers, in this study, the total Chinese population (tp) will be divided into *de jure* insured (ip) and *de jure* uninsured people (up) (Figure 21). Both groups contain a certain part of migrant workers (mw). They are labeled mw$_{ip}$, if found in the group of *de jure* insured people (ip), and mw$_{up}$, if found within the *de jure* uninsured group (up) (Figure 21). The group of *de jure* insured has however been shown to sometimes face severe barriers in accessing

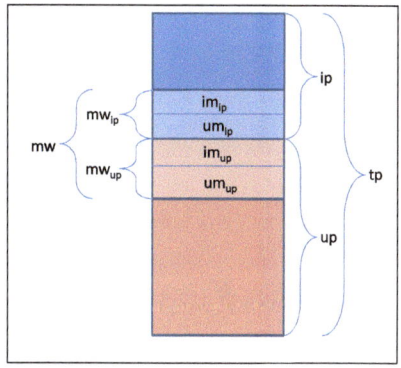

Figure 21: "Insurance status including migrant workers." author's investigation.

health care services (3.3.1.2) with the result of severe health problems (3.3.1.3). In this study, those people will, independent of their *de jure* insurance status, be regarded as *de facto* uninsured. To calculate the amount of *de facto* insured, migrant workers will be regarded as only *de jure*, but not *de facto* insured, except if they were explicitly (re)insured in their new place of working and living. The different percentage values of insured migrant workers found by different scholars and their adaptation to a low, a best, and a high estimate scenario with the respective values of 9.18%, 18.36% and 27.54% (3.3.2.2.1) will be used for further calculations of the number of *de facto* insured migrants (im). They are labeled im$_{ip}$, if found within the group of *de jure* insured (ip) and im$_{up}$, if found within the *de jure* uninsured people (up) (Figure 21). To answer the first research question, it will be necessary to calculate the group of *de facto* insured citizens

117

(ip_{mw}), which includes the dark blue part, as well as the im_{ip}- and im_{up}-part in Figure 21 (see above). An explanation on the math behind can be found in Box 2.

Box 2: Calculating the *de facto* insured citizens (ip_{mw}):

As migrant workers are generally regarded to be *de facto* uninsured, but some migrant workers have been (re)insured within urban insurance schemes (im), the amount of *de facto* insured citizens (ip_{mw}) could be calculated by subtracting the number of migrant workers within the insured part of the population (mw_{ip}) from the number of *de jure* insured people (ip) and adding the amount of (re)insured migrant workers (im):

$$ip_{mw} = ip - mw_{ip} + im.$$

Migrant workers within the *de jure* insured part of the population (mw_{ip}) are, one the other hand, assumed to be distributed the same way than non-migrating people. In other words, migrant workers (mw_{ip} or mw) account for the same relative portion independent from the main unit – e.g. the *de jure* insured part of the population (ip) or the total population (tp):

$$mw_{ip}/ip = mw/tp \Leftrightarrow mw_{ip} = mw/tp*ip.$$

Combining the two formulas, ip_{mw} can be calculated:

$$ip_{mw} = ip-(mw/tp*ip) +im$$

To answer the second research question, some additional steps are necessary. The calculation of the future amount of *de facto* health insured citizens is undertaken by assuming that rural and urban areas enjoy an equal growth rate if no further migration would happen. The change of the urbanization rate is hence interpreted as a result of migration and not of a higher fertility rate of urban citizens. The amount of insured people in the PRC in 2020 (ip_{mw}) builds on the same insurance levels as in 2011 (Box 2) and adds the amount of migrants who will be granted access to urban insurance schemes by receiving urban *hukou*s (新华, 2014, p. 13).

3.3.2.3.2   Detailed investigations on urban health insurance schemes

In order to understand the specific situation of rural and urban areas, further investigations on the population structure are needed. As shown in Figure 22, the Chinese population has been growing since 1980 and will keep on growing until roughly 2030.

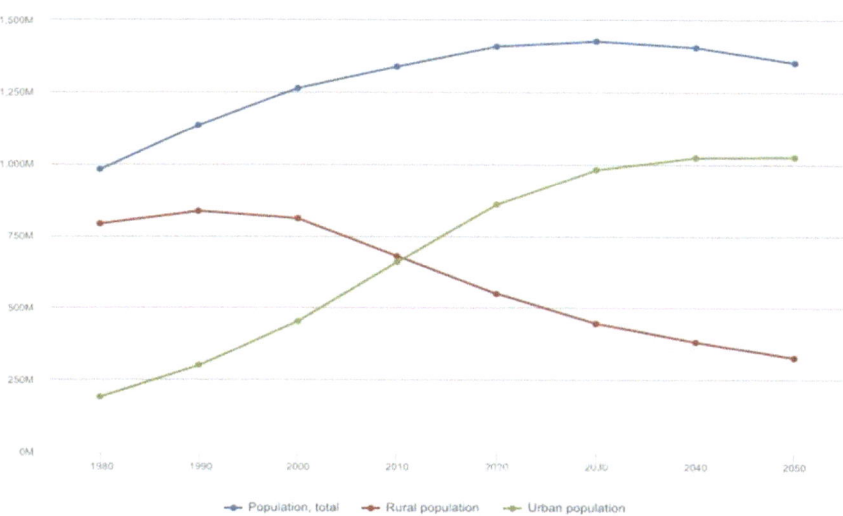

Country : China
Created from: Health Nutrition and Population Statistics: Population estimates and projections
Figure 22: "Population development in China 1980-2050" (World Bank 2014).

Thereafter, it will slowly decrease (blue line in Figure 22). Looking at the relationship between urban (green line in Figure 22) and rural residents (red line in Figure 22), rural residents seem to have had outnumbered urban residents until 2010. After this tipping point, the relationship turned around with urban citizens outnumbering rural citizens (World Bank, 2014b). The magnitude of the growth of these two populations indicates that migration from rural-to-urban areas plays an important role in China. This view is also supported by scholars who find that half of the migrants originate from rural areas and half from urban areas (Ness, 2013). Although it is theoretically possible that some of these migrants aim at rural areas, this analysis assumes that urban areas are the destination point of the migration in China. This is not to oppose that some migrants in urban areas might return back to their rural home places. Those movements would however not count as migration as they lead to reducing the number of migrants by turning former migrant workers into sedentary citizens again.

Two further assumptions have already been outlined in chapter 3.3.2.3.1. Firstly, it was mentioned that this analysis derives the number of *de facto* insured part of the population by assuming that the NHSS data included the same proportional part of migrant workers in the *de jure* insured part of the population as their proportional representation in the total population. Secondly, it was assumed that these proportions would stay constant even if those migrants not belonging to households are included (3.3.2.3.2).

Building on these three assumptions – that migrant workers within the NHSS are distributed proportionally over the different sub groups, that these proportions are constant if further migrant workers are included and that migration in China only happens with urban areas as destination – two observations can be made according the rural insurance system: Firstly, the rural population will shrink because migrant workers mainly leave but do not enter rural areas. Secondly, the rural health insurance coverage rate will not change, because the same proportional amount of *de jure* uninsured migrants as *de jure* insured migrants leaves the countryside. Therefore, a detailed investigation of the rural areas would not lead to any new findings and will hence not be undertaken in this study. It is however possible to state that the rural *de jure* proportion of insured inhabitants is equal to the de facto proportion: 97.4% in 2011 (Meng et al., 2012b; 黄, 2012). As a consequence, it can be concluded that China, in its rural areas, not only reached its 90% goal, but also reached a level that can be labeled universal coverage as it nearly reaches 100% of the rural population. This, however, cannot be stated for the urban part of the population. In that case, effects of migration might be observed more clearly.

In order to better understand the magnitude that migration to urban areas poses to the place of destination, this study will attribute migrant workers to the group of urban inhabitants and consequently the urban medical insurance schemes. The urban medical insurance schemes consist of UEBMI and URBMI (compare 1.4)[80]. The group of urban dwellers (ud_{mw}) involves urbans holding an urban residence permit (ud) as well as migrant workers living and working in cities (mw). Each of these groups is again divided into insured (im and iu) and uninsured (um and uu)

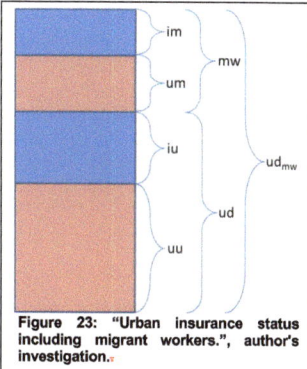

Figure 23: "Urban insurance status including migrant workers.", author's investigation.

sub-groups (Figure 23). Concerning the amount of *de facto* insured urbans within those schemes (iu_{mw}), migrant workers who have been (re)insured within urban insurance schemes (im) have to be added to the insured urban residents (iu) (see Figure 23, Box 3).

Box 3: Calculating the *de facto* amount of urban (iu_{mw}) insured:

The relative amount of *de facto* insured urbans ($iu_{mw\%}$) can be found by dividing the number of *de facto* insured urban people (iu_{mw}) by the number of the *de facto* urban population (ud_{mw}). The first value can be derived by adding the reinsured migrant workers (im) to the *de jure* insured urbans (iu) (iu_{mw} = iu + im); the second value by adding the *de jure* urban population (ud) to the number of migrant workers (mw) (ud_{mw} = ud + mw). Taking into account the low and high estimates proposed by other scholars, the im-value has to be adapted accordingly. For iu_{mw} it therefore follows:

Low estimate: $iu_{mw\%} = iu_{mw}/ud_{mw} = (iu+50\%*im)/(ud+mw)$
Best estimate: $iu_{mw\%} = iu_{mw}/ud_{mw} = (iu+100\%*im)/(ud+mw)$
High estimate: $iu_{mw\%} = iu_{mw}/ud_{mw} = (iu+150\%*im)/(ud+mw)$

---

[80] The UEBMI and URBMI systems are complemented by some minor systems. They are included in the calculations, but not explicitly mentioned here.

121

3.3.2.4 Results

The results of this study will be listed by firstly addressing the total population and secondly the urban population.

3.3.2.4.1 Results for the total part of the population

The calculations of the *de facto* health insured Chinese citizens for 2011 built on different sources: Firstly, the three different scenarios, secondly, findings from the NHSS and thirdly, official numbers from the National Bureau of Statistics of China (compare 3.3.2.2). The approach of calculating the *de facto* insured citizens (ip_{mw}) is outlined in detail in Box 2. Findings for values which fed into this calculation are given in Table 30. The best estimate for the group of *de facto* insured citizens (ip_{mw}) is 1093.91 million people, with a range of roughly 20 million people for the for the low (1070.71 million) and high (1117.12 million) estimate scenarios (see Table 30).

Variable	Low (in million)	Best (in million)	High (in million)	Variable	Low (in million)	Best (in million)	High (in million)
tp	1347.35	1347.35	1347.35	tp	1,407.88	1,407.88	1,407.88
ip	1289.41	1289.41	1289.41	ip	1,347.34	1,347.34	1,347.34
up	57.94	57.94	57.94	up	60.54	60.54	60.54
mw	252.78	252.78	252.78	mw	375.69	375.69	375.69
im	23.21	46.41	69.62	im	134.49	168.98	203.46
um	229.58	206.37	183.17	um	241.20	206.71	172.22
ip_{mw}	1070.71	1093.91	1117.12	ip_{mw}	1,122.30	1,156.79	1,191.27

Table 30 "Insurance status 2011 including migrant workers.", data from the National Bureau of Statistics of China (NBSC 2012), author's investigation.

Table 29: "Insurance status 2020 including migrant workers.", data from the National Bureau of Statistics of China (NBSC 2012) and the World Bank (World Bank 2014), author's investigation.

The calculations of the *de facto* health insured Chinese citizens for 2020 are performed analogous to those for 2011, except for additionally building on the projections that were described in the methodology chapter (3.3.2.3). Building on the methodology above, the best estimate for the *de facto* insured citizens (ip_{mw}) in 2020 is 1.157 billion people, with a range of approximately 35 million people for the low (1.122 billion people) and high (1.191 billion people) estimate scenarios (see Table 29).

Comparing the *de jure* insured Chinese citizens (ip) – calculated on the basis of the NHSS (Meng et al., 2012b; 黄, 2012) – with the *de facto* amount

Scenario	ip (in million)	ip$_{mw}$ (in million)	Difference ip (in million)	ip (in percent)	ip$_{mw}$ (in percent)	Difference (in percentage points)
Low	1,289.41	1,070.71	218.70	95.70%	79.47%	15.37
Best	1,289.41	1,093.91	195.50	95.70%	81.19%	12.79
High	1,289.41	1,117.12	172.29	95.70%	82.91%	10.20

Table 31: "Number of *de jure* (ip) and *de facto* (ip$_{mw}$) insured people in the PRC in 2011", data from the National Bureau of Statistics of China (NBSC 2012), author's investigation.

of insured citizens (ip$_{mw}$), remarkable differences are found. Taking into account the special situation of migrant workers considerably lowers the rate of insured people from 1,289.41 million to 1,093.91 million in the best estimate. The difference is therefore around 200 million people that were formerly accounted to be insured, but actually are not, following this study's calculations. The low and high estimates, again, approximately range by 20 million. Consequently, the aim set by the Chinese government – to insure 90% of the population – is reached only *de jure* (95.7%), but not *de facto* (81.19%). This does not only hold true for the best (81.19%), but also for the low (79.47%) and high (82.91%) estimate scenario (Table 31). In other words, roughly 1/5 of the Chinese population is still left without *de facto* health insurance in 2011, no matter if the low, best or high estimate scenario is applied.

For the 2020 future scenarios nearly the same findings can be made as for the present 2011 scenarios. Once again, the amount of *de facto* insured people drops remarkably after taking into account the lower insurance rate of migrant workers. The difference between *de jure* and *de facto* insured Chinese citizens is about 190 million in the best estimate scenario, with a range of approximately 35 million people for the low and high estimate scenarios. This equals a reduction of approximately 14 percentage points in the best estimate, and 16-11 percentage points in

Scenario	ip (in million)	ip$_{mw}$ (in million)	Difference ip (in million)	ip (in percent)	ip$_{mw}$ (in percent)	Difference (in percentage points)
Low	1,347.34	1,122.30	225.05	95.70%	79.72%	15.98
Best	1,347.34	1,156.79	190.56	95.70%	82.16%	13.54
High	1,347.34	1,191.27	156.07	95.70%	84.61%	11.09

Table 32: "Number of *de jure* (ip) and *de facto* (ip$_{mw}$) insured people in the PRC in 2020.", data from the National Bureau of Statistics of China (NBSC 2012) and the World Bank (World Bank 2014), author's investigation.

the low and high estimates. Also in the future scenarios, the aim set by the Chinese government – to insure 90% or even 100% of the population – is not reached *de facto*, as only 82.16% of the population is insured in the best, 79.72% in the low and 84.61% in the high estimate scenario (see Table 32).

Furthermore, the findings made for the future mean that the policy of 2014 will not reduce the problem of uninsured migrant workers. Despite going in the right direction, the effect of insuring additional 100 million migrant workers through granting them access to urban *hukou*s is not sufficient. The positive effect of this policy is nearly neutralized by the increasing urbanization that the Chinese government wants to achieve until 2020. It can be observed that the effect of granting urban *hukou*s to 100 million more migrant

Scenario	Increase of uninsured Chinese citizens 2011-2020	
	(in million)	(in percentage points)
Low	8.94	0.00
Best	-2.34	-0.01
High	-13.63	-0.02

Table 33: "Increase of uninsured Chinese citizens 2011-2020.", data from the National Bureau of Statistics of China (NBSC 2012) and the World Bank (World Bank 2014), author's investigation.

workers does not change the rate of insured Chinese citizens in either of three scenarios (see Table 33). The rate of uninsured migrant workers is consequently unlikely to change significantly until 2020 and the reform announced by the Chinese government in 2014 must be interpreted as a step towards keeping up the *status quo*, but not as a step towards improving the current situation (see Table 32).

Both goals set by the Chinese government – to reach 90% health insurance coverage in 2011 and 100%

Year	90% goal for $ip_{mw\%}$	ip_{mw}	100% goal for $ip_{mw\%}$	ip_{mw}	Difference status quo-90%	Difference 90%-100%
	(in percent)	(in million)	(in percent)	(in million)	(in million)	(in million)
2011	90.00%	1,212.62	100.00%	1,347.35	118.70	134.74
2020	90.00%	1,267.10	100.00%	1,407.88	110.31	140.79

Table 34: "Gaps to reaching the 90% and 100% goal in 2011 and 2020.", data from the National Bureau of Statistics of China (NBSC 2012) and the World Bank (World Bank 2014), author's investigation.

in 2020 – could only have been reached and will only be reached if a higher amount of people is insured. For 2011, nearly an additional 120 million people would have had to be insured. For the year 2020, the Chinese government will have to insure 110 million more to reach the 90% goal and 250 million more[81] to reach nearly 100% insurance coverage (see Table 34).

---

[81] The 250 million value is the sum of the two differences with the values of approximately 110 million and 140 million (see Table 34).

3.3.2.4.2 Results for the urban part of the population

Building on the methodology described in 3.3.2.3.2, the *de facto* amount of urban insured (iu_{mw}) can be calculated (see Table 35). Comparing *de jure* and *de facto* values of health insurance coverage, it is found that the attribution of migrant workers to urban insurance schemes – the only schemes that could change the *e* percentage – drops by approximately 20 percentage points to an insurance rate of roughly 70% (69% for the low and 74% for the high insurance scenario) (see Table 35). The formulas used for these calculations are shown in Box 3.

Scenario	iu (in million)	iu_{mw} (in million)	Difference (in million)	$iu_\%$ (in percent)	$iu_{mw\%}$ (in percent)	Difference (in percentage points)
Low	627.93	651.13	-23.21	90.90%	69.01%	21.89
Best	627.93	674.34	-46.41	90.90%	71.47%	19.43
High	627.93	697.54	-69.62	90.90%	73.93%	16.97

Table 35: "Number of *de jure* (ip) and *de facto* (ip_{mw}) insured urban citizens in 2011.", data from the National Bureau of Statistics of China (NBSC 2012) and the World Bank (World Bank 2014), author's investigation.

This means first of all: As migrant workers migrate from urban or rural places to urban areas, the insurance schemes of the target places are highly stressed, leading to low rates of *de facto* insurance rates. Secondly, it becomes obvious that migrant workers make up the biggest share of uninsured urban inhabitants. Depending on the scenario, for every uninsured urban resident there are 3.65 (low), 3.28 (best) or 2.91 (high) migrant workers without servable health insurance. As an approximation, it can be said that ¾ of all uninsured urban inhabitants are migrants (see Table 36).

Scenario	um (in million)	uu (in million)	Ratio (um/uu)
Low	229.58	62.86	3.65
Best	206.37	62.86	3.28
High	183.17	62.86	2.91

Table 36: "Comparison of uninsured migrant workers in cities (um) and uninsured urban residents (uu)", author's investigation.

Combining these two findings, it can be stated that the existing gap between rural and urban insurance status mainly arises from the amount of migrant workers pouring into the cities. It is primarily them who are suffering from the lack of *de facto* health insurance coverage.

In the year 2020, the lack of *de facto* health insurance in urban areas will, very likely, still be a migrant workers' problem. Calculations show that the inclusion of the

Scenario	iu (in million)	iu_{mw} (in million)	Difference (in million)	$iu_\%$ (in percent)	$iu_{mw\%}$ (in percent)	Difference (in percentage points)
Low	767.86	902.35	-134.49	90.90%	73.94%	16.96
Best	767.86	936.84	-168.98	90.90%	76.76%	14.14
High	767.86	971.32	-203.46	90.90%	79.59%	11.31

Table 37: "Number of *de jure* (ip) and *de facto* (ip_{mw}) insured urban citizens in 2020.", data from the National Bureau of Statistics of China (NBSC 2012) and the World Bank (World Bank 2014), author's investigation.

migrant workers group reduces the health insurance rate from roughly 90% to 75% – the exact values for the three scenarios are listed in Table 37.

Although showing similarities in the main findings with the present scenarios, the future scenarios make clear that the policy of 2014 will have a slight but visible impact on the situation in urban areas. While the 2011 findings indicate a *de jure* health insurance rate of 72%, 69% and 74% for the best, the low and the high estimates (see Table 36), the projections for 2020 show an increase of roughly 5 percentage points, granting about 77%, 74% and 80% of urban inhabitants access to health insurance schemes (compare Table 36 and Table 37). Therefore, the findings of chapter 3.3.2.4.1 have to be slightly corrected. Small positive effects of the policy of 2014 of insuring additional 100 million urban inhabitants become evident if the situation of the whole country (4.2) is compared with the situation of the urban population (5.3). The policy goal to insure another 100 million migrant workers by issuing urban *hukou*s, must therefore be interpreted as slightly improving the insurance situation in urban areas. It is therefore not merely a policy to maintain, but to slightly improve the current *status quo*.

Nonetheless, these positive effects are only minor and large challenges still remain. In order to also reach the 90% goal in 2011 in urban areas, the Chinese government would

Year	90% goal for $iu_{mw\%}$ (in percent)	iu_{mw} (in million)	100% goal for $iu_{mw\%}$ (in percent)	iu_{mw} (in million)	Difference status quo-90% (in million)	Difference 90%-100% (in million)
2011	90.00%	849.21	100.00%	943.57	174.87	94.36
2020	90.00%	1,098.38	100.00%	1,220.42	161.54	122.04

Table 38: "Gaps to reaching the 90% and 100% goal in 2011 and 2020 in urban areas.", data from the National Bureau of Statistics of China (NBSC 2012) and the World Bank (World Bank 2014), author's investigation.

have had to insure 175 million more urban people than it actually did. In order to reach the 90% target in 2020, it will have to insure more than 160 million more migrants than it is already planning to insure through the policy of 2014. The aim to reach universal coverage in 2020 could only be met if more than another 280 million people would get access to health insurance, already accounting for those targeted by the policy of 2014 (see Table 38).

It might be questioned why some of the results in the paragraph above are higher than those presented for the total population. Comparing the result values for the urban with those for the total population (as a difference taken as total minus urban), a negative result is found for the difference between the status quo and the 90% target, for both the 2011 and the 2020 scenario. This points towards the slightly puzzling result that a lower additional amount of people has to be insured in the total than in the partial urban population (see Table 39). One explanation of this finding is that the total population includes the rural part where *de facto* coverage is already above 90%. In this case, the deficiencies of the urban locations are partly neutralized and hence better than the results for the urban population. The difference between the 90% goal and the 100% goal show, as expected, that the amount of people which have to be reinsured in urban areas is smaller than that of the total population (see Table 39). This, of course, appears because gaps have to be filled in rural as well as in urban areas.

Comparison of the total and the urban area	
Difference status quo-90% (in million)	Difference 90%-100% (in million)
-56.17	40.38
-51.23	18.75

Table 39: "Gaps to reaching the 90% and 100% goal in 2011 and 2020 as a comparison of the total and the urban area.", data from the National Bureau of Statistics of China (NBSC 2012) and the World Bank (World Bank 2014), author's investigation.

3.3.2.6 Conclusion and policy implications

This analysis could give new insights into the *de facto* health insurance coverage rate in the PRC by analyzing the situation in 2011 and the future situation (through aspired numbers for 2020). The year 2011 was chosen because of two reasons: Firstly, it is the latest year of the NHSS study which contributed outstanding insights into the *de jure* health insurance coverage rate (Meng et al., 2012b; 黄, 2012). Secondly, the Chinese government announced to reach more than 90% coverage rate in 2011 (PRC, 2011, 2009). The year 2020 was chosen to represent the future because the Chinese government has announced to grant urban *hukou*s to 100 million people by 2020 and thereby allow them to access urban health insurance schemes (新华, 2014).

The year 2011 as well as the future analysis were undertaken by building on three different scenarios: A best estimate scenario, where roughly 20% of all migrants own servable, and therefore *de facto*, health insurance, as well as a low and high estimate scenario with approximately 10% and 30% of insured migrant workers.

The two approaches – for the year 2011 and for 2020 – and the three scenarios – low, best and high – where able to answer both research questions identified in part 1:

The first research question, "Did the Chinese government succeed with insuring more than 90% of its population to health insurance plans in 2011?", can be answered negatively. Although the government managed to *de jure* insure 95.7% of the total population – that is 97.4% of the rural and 90.9% of the urban population – the *de facto* insurance rates are lower. By taking into account the special situation of migrant workers, health insurance coverage rates drop to 81.19% (best estimate) for the total population and to 71.47% for the urban population. The rural population is not negatively affected, keeping its high insurance level of 97.4%.

Also the second research question, "Is universal health insurance coverage reached with the policy of 2014 targeting migrant workers' *hukou* status", must be answered negatively. Analyzing the possible effects of this reform for the whole population, this study finds that the reform initiated in 2014 does not change the situation that was found in 2011. Granting urban *hukou*s, and thereby access to health insurance, to further 100 million migrants does not show any significant positive effects for the total population and only slightly positive effects for the urban population. Although steering into the right direction, the higher amount of insured people that can be anticipated according to the policy of 2014 is neutralized by the higher total number of migrant workers that must be expected in 2020. Nonetheless, both comparisons, the one with the total (3.3.2.4.1) and the one with the urban population (3.3.2.4.2) find insurance coverage rates – 77% and 82% respectively – that are significantly below the 90% goal of the Chinese government and even more below universal coverage.

128

The final conclusion for both research questions is therefore that the government of the PRC has only managed to *de jure* insure more than 90% of its population, but fails to insure *de facto* – meaning including migrant workers – more than 90%, even more so 100%. This holds true for the year 2011 as well as the future analysis, all three scenarios and the situation for the total and the urban population. An exemption to this is the situation in rural areas, where nearly 100% of the people *de facto* own health insurance already since 2011.

This chapter (3.3.2.6) points towards policy implications that arise from the findings above. In order to reach the target of universal coverage by 2020, the Chinese government would not only have to insure the additional 100 million migrants planned by the policy of 2014, but also further 250-280 million people depending on the reference point (the total population or the urban population) (see 3.3.2.4.1 and 3.3.2.4.2). The policy suggestion therefore is to enlarge the planned number of new urban *hukou*s to 350 million or 380 million and not "only" 100 million. According to the numbers found in official Chinese data sets and data sets of international organizations, this number would ensure to reach the goals laid out in the 2009 "Implementation Plan for the Recent Priorities of the Health Care System Reform (2009-2011)" (PRC, 2009) and the 12th Five-Year Plan issued in 2011 (PRC, 2011).

Although enlarging the number of new urban *hukou* holders specified in the Chinese policy of 2014 (新华, 2014) will ensure to reach the goal of universal health care in 2020, this way of dealing with the problem is not a structural one, but rather a repair solution. The structural issue which leads to the problem of uninsured migrants in urban areas is the barriers which prohibit the use of health insurance contracts that are issued in the home place of the migrants. This problem has already been addressed by the Chinese government itself. In 2009, the Chinese Ministry of Human Resources and Social Security, the Chinese Ministry of Health and the Chinese Ministry of Finance jointly issued a document called "Notification on a professional method to continue health insurance of the floating and work seeking population" ("关于印发流动就业人员基本医疗保障关系转移接续暂行办法的通知") (人力资源和社会保障部 et al., 2009). In this document, the three ministries laid ground for a policy that can issue a so called "All-in-One Card" and thereby allow migrant workers to move between cities and areas and still receive health care within their area of living and working. The policy explicitly aims to offering flexibility through the possibility of transferring personal accounts from one insurance scheme to another and not discriminating people according to their *hukou* (人力资源和社会保障部 et al., 2009). This policy would equally well lead to universal health insurance in 2020 as the above proposed policy, if it would be applied nation-wide. An appealing aspect of the "All-in-One Card" would hence be that it offers a solution which would not need to adapt to changing amounts of migrant workers. It would solve the underlying problem in a systematic way.

4 Summary and conclusion

The objective of the study at hand is to give an insight into the situation of UHC in China from a health economic perspective. Therefore, in the first chapter, the author introduced into the historical background, analyzed the relevance of UHC today and shed a first light on the health insurance status in the People's Republic.

In the second chapter, "Definition and concept", the structure of this study was laid out. It was shown that UHC is made up of three dimensions of health insurance. Firstly, the height dimension with the leading question "What proportion of the costs is covered?", secondly, the depth dimension that is concerned with the question "Which benefits are covered?" and thirdly, the breadth dimension which investigates "Who is insured?". Due to limited resources however, these three dimensions are not achievable to their full extent in every state of the PRC. Hence, three further questions have been found to arise on the way of implementing UHC. They are: 1. "How to shift from out-of-pocket payment toward pre-payment?", 2. "Which services to expand first?" and 3. "Whom to include first?". A guiding principle for this second set of questions is the need of the people which was defined as the gap between actual and normal health levels (2.1.2.2).

From a conceptual point of view, the first dimension (height) was structured by looking at health economic theory and practical approaches from the international community (2.1). Both approaches have shown that UHC should strive to separate the use of health services from the payment of services in order to achieve financial risk protection

130

and access to medical services. These goals have been shown to be achievable through the implementation of prepayment mechanisms and sharing risks through pooling them on a population basis. A measurable outcome of such interventions is the rate of OOP which should at least fall below 15-20% of total health expenditure. In addition, a need oriented, equitable health service consumption level (benefits) among the income quintiles as well as a need oriented and equitable fundraising (payments) is demanded to be assured (2.1.2.2).

Also, the second dimension (depth) is taking into account health economic theory and practical approaches of the international community (2.2). In reference to health economic theory, it concludes that the amount of consumed health care does not necessary lead to a higher health output. The reason for this observation is founded on the insight that health services have to be appropriate for the situation of the individual patient. The appropriateness of health care services can in turn be measured through practical approaches such as cost-effectiveness (CEA) and cost-benefit analyses (CBA), in which the financial investment is compared to health outputs like DALYs and their monetary value. Within the CEA, available tools allow to rank potential services into high, middle and low categories which facilitate priority setting for the inclusion of health interventions into a catalogue of benefits.

The third dimension (breadth) investigated findings of the scientific community (chapter 2.3). It was found that states tend to insure rich income quintiles of the population first, in order to quickly expand the coverage rate. Unfortunately, through this approach low income quintiles are often marginalized and not easily included later on. As lower income quintiles often have a higher need for health services, medical care consumption is often inversely correlated with the need of the population (inverse care law). The conclusion drawn from this dimension was therefore to include vulnerable groups from the very beginning.

The third chapter of this study described the situation in the People's Republic of China by using the three dimensions as a guiding structure. Concerning the first of the three dimensions (height) (chapter 3.1), it was found that the amount of OOP has not reached the lowest requirement of 15-20% until 2012, but still ranges at least around 35%. It is therefore not surprising that catastrophic health payments still affect about 13% of all Chinese households and roughly one third of all self-discharges happen due to financial reasons (nearly 10% of all inpatients). Despite these alarming observations, it is generally pointed out that OOP and the rate of self-discharge are shrinking. The constancy of the rate of households that experience catastrophic health expenditures (13%) can be explained by the underlying health economic theory, which states that higher financial support (and hence lower OOP) increases the access to health services and the amount of consumption and money spent. Although pointing to a positive aspect (increased access), the constant rate of catastrophic health expenditure is nonetheless a sign for a high need of improvement in the Chinese health insurance system.

With respect to the distribution of benefits, measured as reimbursement rates, an inequitable distribution was found wherever differentiable. In detail, these findings (listed in Table 40) are: (1) The reimbursement rates between the three big social health insurance schemes (UEBMI, URBMI, NCMS) proved to be inequitable as the Chinese system does not include structures which redistribute according to the need levels of the participants. (2) Due to a lack of data, it was not possible to investigate in how far such structures exist within the schemes. (3-4) Regarding the inpatient reimbursement rates, the situation was found to be mostly inequitable as more benefits were enjoyed by the economically stronger party. The inequality between the schemes arises from favoring the urban (UEBMI and URBMI) schemes compared to the rural (NCMS) scheme and the urban working population (UEBMI) compared to the non-working population (URBMI). Within the schemes, high income groups, those living in urban areas and, with one exception, those living in wealthier regions are favored in the Chinese health insurance system. (5) Looking at outpatient services, the lack of data unfortunately prohibits judging the level of equity between the schemes. (6) Within the schemes, an inequitable situation has been found, because the redistribution rate correlates positively with the income level of the population (Table 40).

distribution system	field of analysis		effect of distribution
SHI	(1)	reimbursement rates (social redistribution-between)	inequity
	(2)	reimbursement rates (social redistribution-within)	not distinguishable
	(3)	reimbursement rates (inpatient-between)	inequity
	(4)	reimbursement rates (inpatient-within)	inequity
	(5)	reimbursement rates (outpatient-between)	not distinguishable
	(6)	reimbursement rates (outpatient-within)	inequity

Table 40: "Summary of benefit related equity issues in the Chinese health insurance system", author's investigation.

Regarding the equitable raising of payments, a more differentiated result was found (Table 41). Similar to the findings of the benefits section, (1) the pre-payments between the schemes cannot be redistributed between the social groups as the schemes are not connected. This issue is hence labeled inequitable. Also parallel to the benefits section, (2) no data was available for social redistribution within the schemes and the level of equity is hence not distinguishable. (3) Between the three social insurance schemes, pre-payments are however raised in an equitable way as participants of the less privileged schemes have to pay lower rates than those of the more privileged ones. (4) An equitable situation was also found within the social health insurance schemes as richer provinces pay more than poorer ones. Investigating the Chinese tax system has shown that (5) the collection of taxes must be labeled inequitable as richer provinces pay less than poorer provinces. (6) The distribution between localities however is equitable, as the distribution mechanism in place favors those provinces with higher financial needs. (7) The same can be said about the tax distribution between social groups. As the government supports those people with financial needs, this mechanism can be labeled equitable as well (Table 41).

distribution system	field of analysis		effect of distribution
SHI	(1)	pre-payments (social redistribution-between)	inequity
	(2)	pre-payments (social redistribution-within)	not distinguishable
	(3)	pre-payments (between)	equity
	(4)	pre-payments (within)	equity
tax	(5)	collection	inequity
	(6)	distribution between localities	equity
	(7)	distribution between social groups	equity

Table 41: "Summary of payment related equity issues in the Chinese health insurance system", author's investigation.

In order to structure the diverse findings pointed out above, studies were analyzed which compare the payment and benefit sides. It has been found that Chinese high income households contribute more financial resources to the health system, but also consume more health services. The health system of the PRC therefore in total distributes health services according to the ability to pay and has not yet managed to fully separate the payment of health services from its consumption. Although it can be observed that the pro-rich government funding strengthens the access to health services of the poor, an equitable funding would require directing resources according to individual needs.

The second dimension of UHC, the depth dimension (chapter 3.2), investigated the situation of appropriate health care in China as it appears today and looked at one specific example for appropriate health interventions in the field of NCDs. The current situation in China regarding appropriate health care showed several systematic problems. Firstly, the unclear clarification of the roles of the different ministries involved leads to over- as well as under-provision of health care. Secondly, the financing structure overburdens lower administrative levels which often cannot provide adequate health services to the people. Thirdly, the benefit package only *de jure* applies cost sharing tools to inappropriate health services. *De facto*, these principles are not followed in Chinese hospitals because of the fee for service system, corruption and missing

134

alternative financing resources. The financial pressure resulting from the fee for service system also ties revenues and bonuses of the staff to these profits. Corruption of pharmaceutical companies and individuals are estimated to account for roughly 50% of the total income of senior physicians. Hospitals generate more than 90% of their revenues through the selling of drugs and services. As many of these wrong incentives lie outside the insurance system and UHC, it was concluded that a health insurance system that builds on the provision of appropriate health care cannot be achieved without reforming the payment system of Chinese hospitals and health providers (3.2.1).

The focus on NCDs as one example of appropriate health service provision has been chosen due to three reasons. Firstly, NCDs are responsible for most of the death incidents in middle-income countries like China. Secondly, their underlying risk factors and physiological risk markers are directly linked to these deaths. Thirdly, the monetary burden from the resulting health problems are huge and mainly growing (chapter 3.2.2). Appropriate interventions to reduce the NCD related health burden have focused on individual based health interventions directed towards the four behavioral risk factors tobacco use, unhealthy diet, physical inactivity and high alcohol consumption, and their four associated physiological risk markers – high blood pressure, overweight and obesity, high blood glucose level and high cholesterol level (chapter 3.2.3). The most appropriate health interventions included skill enhancement of care givers, screening of patients and the actual intervention (they were described in chapter 3.2.4 and summarized in Table 17). The costs for these interventions were calculated (Table 20 and Table 21) building on the number of people at risk (Table 18 and Table 19). They amounted to roughly USD 45 billion for tobacco related interventions, USD 8 billion for diet and physical inactivity related interventions and USD 3 billion for alcohol related interventions (Table 21). Comparing these costs to health outcomes measured in DALYs (chapter 3.2.4.3), a cost-efficiency analysis showed that all four risk factors and all four physiological risk markers qualify for the Chinese catalogue of benefits with the highest priority. All of them, except the risk factor smoking, were furthermore grouped within the high priority section that has no overlapping with the middle priority category and is therefore unequivocally assigned to the highest of the three classes (Figure 19). The risk factor smoking should further be judged according to its influence on the health of the worse off and on financial risk protection, in order to decide if it is to be categorized as high or middle. Comparing the interventions referring to the risk factors and physiological risk markers with other health interventions, it was found that in a worst case scenario the risk factors diet and alcohol as well as the physiological marker high blood pressure would rank among the top ten cost-effective interventions. Under more optimistic assumptions even the interventions relating to physical inactivity and to the other physiological risk markers would be included in the top ten group. Once again, only the risk factor smoking shows less positive results (Figure 20). The reason for the gap between the latter and the other risk factors might foremost be the high intervention costs arising from the recommended treatment via nicotine replacement medication. If a program could produce good results without the help of medication, then the findings in this study would probably be closer to those of the other risk factors.

An additional cost-benefit analysis (chapter 3.2.4.4) compared monetary values for cost and benefits. It showed that investing in individual based medical interventions is highly beneficial and recommendable: Benefits from the four risk factors tobacco, alcohol, diet and physical inactivity were found to surpass the calculated costs by 10-250 times. This means, that policy makers can expect to generate a social value worth USD 10-250 for every USD they invest in the described health interventions. For the associated factors high blood pressure, high BMI, high fasting plasma glucose and high total cholesterol, benefits were 30-210 times higher than the associated costs. Regarding the net benefit of the four risk factors, these positive results translate into a monetary value of USD 0.1-1.9 trillion. For the four physiological risk markers, the net benefits amount to USD 0.2-2.6 trillion. Both analyses, cost effectiveness and cost-benefit, consequently suggest to include individual based interventions in the catalogue of benefits of the Chinese health insurance system (Table 27 and Table 28).

The final dimension (breadth) (chapter 3.3) extracted from a literature review that migrant workers are more severely exposed to various risks than their sedentary counterparts. Sources of this higher risk lie in environmental pollution, the working environment, the housing situation, a low vaccine status, a higher exposure to communicable diseases as well as sexually transmittable diseases (chapter 3.3.1.1). They furthermore suffer from worse health care access due to the fact that rural insurances are not portable to urban settings and urban insurance schemes are only open to those owning the specific *hukou*. Hence, 40% of migrant workers do not seek health care when ill due to financial reasons, and 60% out of those who seek health care choose the cheaper, unauthorized and unqualified health institutions. High medical expenses are also the reason for more than half of the 63.2% who chose to return to their rural homes for inpatient care (chapter 3.3.1.2). Although it was reported that the subjective health rating of migrant workers does not show negative influences, their objectively measurable health status shows the negative effects of higher risk and lower health care access. The health status of migrant workers was found to lack concerning diverse communicable diseases (including sexually transmittable diseases), mental health related diseases, work-related accidents as well as suicides. Due to the additional lack of treatment it is generally stated that these discrepancies will widen in the future (chapter 3.3.1.3).

In order to gain more information about the health insurance coverage of migrant workers in China, an analysis was conducted for the state of 2011 as well as the near future (2020) (chapter 3.3.2). For both points of time, different scenarios were applied: a low coverage scenario which assumes that 9.18% of all migrant workers still own servable health insurance, a best estimate scenario with the value of 18.36% and a high coverage scenario assuming a value of 27.54%. The calculated coverage rate for the Chinese population (including migrant workers) – the *de facto* insured citizens (ip_{mw}) (chapter 3.3.2.4.1) – is 1.094 billion people for the best estimate. This value ranges by roughly 20 million people for the low (1.070 billion) and high (1.117 billion) estimate scenarios (see Table 30 in the main text). For the year 2020, the best estimate for *de facto* insured citizens (ip_{mw}) is 1.157 billion people, with a range of approximately 35 million people for the low (1.122 billion people) and high (1.191 billion people) estimate scenarios (Table 29 of the main text). The calculated best estimates for both years showed that official numbers which do not include migrant workers overestimate the amount of insured people in China by nearly 200 million people (with ranges by roughly 20 million in 2011 and 35 million in 2020 for the low and high estimates). These numbers translate into relative coverage rates of 81.19% for the best estimate, 79.47% for the low and 82.91% for the high estimate scenario in 2011 (Table 31). In other words, roughly 1/5 of the Chinese population is still left without *de facto* health insurance in 2011, no matter if the low, best or high estimate scenario is applied. For 2020 only 82.16% of the population is insured assuming the best, 79.72% the low and 84.61% the high estimate scenario (Table 32). It was hence concluded that the two goals of the Chinese government, to insure 90% of the Chinese population by 2011 and reach universal coverage by 2020, have not been and will not be achieved. In order to achieve these goals, additional 120 million people would have had to be insured in 2011 and the Chinese government would have to insure 110 million more to reach the 90% goal and 250 million more to reach nearly 100% coverage in 2020 (Table 34).

A similar investigation was undertaken for the urban part of the Chinese population (chapter 3.3.2.4.2), as the *de facto* status of health insurance of migrant workers can only be changed by the urban insurance schemes. Here, it was found that the former *de jure* insurance coverage rate went down by approximately 20 percentage points to roughly 70% in the best estimate scenario, 69% in the low and 74% in the high estimate scenario. It was furthermore found that in e2011 approximately three quarters of all uninsured urban dwellers were migrant workers and the biggest stress within urban populations was therefore borne by migrant workers. The same observation was made for the year 2020. Although an additional 100 million migrant workers are planned to be insured by then, the current insurance rate of 90% was found to drop to approximately 75% accounting for the special situation of migrant workers. Compared to the situation in 2011, these findings suggest that the situation of uninsured urban inhabitants will slightly improve by 5 percentage points. The new policy of issuing *hukous* to 100 million additional migrant workers will therefore have a slight positive effect on the *de facto* insurance level of Chinese cities. Nonetheless, large gaps remain between the estimated situation and the two goals that were set by the Chinese government. To reach the 90% goal in 2011 in urban areas, the Chinese government would have had to insure 175 million more urban people than it actually did. In order to reach the 90% target in 2020, it will have to insure more than 160 million more migrants than it is already planning to insure through the new policy. The aim to reach universal coverage in 2020 could only be met, if more than 280 million more people than planned by the new policy get *de facto* access to health insurance.

5 Boundaries and discussion

This thesis, like any other study, had to limit its field of research in order to be able to manage the information of the major field of interest. When judging the results of this study, its limitations have to be kept in mind. First and foremost, the size of China as a country as well as the complexity of the health insurance system make it impossible to cover every aspect in depth. Therefore, a decision had to be made between an all-encompassing and an in-depth approach. In order to deliver a detailed analysis of the fields under investigation, this study focused on the investigation of central aspects of the Chinese health insurance system in a spotlight manner. Although this choice makes the study vulnerable to critique that demands a holistic approach, the investigated topics were chosen in such a way that they might serve the reader by giving a good understanding of the general character of the Chinese health insurance system and also of its future potentials.

Beyond these general boundaries, the three dimensions that were central in this study rely on implicit and explicit assumptions that will be described in detail in order to enable further discussions about the topic.

5.1 Analysis of the first dimension (height)

Concerning the first dimension (height), two aspects were discussed: (1) low user fees and OOP and (2) the separation of benefits and payments (especially focusing on equity and vulnerable groups). Although the first point of discussion showed clearly that China has not reached the goals set for the maximum acceptable rate of OOP (at least below 15-20%, better below 10%), the more detailed description showed that clear statements can hardly be made. It was for example found that the rate of OOP, and even the tendency over time, differs depending on the research material consulted. This issue was not analyzed in detail as it is only secondary to the focus of the study at hand. It is however obvious that comparative research work is necessary at this area if detailed information is aspired about the rate of OOP and its development tendency.

A similar statement can be made concerning the findings that were presented looking at the state of equity within the health insurance system and between the different programs. Despite the relatively clear general tendencies[82], details were often unclear and would need further investigation if the research focus would demand it.

The study furthermore gave an interpretation of the unchanged rate of catastrophic health payments in China. This tendency was found to be especially interesting as other indicators such as total OOP (as measured by World Bank), the rate of health insurance and inpatient reimbursement rates steadily increased and therefore seemed to be in contrast with the unchanged rate of catastrophic health payments. The interpretation given in the paper has its roots in health economic theory and can therefore be regarded as worth considering. For researchers with deeper interest in this issue, it might therefore be interesting to test the statement with other data sources and methods. In this work, a deeper investigation was not carried out as this aspect was not of primary interest.

At last, in the summary of this study it could only be referred to one study which weighs payments and benefits. The former investigation brought to light partly confusing findings which showed that payments were generally collected in an equitable way while benefits are distributed inequitably. Building on only one study that investigates this discrepancy might be enough to draw an interim conclusion (as done in this study), but it is by no means sufficient to describe the Chinese situation with a high degree of certainty. Also here, further research such as a systematic literature search and meta analyses would be mandatory if this issue was of greater importance within the research focus.

5.2 Analysis of the second dimension (depth)

The reader might ask if the high CBA results shown above are trustworthy. The reasons for the high values are twofold. Firstly, VSL studies in general produce higher results than other approaches like the VOLY or HTA approach[83] (Pearce and Howarth, 2000). The reason for this might be that the VSL approach asks for people's preferences and

---

[82] In two cases, (1) the pre-payments redistribution mechanisms within the insurance schemes and (2) the outpatient reimbursement rates between the insurance schemes, the lack of data did not allow to draw a clear conclusion. Here, data sources would be needed even for the research question at hand. They could however not be found.
[83] For a deeper discussion on using the VSL please see Annex 5.

health is generally valued as the most important good, even more important than achieving a high economic or social status (WHO, 2010a, p. ix). Secondly, the interventions which are described in this work – individual based, mostly non-medical interventions – are extremely inexpensive. In the context of the CBA, this consequently leads to high positive values. Hence, the high results do not only arise because of high benefits due to the VSL approach but also because of interventions that are very cost-efficient. Despite critique that might still arise concerning the amount of benefits presented in this study, it might be agreed that the magnitude of the presented results clearly shows that investing in individual-based interventions related to the "deadly quartet" is highly profitable, even if the profit was partially smaller than described here.

The possible health interventions to reduce the burden of disease laid out in chapter 3.2.3 might be discussed in terms of the reduction values that were presented. First of all, the studies used in the named chapter mainly focus on northern European populations and it might be argued that the Chinese population, due to different genetics, might show different outcomes from those considered in this study. However, as intercultural studies do exist that stress the importance of socioeconomic, cultural and family characteristics more than those determined by genetics (Zilanawala et al., 2015), this argument is not taken into account here. In how far the behavioral differences might lead to a different compliance and require an adaptation of the programs presented here, is outside of the scope of this study. Intercultural studies concerning this issue would be most interesting.

A further question arising from chapter 3.2.3 might be, if the observed results on mortality would be similar on morbidity or combined measurements like DALYs. As this is solely a question of the specific relation between mortality and morbidity, this discussion will however not alter the overall tendency which was shown in this thesis.

It might also be discussed why the results of individual interventions targeting tobacco smoking are relatively small compared to the other three risk factors. This is foremost the result of this study strictly following the recommendations found in the literature research underlying chapter 3.2.3. It is explicitly stated that tobacco smoking is best to quit with the help of medication. As all other risk factors are treated without medicinal help and as pharmaceuticals are more than twice as expensive as non-medicinal interventions, the costs of tobacco interventions are by far highest among the four risk factors. It would be interesting to include studies that describe a non-pharmaceutical approach of quitting smoking. The corresponding cost-effectiveness and cost-benefit values might be higher than those presented above.

5.3 Analysis of the third dimension (breadth)

The analysis undertaken for the breadth dimension used three different scenarios – a low, a best and a high estimate scenario – to calculate the *de jure* amount of health insured Chinese citizens. Certain aspects might lead to criticizing the values that are used for these scenarios: Firstly, only a few studies investigate the insurance rate of migrant workers which therefore might not be built on sufficient research evidence. Secondly, these studies build their findings on sample cities with special characteristics, such as size and economic power. They might therefore not represent the situation of the whole country. These weaknesses are however already accounted for as the study does not take up a position but includes all different perspectives into its three estimate scenarios and thereby offers a sensitive analysis which includes uncertainties arising from above reservations (chapter 3.3.2.2).

It is unclear how many migrant workers were included in the NHSS and how they were distributed between the insured and the uninsured group. The above solution for this lack of information is assuming a proportional equal distribution (3.3.2.3). This solution might be prone to critique if new information should appear. So far, this approach can be regarded as a solution that builds on relatively current findings and logical reasoning.

Finally, the assumption that migrant workers do not migrate to rural locations might be criticized. It is however important to understand that migrant workers who return to their hometowns are included in the calculations as they would not count as migrants after having returned home. The above assumption only excludes those people that migrate from urban and rural areas to other rural areas and do not return home. Although this assumption might be criticized, the study showed evidence that this number, if existent, must be very small (3.3.2.3.2).

142

6 Outlook

The outlook of this study will focus on two aspects. Firstly, the new aspects that were described in detail in chapter 1.5 will be picked up and it will be investigated in how far they might be developed further by other scholars (6.1). Secondly, the findings of this study will be put in relation to the international situation. Based on these insights, potential influences of the results are examined (6.2).

6.1 New aspects

The boundaries and discussion chapter (chapter 5) already pointed out some areas where further research could enhance the findings of this thesis. Looking at the four contributions that this study can add to the scientific literature (compare chapter 1.5), more potential areas for enhancement can be found.

The contribution of providing a first analysis of the Chinese health insurance system which looks at the three WHO dimensions of UHC offers the opportunity to give inputs to national (upcoming 13th Five-Year Plan) as well as international (upcoming Sustainable Development Goals (SDG)) policy processes (compare next chapter 6.2) targeting the achievement of UHC.

With regard to health economic theory, further investigations and modeling as well as critical inputs might help to improve the appropriateness approach and lead to a richer health economic theory. The approach undertaken here has moreover kept the wording of "moral hazard" and "access to health services" in order to refer to the original works. Both concepts, in the light of including positive and negative effects depending on the appropriateness of health care, might need renaming and reclassifying within the appropriateness approach in order to increase its consistency. Further work on the side of classifications and modeling is absolutely encouraged. Due to the theoretical (2.1.1, 2.2.1 and 3.2.3) as well as the cost-effective and cost-benefit results (3.2.4), a further investigation of this approach could lead to the inclusion of preventive care[84] into

---

[84] "Preventive care" in this context also includes the strengthening of individual health interventions as discussed in chapter 3.2.3.

standard health economic theory, into concepts of international organizations and into countries' catalogues of benefits.

Although migrant workers already receive notable attention within the scientific community, this analysis was able to show that they *de facto* still remain a marginalized group that is hidden by reporting *de jure* health insurance coverage rates which are too high compared to the *de facto* health insurance rates. This discovery together with the finding that planned interventions by the Chinese government will not improve the current situation, but only keep the status quo, are alarming results. It is hoped that the presented results are taken up by other scholars and taken into account by policy makers of the People's Republic of China.

6.2 International context

Analyses such as undertaken in chapter 3.1.1 and Annex 6 show clearly that the results presented in this study can additionally be judged by comparison to other countries.

Chapter 3.1.1 for example could point out that China does not reach the goals set by international organizations and scholars, most visible in the rate of OOP. Comparing its situation to other low- and middle-income countries, it was however found that missing this goal is rather the norm in certain areas of the world. Hence, the member states of the WHO Western Pacific Region (which China is part of) have set their target to 30-40% (WHO, 2010a, p. xiv), which China already managed to achieve between 2008 and 2009 (Table 4).

Furthermore, the negative findings regarding the appropriateness of health services within the Chinese catalogue of benefits (3.2.1) and the resulting unrealized benefits from individual NCD interventions (3.2.4) are put into perspective if compared with other countries. Comparing the outcomes of the four NCD risk factors in China to those in Europe and the USA (see Annex 6) it is found that the negative effects of tobacco use, unhealthy diet and physical inactivity are less severe in China than in Europe and the USA. For the risk factor alcohol, China is still doing better than Europe, however as bad as the US (see Table 45 and Figure 26-Figure 29 in Annex 6). This might be because NCDs are often related to people's lifestyles and therefore mainly a phenomenon of highly developed countries (Herd et al., 2010, p. 2). The situation in China might hence deteriorate in the years to come although it currently shows comparably good results compared to the more developed countries in Europe and to the USA (compare chapter 3.2.2 and especially Figure 11 and Figure 12). The interpretation that the burden of NCDs is linked to the development status of a country is also supported by the finding that the situation in China, unlike Europe and the USA, is steadily worsening concerning dietary risks and physical activity and only slightly getting better for tobacco and alcohol abuse in recent years (Table 45, Figure 26–Figure 29 in Annex 6). Even beyond the particular findings of this study, other sources such as OECD attest an overall worsening of NCDs in China (Herd et al., 2010, p. 6) and hence support the above statement and the raise of awareness.

New insights through country comparison can also be gained in the last of the three dimensions which concerns the coverage rate of health insurance systems. Looking at the USA, it can be found that the percentage of people with health insurance has clearly been below 90% until 2013 (86.7%) and only came close to 90% in 2014 (89.6%) (US Census Bureau, 2015). This is considerably less than the 95.7% ratio that was calculated for China in 2011 (Meng et al., 2012b). It might be argued, that the official ratio of the USA should rather be compared to the *de jure* insured best estimate of 81.19% found in chapter 3.3.2.4. However, such a comparison might be misleading as the USA are hosting a large number of unauthorized immigrants that make up about 3.5% of the US population (slightly above 11 million in real numbers and roughly constant between 2009 and 2014) (Baker and Rytina, 2012; Krogstad and Passel, 2015). It is beyond the feasibility of this study to judge in how far the unauthorized immigrants in the US might have similar effects on the official coverage rate than the migrant workers in China. It is also above the horizon of this thesis to make a comparison with Europe, as it is too fragmented to be discussed in detail here. However, Europe was found to have nearly entirely reached the state of UHC by 2009 (Stuckler et al., 2010) and might therefore perform better than China and the USA. Nevertheless, this remark must be interpreted as indicative and by no means conclusive.

Another interesting finding in this study which shows the results of China in a different light is the development speed of western countries. Chapter 1.1 and 1.2 clearly stated

145

that a large number of developed European countries only reached UHC in the late 1970s or even in recent years (1.1) and the USA did qualify as a UHC country in the 2010 study of Stuckler and colleagues (Stuckler et al., 2010). In addition, many low- and middle-income countries are moving significantly faster towards UHC than industrialized countries did in the past (WHO and Lerberghe, 2008, pp. 25, 26) (1.2). China might therefore, in terms of development speed, be judged to perform better than many of the developed countries.

Despite having shown that many of the negative findings regarding the three dimensions (chapters 3.1, 3.2 and 3.3) might be relativized if compared with the situation in selected countries, it also has to be stated that examples cannot negate a principle tendency as they might always be opposed by other examples stating the contrary. The findings described for the three dimensions in chapter 3 and 4 therefore remain valid, in spite of the international comparisons undertaken above. Instead of seeking orientation on countries that do worse, this thesis aims to support the strive for the highest outcome possible and to increase the livelihood of the Chinese people. In this regard, the coming years from 2016 onwards offer an extraordinary chance for implementing UHC and realizing the related social benefits. Firstly, the new Five-Year Plan (2016-2020) contains the possibility to focus on the prosperity of the Chinese society and on long-term developments as advertised by Premier Li Keqiang (Xinhua, 2014). Secondly, the upcoming SDG program of the United Nations for the period of 2016-2030 supports the current developments observed in China. Within the SDGs, goal number 3.8[85], one of the goals is especially targeting UHC:

"Achieve universal health coverage, including financial risk protection, access to quality essential health-care services and access to safe, effective, quality and affordable essential medicines and vaccines for all" (UN, 2015)

The similarity between goal 3.8 and the content of this thesis adds importance to the research undertaken above and shows the importance within the international context. This shall be described in more detail. Looking at the two targets of goal 3.8,

---

[85] The superordinate goal three is "Ensure healthy lives and promote wellbeing for all at all ages" (UN, 2015; WHO, 2015, p. 4).

1. "By 2030, all populations, independent of household income, expenditure or wealth, place of residence or sex, have at a minimum 80% essential health services coverage."
2. "By 2030, everyone has 100% financial protection from out-of-pocket payments for health services." (WHO, 2015, p. 15),

the similarities become more obvious. The focus on "all populations" (target 1) and "everyone" (target 2) clearly shows a link to the above discussed breadth dimension (especially chapters 2.3 and 3.3). Target 1 furthermore focuses on "essential health services coverage" which points to the importance of implementing the above discussed depth dimension (especially chapters 2.2 and 3.2). Target 2 completes the three dimensions by emphasizing the need of "100% financial protection from out-of-pocket payments" which was analyzed in the height dimension (especially chapters 2.1 and 3.1).

Analyzing the indicators which are planned to describe these two targets (see Annex 9 for all indicators of goal 3.8), the importance of this thesis is once again strengthened. On the one hand, many of the issues included in this thesis are also recommended by the SDG indicators. On the other hand, the thesis points to important fields of research that have not been taken up by the SDG indicators. Concerning target 1, "health services coverage", it is remarkable that the SDGs include the wording "adequate" and "skilled " (Annex 9) which point towards quality and appropriateness considerations as discussed in the depth dimension (2.2.1 and 3.2.1). With "non-tobacco use" as a preventive and "diabetes treatment and hypertension treatment" as treatment indicators (Annex 9), the SDG process includes one of the discussed risk factors and two of the discussed physiological risk markers of chapter 3.2. Unfortunately however, by focusing on tobacco as a preventive indicator, the SDGs include the least effective individual intervention possible. Together with the fact that diabetes and hypertension treatment are only included as treatments, but not as preventive interventions, can be interpreted as focusing on population based interventions and neglecting the possibilities of individual based preventive interventions. This again indicates that the research gap identified in this study – individual based preventive interventions (3.2.3) – is also

147

prevalent in the target setting of the UN and hence very important to address by the scientific community.

The height dimension of chapter 2.1 and 3.1 is reflected in the second target "financial protection coverage". As in the above analyses, a strong focus is set on OOP, which is discussed as "impoverishing expenditure" and "catastrophic expenditure" (Annex 9).

In target 1 as well as in target 2, the SDG indicators include equity concerns. Although their stratification groups are not the exact same than those discussed in chapter 3.1 (height dimension) and 3.3 (breadth dimension)[86], common stratification groups, such as wealth groups (3.1) and the place of residence (3.1 and 3.3), have a large share.

A last aspect that was discussed in this thesis but is not obvious in the SDG target setting, is the partially opposing trend of the two targets of goal 3.8. As described in the health theory section of chapter 2.2.1, an increase of "essential health services coverage" (target 1) tends to lead to less, not more "financial protection from out-of-pocket payments" (as aspired by target 2) (Nyman, 1999, pp. 143–145). Pursuing target 1 therefore demands countries to intensify their efforts to achieve target 2 if they do not want to experience loss of social achievements made before.

Overall, it can be stated that the upcoming 13th Five-Year Plan of the Chinese government and the new SDG agenda offer a great opportunity for China to intensify its efforts to finally achieve UHC.

---

[86] The SDG indicators focus on "wealth quintile, place of residence and sex" as stratification groups (see Annex 9).

Bibliography

Aalto, M., 2001. Brief intervention for male heavy drinkers in routine general practice: a three-year randomized controlled study. Alcohol Alcohol 36, 224–230. doi:10.1093/alcalc/36.3.224

Alberini, A., Cropper, M., Krupnick, A., Simon, N., 2004. Does the value of a statistical life vary with age and health status? Evidence from the US and Canada. J. Environ. Econ. Manag. 769–792.

Alcorn, T., Bao, B., 2011. China progresses with health reform but challenges remain. The Lancet 377.

Amann, M., Borken-Kleefeld, J., Cofala, J., Hettelingh, J., Heyes, C., Höglund-Isaksson1), L., Holland, M., Kiesewetter, G., Klimont, Z., Rafaj, P., Posch, M., Sander, R., Schöpp, W., Wagner, F., Winiwarter, W., 2014. The final policy scenarios of the EU Clean Air Policy package (TSAP Report #11, Version 1.1a). DG-Environment, European Commission, Brussels.

Arrow, K., 1963. Uncertainty and the welfare economics of medical care. Am. Econ. Rev. 5.

Austrian Information, 2012. Austria's health care system [WWW Document]. Austrian Inf. URL http://www.austrianinformation.org/summer-2012/2012/8/21/austrias-health-care-system.html (accessed 12.15.14).

Bai, C.-E., Wu, B., 2014. Health insurance and consumption: evidence from China's new cooperative medical scheme. J. Comp. Econ. 42, 450–469.

Baker, B., Rytina, N., 2012. Estimates of the unauthorized immigrant population residing in the United States: January 2012.

Bärnighausen, T., Sauerborn, R., 2002. One hundred and eighteen years of the German health insurance system: are there any lessons for middle- and low-income countries? Soc. Sci. Med. 54, 1559–1587. doi:10.1016/S0277-9536(01)00137-X

Batra, A., 2011. Treatment of tobacco dependence. Dtsch. Aerzteblatt Online. doi:10.3238/arztebl.2011.0555

Batra, A., Hering, T., Arbter, P., 2013. Curriculum „Qualifikation Tabakentwöhnung". Bundesärztekammer.

Bertholet, N., 2005. Reduction of alcohol consumption by brief alcohol intervention in primary care: systematic review and meta-analysis. Arch. Intern. Med. 165, 986. doi:10.1001/archinte.165.9.986

Biao, X., 2003. Migration and health in China: problems, obstacles and solutions.

Biausque, V., 2012. The Value of Statistical Life: A Meta-Analysis. Ecole Nationale de la Statistique et de l'Administration Economique, Paris.

Blendon, R., Donelan, K., Leitman, R., Epstein, A., Cantor, J., Morrison, A.C.I., Moloney, T., Koeck, C., 1993. Health reform lessons learned from physicians in three nations. Health Aff. (Millwood) 3.

Boardman, A.E., Greenberg, D.H., Vining, A.R., Weimer, D.L. (Eds.), 2011. Cost-benefit analysis: concepts and practice, 4. ed., intern. ed. ed, The Pearson series in economics. Prentice Hall, Boston, [Mass.].

Bobadilla, J.L., Cowley, P., Musgrove, P., Saxenian, H., 1994. Design, content and financing of an essential national package of health services. Bull. World Health Organ. 72, 653–662.

Braathen, N., 2012. Valuation of human lives: Presentation at an Informal Joint Workshop of the Regulatory Policy Committee and the Annual Meeting of Sustainable Development Experts on The Role of Impact Assessments in Policy Making.

Brixi, H., Mu, Y., Targa, B., Hipgrave, D., 2011. Equity and public governance in health system reform: Challenges and opportunities for China. The World Bank, Washington DC, USA.

Brown, P., De Brauw, A., Du, Y., 2007. Can health insurance mitigate shocks to consumption? Evidence from China., in: Evidence from China (July 2007). iHEA 2007 6th World Congress: Explorations in Health Economics Paper.

Bruce Hillman, C.J., Griffith, P., Nelson, W., Bernhardt, L., 1992. Physicians' utilization and charges for outpatient diagnostic imaging in a Medicare population. J. Am. Med. Assoc.

Bundesärztekammer, 2001. Frei von Tabak - Ein Stufenprogramm zur Raucherberatung und Rauchertherapie in der Arztpraxis. Bundesärztekammer und Kassenärztliche Bundesvereinigung.

Camenzind, P., 2013. International Profiles of Health Care Systems, 2013 - Switzerland. The Commonwealth Fund, New York.

Casey, J., Koleski, K., 2011. Backgrounder: China's 12th Five-Year Plan.

CBI, 2013. Fit for purpose: Absence and workplace health survey 2013. Confederation of British Industry, London.

CBI, 2011. Healthy returns? Absence and workplace health survey, 2011. Confederation of British Industry, London.

CBI, 1998. Missing out: 1998 absence and labour turnover survey. Confederation of British Industry, London.

Chandra, A., Gruber, J., McKnight, R., 2010. Patient Cost-Sharing and Hospitalization Offsets in the Elderly. Am. Econ. Rev. 100, 193–213. doi:10.1257/aer.100.1.193

Chanel, O., 2011. Guidelines on monetary cost calculations related to air-pollution health impacts (No. 2007105). National Center for Scientific Research, Marseilles.

Chan, J., Pun, N., 2010. Suicide as Protest for the New Generation of Chinese Migrant Workers: Foxconn, Global Capital, and the State. The Asia-Pacific Journal 37.

Cheng, L., Liu, H., Zhang, Y., Shen, K., Zeng, Y., 2014. The Impact of Health Insurance on Health Outcomes and Spending of the Elderly: Evidence from China's New Cooperative Medical Scheme. Health Econ.

Chen, J., Chen, S., Landry, P.F., 2013. Migration, environmental hazards, and health outcomes in China. Soc. Sci. Med. 80, 85–95.

Chen, Y., Jin, G.Z., 2012. Does health insurance coverage lead to better health and educational outcomes? Evidence from rural China. J. Health Econ. 31, 1–14.

Chestnut, L., De Civita, P., 2009. Economic Evaluation of Mortality Risk Reduction: Review and Recommendations for Policy and Regulatory Analysis. Policy Research Initiative, Government of Canada, Ottawa.

Chestnut, L., Mills, D., Agras, J., 2000. National costs of asthma for 1997.

China.org.cn, 2012. The Development of China's New Rural Cooperative Medical Scheme [WWW Document]. China.org.cn. URL http://www.china.org.cn/china/2012-09/17/content_26545922.htm (accessed 11.11.14).

Chinese Embassy, 2011. Premier Wen targets causes of instability, stresses fair treatment of disadvantaged groups.

Chisholm, D., Abegunde, D., Mendis, S., World Health Organization, 2011. Scaling up action against noncommunicable diseases: how much will it cost? World Health Organization, Geneva, Switzerland.

Corens, D., 2007. Health Systems in Transition - Belgium Health System Review, The European Observatory on Health Systems and Policies. WHO Regional Office for Europe, Copenhagen.

Cropper, M., Aydede, S., Portney, P., 1994. Preferences for savig live-saving programs: how the public discount time and age. J. Risk Uncertain. 243–265.

Daley, C., Gubb, J., Clarke, E., Bidgood, E., 2013. Healthcare Systems: The Netherlands. CIVITAS, Delft.

Danzon, P.M., Pauly, M.V., 2002. Health Insurance and the Growth in Pharmaceutical Expenditures. J. Law Econ. 45, 587–613.

de Meza, D., 1983. Health insurance and the demand for medical care. J. Health Econ.

DGNTF, 2014. Programmbeschreibung Für immer rauchfrei! - Deutsche Gesellschaft für Nikotin und Tabakforschung [WWW Document]. URL http://www.dgntf.de/programmbeschreibung-fuer-immer-rauchfrei.html (accessed 10.24.14).

DiabetesStiftung DDS, 2007. Diabetes-Risiko: Diabetes FINDRISK [WWW Document]. URL http://diabetes-risiko.de/diabetes-risikotest.html (accessed 12.7.14).

Doll, R., 2004. Mortality in relation to smoking: 50 years' observations on male British doctors. BMJ 328, 1519–0. doi:10.1136/bmj.38142.554479.AE

Donatitini, A., 2013. International Profiles of Health Care Systems, 2013 - Italy. The Commonwealth Fund, New York.

Dong, M., 2011. China's 12th Five-Year Plan: Healthcare Sector.

Doorslaer, E. van, O'Donnell, O., 2008. Measurement and Explanation of Inequality in Health and Health Care in Low-Income Settings. U. N. Univ. - World Inst. Dev. Econ. Res.

Dranove, D., White, W., 1987. Agency and the organization of health care delivery. Inquiry 4.

Durand-Zaleskiki, I., 2013. International Profiles of Health Care Systems, 2013 - Italy. The Commonwealth Fund, New York.

EC, 2013. Proposal for a Directive of the European Parliament and of the Council on the reduction of national emissions of certain atmospheric pollutants and amending Directive 2003/35/EC. European Commission, Brussels.

Epstein, A., Begg, C., McNeil, B., 1986. The use of ambulatory testing in prepaid and fee-for-service group practices: relation to perceived profitability. N. Engl. J. Med.

ERC, 2013. ERC: International Drug Price Indicator Guide [WWW Document]. URL http://erc.msh.org/dmpguide/searchresult.cfm?year=2013&byletter=yes&languag e=english&word=n (accessed 12.9.14).

Erdmann, J., Christ, S., Hausmann, M., Schusdziarra, V., 2008. Von der Regulation der Nahrungsaufnahme zur Adipositas-Therapie. Med Welt 59, 83–92.

FAO, 2006. The double burden of malnutrition Case studies from six developing countries. Food and Agriculture Organization of the United Nations, Rome.

Feldman, R., Dowd, B., 1991. A new estimate of the welfare loss of excess health insurance. Am. Econ. Rev.

Feldstein, M., 1971. Hospital cost inflation: a study in nonprofit price dynamics. Am. Econ. Rev.

Feldstein, M.S., 1973. The Welfare Loss of Excess Health Insurance. J. Polit. Econ. 81, 251–280.

Fischer, G., Kuhlmey, A., Lauterbach, K., Rosenbrock, R., Schwarz, F., Scriba, P., Wille, E., 2003. Gutachten 2003 des Sachverständigenrates für die Konzertierte Aktion im Gesundheitswesen - Finanzierung, Nutzenorientierung und Qualität. Sachverständigenrat Für Konzertierte Aktion Im Gesundheitswesen.

Fleurbaey, M., Schokkaert, E., 2011. Equity in Health and Health Care. Univ. Cathol. Louvain.

Friedman, B., 1974. Risk aversion and the consumer choice of health insurance option. Rev. Econ. Stat.

Fu, C., Xu, J., Liu, W., Zhang, W., Wang, M., Nie, J., Rüdiger, von K., 2010. Low measles seropositivity rate among children and young adults: A seroepidemiological study in southern China in 2008. Vaccine 28, 8219–8223. doi:10.1016/j.vaccine.2010.07.071

Gaynor, M., Li, J., Vogt, W.B., 2007. Substitution, Spending Offsets, and Prescription Drug Benefit Design. Forum Health Econ. Policy 10. doi:10.2202/1558-9544.1084

Gibson, T.B., Ozminkowski, R.J., Goetzel, R.Z., 2005. The Effects of Prescription Drug Cost Sharing: A Review of the Evidence. Am. J. Manag. Care 11, 730–740.

Giles, J., Wang, D., Park, A., 2013. Expanding social insurance coverage in Urban China. Emerald Group Publishing Limited.

Gilman, B.H., Kautter, J., 2008. Impact of Multitiered Copayments on the Use and Cost of Prescription Drugs among Medicare Beneficiaries. Health Serv. Res. 43, 478–495. doi:10.1111/j.1475-6773.2007.00774.x

Gilman, B.H., Kautter, J., 2007. Consumer Response to Dual Incentives Under Multitiered Prescription Drug Formularies. Am. J. Manag. Care 13, 353–359.

Glazer, J., 1993. Should physicians be permitted to "balance bill" patients? J. Health Econ. 3.

Glenngård, A., Hjalte, F., Svensson, M., Anell, A., Bankauskaite, V., 2005. Health Systems in Transition - Sweden (European Observatory on Health Care Systems). WHO, Copenhagen.

Goldman, D.P., Joyce, G.F., Zheng, Y., 2007. Prescription Drug Cost Sharing: Associations With Medication and Medical Utilization and Spending and Health. JAMA 298, 61. doi:10.1001/jama.298.1.61

Gong, P., Liang, S., Carlton, E.J., Jiang, Q., Wu, J., Wang, L., Remais, J.V., 2012a. Urbanisation and health in China. The Lancet 379, 843–852. doi:10.1016/S0140-6736(11)61878-3

Gong, P., Liang, S., Carlton, E.J., Jiang, Q., Wu, J., Wang, L., Remais, J.V., 2012b. Urbanisation and health in China - Appendix. The Lancet 379, 843–852. doi:10.1016/S0140-6736(11)61878-3

Gravelle, H., Morris, S., Sutton, M., 2006. Economic studies of equity in the consumption of health care, in: The Elgar Companion To Health Economics. Edward Elgar Publishing Limited, Cheltenham, UK.

154

Greenfield, S., Nelson, E., Zubkoff, M., Manning, W., Rogers, W., Kravitz, R., Keller, A., Tarlov, A., Ware, J., 1992. Variations in resource utilization among medical specialties and systems of care: results of the medical outcome study. J. Am. Med. Assoc.

Grossman, M., 1972. On the concept of health capital and the demand for health. J. Polit. Econ. 2.

Gu, D., 2006. Body Weight and Mortality Among Men and Women in China. JAMA 295, 776. doi:10.1001/jama.295.7.776

Guo, Y., Shibuya, K., Cheng, G., Rao, K., Lee, L., Tang, S., 2010. Tracking China's health reform. The Lancet 375, 1056–1058. doi:10.1016/S0140-6736(10)60397-2

Hambrecht, R., 2004. Sport als Therapie. Herz 29. doi:10.1007/s00059-004-2583-3

Haustein, K., Voigt, M., Haustein, H., Meigen, C., 2004. Die Behandlung der Tabakabhängigkeit mit Nikotin - Erfahrungen aus dem Raucherberatungszentrum Erfurt. ZFA - Z. Für Allg. 80, 108–112. doi:10.1055/s-2004-823019

Heatherton, T., Kozlowski, L., Frecker, R., Fagerström, K., 2014. Fagerstrom Test [WWW Document]. Nicotine Freedom. URL http://nicotinefreedom.com/articles/fagerstrom (accessed 12.7.14)

Hemenway, D., Killen, A., Cashman, S., Parks, C., Bicknell, W., 1990. Physician responses to financial incentives: evidence from a for-profit ambulatory care center. N. Engl. J. Med.

Herd, R., Koen, V., Hu, Y.-W., 2010. Improving China's Health Care System (OECD Economics Department Working Papers No. 751).

Hermanns, N., Gorges, D., 2009. Primary Diabetes Prevention PREDIAS – A structured Treatment and Education Programme for Prevention of Type 2 Diabetes.

Hesketh, T., Jun, Y.X., Lu, L., Mei, W.H., 2008a. Health status and access to health care of migrant workers in China. Public Health Rep. 123, 189.

Hesketh, T., Ye, X.J., Li, L., Wang, H.M., 2008b. Health status and access to health care of migrant workers in China. Public Health Rep. Wash. DC 1974 123, 189–197.

155

Hilless, M., Healy, J., 2001. Health Care Systems in Transition - Australia (European Observatory on Health Care Systems). WHO Regional Office for Europe, Copenhagen.

Hillman, B., Joseph, C., Mabry, M., Sunshine, J., Kennedy, S., Noether, M., 1990. Frequency and costs of diagnostic imaging in office practice - a comparison of self-referring and radiologist-referring physicians. N. Engl. J. Med.

Hoch, E., Mühlig, S., Höfler, M., Sonntag, H., Pittrow, D., Wittchen, H.-U., 2004. Raucherentwöhnung in der primärärztlichen Versorgung: Ziele, Design und Methoden der "Smoking and Nicotine Dependence Awareness and Screening (SNICAS)"-Studie. Suchtmed 6, 32–46.

Holdaway, J., 2010. Environment and Health in China: an introduction to an emerging research field. J. Contemp. China 19, 1–22. doi:10.1080/10670560903335728

Holdaway, J., 2008. Migration and Health in China: An Introduction to Problems, Policy, and Research. Yale-China Health J. 5, 7–21.

Holland, M., 2014. Cost-benefit analysis of final policy scenarios for the EU Clean Air Package. (IIASA TSAP report no.11). DG-Environment, European Commission, Brussels.

Holland, M., Hurley, F., Hunt, A., Watkiss, P., 2005. Methodology for the Cost-Benefit Analysis for CAFE: Volume 3: Uncertainty in the CAFE CBA: Methods and First Analysis. AEA Technology Environment, Didcot.

Holland, M., Taylor, T., Martuzzi, M., George, F., 2014a. Environmental Health Economics for Policy Makers, Environmental Health and Economics Network Reflection Paper No. 4. WHO Regional Office for Europe, Copenhagen.

Holland, M., Taylor, T., Martuzzi, M., George, F., 2014b. Economic Assessment of the Environmental Health Burden in Europe, Environmental Health and Economics Network Reflection Paper No. 3. WHO Regional Office for Europe, Copenhagen.

Hong, Y.Z., 2010. The Impact of Fiscal Decentralisation and Market Transition on Local Public Finance in China: Fiscal Inadequacy and and Unmet Social Security Needs. Univ. Colledge Lond.

Hou, Z., Van de Poel, E., Van Doorslaer, E., Yua, B., Menge, Q., 2012. Effects of NCMS coverage on access to care and financial protection in China.

Hunt, A., 2011. Policy Interventions to Address Health Impacts Associated with Air Pollution, Unsafe Water Supply and Sanitation, and Hazardous Chemicals" (No. 35), OECD Environment Working Papers. OECD, Paris.

Hunt, A., Ferguson, J., 2010. A Review of Recent Policy-Relevant Findings from the Environmental Health Literature. OECD Secretary-General, Paris.

Huskamp, H.A., Deverka, P.A., Epstein, A.M., Epstein, R.S., McGuigan, K.A., Frank, R.G., 2003. The Effect of Incentive-Based Formularies on Prescription-Drug Utilization and Spending. N. Engl. J. Med. 349, 2224–2232. doi:10.1056/NEJMsa030954

Huskamp, H.A., Deverka, P.A., Epstein, A.M., Epstein, R.S., McGuigan, K.A., Muriel, A.C., Frank, R.G., 2005. Impact of 3-Tier Formularies on Drug Treatment of Attention-Deficit/Hyperactivity Disorder in Children. Arch. Gen. Psychiatry 62, 435. doi:10.1001/archpsyc.62.4.435

IHME, 2014a. ownCloud - Global Burden of Disease Study 2010 (GBD 2010) Results by Risk Factor - Country Level [WWW Document]. URL https://cloud.ihme.washington.edu/public.php?service=files&t=5a680ed82f7be84 d10b32052099fb617&path= (accessed 10.13.14).

IHME, 2014b. Global Burden of Disease (GBD) | Institute for Health Metrics and Evaluation [WWW Document]. URL http://www.healthdata.org/gbd (accessed 9.15.14).

John, U., Hapke, U., Rumpf, H.-J., 2001. Alkoholismus: Missbrauch oder Abhängigkeit von Alkohol 98, 2438–2442.

Jolliffe, J., Rees, K., Taylor, R.R., Thompson, D.R., Oldridge, N., Ebrahim, S., 2001. Exercise-based rehabilitation for coronary heart disease, in: The Cochrane Collaboration (Ed.), The Cochrane Database of Systematic Reviews. John Wiley & Sons, Ltd, Chichester, UK.

Jung, J., Liu, J., 2011. Does health insurance decrease health expenditure risk in developing countries? The case of China.

Keeler, E., 1987. Effect of cost sharing on physiological health, health practices and worry. Health Serv. Res.

Keeler, E.B., Rolph, J.E., 1988. The demand for episodes of treatment in the health insurance experiment. J. Health Econ. 7, 337–367. doi:10.1016/0167-6296(88)90020-3

Keeler, E., Brook, R., Goldberg, G., Kamberg, C., Newhouse, J., 1985. How free care reduced hypertension in the health insurance experiment. JAMA.

Kessler, D., McClellan, M., 1996. Do doctors practice defensive medicine? Q. J. Econ.

Kieny, M.-P., Evans, D., 2013. Universal health coverage. East. Mediterr. Health J. 19, 305–306.

Kolenda, K.-D., 2012. Verhaltenspräventive Maßnahmen bei Behandlung der Hypertonie. Aerzteblatt SH.

Kolenda, K.-D., Ratje, U., 2013. Mehr Prävention - Vorbeugung und Behandlung lebensstilbedingter Krankheiten. Marseille Verlag, München.

Krogstad, J., Passel, J., 2015. 5 facts about illegal immigration in the U.S. [WWW Document]. Fact Tank Pew Res. Cent. URL http://www.pewresearch.org/fact-tank/2015/07/24/5-facts-about-illegal-immigration-in-the-u-s/ (accessed 11.14.15).

Kronsbein, P., Fischer, M.R., Tolks, D., Greaves, C., Puhl, S., Stych, K.E., EH Schwarz, P., on behalf of the IMAGE Study group, 2011. IMAGE: Development of a European curriculum for the training of prevention managers. Br. J. Diabetes Vasc. Dis. 11, 163–167. doi:10.1177/1474651411411256

Krupnick, A., 2007. Mortality-risk valuation and age: state preference evidence. Rev. Environ. Econ. Policy 261–282.

Krupnick, A., Alberini, A., Cropper, M., Simon, N., O'Brien, B., Goeree, R., Heintzelmann, M., 2002. Age, health and the willingness to pay for mortality risk reductions: a contingent valuation survey of Ontario residents. J. Risk Uncertain. 161–186.

Kuhnle, S., Hort, S., 2004. The Developmental Welfare State in Scandinavia Lessons for the Developing World. UNRISD, Geneva.

Lagarde, M., 2008. The impact of user fees on health service utilization in low- and middle-income countries: how strong is the evidence? Bull. World Health Organ. 86, 839–848. doi:10.2471/BLT.07.049197

Landon, B.E., Rosenthal, M.B., Normand, S., Spettell, C., Lessler, A., Underwood, H.R., Newhouse, J.P., 2007. Incentive formularies and changes in prescription drug spending. Am. J. Manag. Care 13, 360.

Lau, J.T.F., Cheng, Y., Gu, J., Zhou, R., Yu, C., Holroyd, E., Yeung, N.C.Y., 2012. Suicides in a mega-size factory in China: poor mental health among young migrant workers in China. Occup. Environ. Med. 69, 526–526. doi:10.1136/oemed-2011-100593

Lawthers, A., Laird, N., Lipsitz, S., Hebert, L., Brennan, T., 1992. Physicians' perceptions of the risk of being sued. J. Health Polit. Policy Law 3.

Liang, Y., Guo, M., 2014. Utilization of health services and health-related quality of life research of rural-to-urban migrants in China: a cross-sectional analysis. Soc. Indic. Res. 1–19.

Li, L., Morrow, M., Kermode, M., 2007. Vulnerable but feeling safe: HIV risk among male rural-to-urban migrant workers in Chengdu, China. AIDS Care 19, 1288–1295. doi:10.1080/09540120701402855

Lindhjem, H., Navrud, S., Braathen, N., 2010. Valuing Lives Saved from Environmental, Transport and Health Policies: A Meta-Analysis of Stated Preference Studies. OECD Secretary General, Paris.

Liu, X., Yi, Y., 2004. The Health Sector in China Policy and Institutional Review. World Bank, Beijing.

Li, X., Stanton, B., Fang, X., Lin, D., 2006. Social stigma and mental health among rural-to-urban migrants in China: A conceptual framework and future research needs. World Health Popul. 8, 14.

Li, Y., 2013. Understanding Health Constraints Among Rural-to-Urban Migrants in China. Qual. Health Res. 23, 1459–1469. doi:10.1177/1049732313507500

Lohr, K., Brook, R., Kamberg, C., Goldberg, G., Liebowitz, A., Keesey, J., Reboussin, D., Newhouse, J., 1986. Use of medical care in the Rand Health Insurance Experiment. Diagnosis- and service-specific analyses in a randomized controlled trial. Med. Care 9.

Lopez, G., Planas, I., Costa i Font, J., 2004. Diversity and Regional Inequalities: Assessing the Outcomes of the Spanish "System of Health Care Services." SSRN Electron. J. doi:10.2139/ssrn.563343

Ma, C., McGuire, T., 1997. Optimal Health Insurance and Provider Payment. Am. Econ. Rev. 4.

Maioni, A., 1998. Parting at the crossroads: the emergence of health insurance in the United States and Canada, Princeton studies in American politics. Princeton University Press, Princeton, N.J.

Manning, W., Marquis, S., 1996. Health insurance: The tradeoff between risk pooling and moral hazard. J. Health Econ. 5.

Manning, W., Marquis, S., 1989. Health insurance: Trade-off between risk pooling and moral hazard. The RAND Corporation, Santa Monica.

Marten, R., McIntyre, D., Travassos, C., Shishkin, S., Longde, W., Reddy, S., Vega, J., 2014. An assessment of progress towards universal health coverage in Brazil, Russia, India, China, and South Africa (BRICS). The Lancet. doi:10.1016/S0140-6736(14)60075-1

Mayer-Foulkes, D.A., Pescetto-Villouta, C., 2012. Economic Development and Non-Communicable Chronic Diseases. Glob. Econ. J. 12. doi:10.1515/1524-5861.1889

McCall, T., 1996. Examining Your Doctor. Citadel Press, Seacaucus.

McGuire, T., 2000b. Physician Agency, in: Handbook of Health Economics. Elsevier, Amsterdam.

McGuire, T., 2000a. Demand for Health Insurance, in: Handbook of Health Economics. Elsevier, Amsterdam.

Meng, Q., Xu, L., Zhang, Y., Qian, J., Cai, M., Xin, Y., Gao, J., Xu, K., Boerma, J.T., Barber, S.L., 2012a. Trends in access to health services and financial protection in China between 2003 and 2011: a cross-sectional study - Supplementary appendix. The Lancet 379, 805–814. doi:10.1016/S0140-6736(12)60278-5

Meng, Q., Xu, L., Zhang, Y., Qian, J., Cai, M., Xin, Y., Gao, J., Xu, K., Boerma, J.T., Barber, S.L., 2012b. Trends in access to health services and financial protection in China between 2003 and 2011: a cross-sectional study. The Lancet 379, 805–814. doi:10.1016/S0140-6736(12)60278-5

Meng, Q., Xu, L., Zhang, Y., Qian, J., Cai, M., Xin, Y., Gao, J., Xu, K., Boerma, J.T., Barber, S.L., 2012a. Trends in access to health services and financial protection in China between 2003 and 2011: a cross-sectional study. The Lancet 379.

Middeke, M., 1998. Ernährung bei Hypertonie. DBI 18, 246–254.

Mitchell, J., Cromwell, J., 1982. Physician behavior under the Medicare assignment option. J. Health Econ.

MKL, 2011. China's Education System, Chinese Students, and the Foreign English Teacher [WWW Document]. Foreign Teach. Guide Living Work. China. URL http://middlekingdomlife.com/guide/chinese-education-system-students-english-teacher.htm (accessed 12.9.14).

MoH UK, 1948. The New National Health Service Leaflet.

Mooney, G., Ryan, M., 1993. Agency in health care: getting beyond first principles. J. Health Econ.

Moreno-Serra, R., Smith, P.C., 2012. Does progress towards universal health coverage improve population health? The Lancet 380, 917–923. doi:10.1016/S0140-6736(12)61039-3

Mou, J., Griffiths, S.M., Fong, H., Dawes, M.G., 2013. Health of China's rural-urban migrants and their families: a review of literature from 2000 to 2012. Br. Med. Bull. 106, 19–43. doi:10.1093/bmb/ldt016

Mou, J., Griffiths, S.M., Fong, H.F., Hu, Q., Xie, X., He, Y., Ma, H., Cheng, J., 2010. Seroprevalence of rubella in female migrant factory workers in Shenzhen, China. Vaccine 28, 7844–7851. doi:10.1016/j.vaccine.2010.09.082

Muckle, W., Muckle, J., Welch, V., Tugwell, P., 2012. Managed alcohol as a harm reduction intervention for alcohol addiction in populations at high risk for substance abuse, in: The Cochrane Collaboration (Ed.), Cochrane Database of Systematic Reviews. John Wiley & Sons, Ltd, Chichester, UK.

Mühlig, S., Nowak, D., 2004. Neun Thesen zur Raucherentwöhnung.

Narayan, K.M.V., Ali, M.K., Koplan, J.P., 2010. Global Noncommunicable Diseases — Where Worlds Meet. N. Engl. J. Med. 363, 1196–1198. doi:10.1056/NEJMp1002024

Nationales Programm Alkohol, 2014. Selbsttest (CAGE) [WWW Document]. Natl. Aktionstag Alkohol. URL http://www.aktionstag-alkoholprobleme.ch/index.php?lg=D&pg=14 (accessed 12.7.14).

NBSC, 2012. Statistical Communiqué on the 2011 National Economic and Social Development [WWW Document]. URL http://www.stats.gov.cn/english/newsandcomingevents/t20120222_402786587.ht m (accessed 7.21.12).

NBSC, 2009. Statistical Communiqué on Labor and Social Security Development in 2008 [WWW Document]. URL http://www.stats.gov.cn/english/newsandcomingevents/t20090522_402560900.ht m (accessed 7.21.12).

Ness, I. (Ed.), 2013. The Encyclopedia of Global Human Migration. Blackwell Publishing Ltd, Oxford, UK.

New-Ext, 2004. New Elements for the Assessment of External Costs from Energy Technologies: Publishable Report to the European Commission, DG Research, Technological Development and Demonstration. Institute for Energy Economics and the Rational Use of Energy (IER), Stuttgart.

Newhouse, J., 2004. Consumer-Directed Health Plans and the RAND Health Insurance Experiment. Health Aff. (Millwood) 6, 107-13.

Newhouse, J., 1996. Free for all? - Lessons from the RAND Health Insurance Experiment. Harvard University Press, Harvard.

NHI, 2012. Universal Health Coverage in Taiwan. Bureau of National Health Insurance, Department of Health, Executive Yuan, Taiwan, Yuan.

Nowak, D., Hoch, E., 2005. Raucherentwöhnung – Pharmakologie, Effizienz und Hemmnisse. Bay Int 25, 118–126.

Nyman, J.A., 1999. The value of health insurance: the access motive. J. Health Econ. 18, 141–152. doi:10.1016/S0167-6296(98)00049-6

162

O'Connor, G.T., Buring, J.E., Yusuf, S., Goldhaber, S.Z., Olmstead, E.M., Paffenbarger, R.S., Hennekens, C.H., 1989. An overview of randomized trials of rehabilitation with exercise after myocardial infarction. Circulation 80, 234–244. doi:10.1161/01.CIR.80.2.234

OECD, 2014a. The Cost of Air Pollution. OECD Publishing, Paris.

OECD, 2014b. The cost of air pollution: Health impacts of road transport. OECD, Paris.

OECD, 2012. Mortality Risk Valuation in Environment, Health and Transport Policies. OECD Publishing, Paris.

Ornish, D., 1998. Intensive Lifestyle Changes for Reversal of Coronary Heart Disease. JAMA 280, 2001. doi:10.1001/jama.280.23.2001

Page, S., 2006. Path Dependence. Qarterly J. Polit. Sci. 1, 87–115.

Pauly, M., 1983. More on moral hazard. J. Health Econ. 1.

Pauly, M., 1968. The Economics of Moral Hazard: Comment. Am. Econ. Rev. 3.

Pearce, D., Howarth, A., 2000. Technical Report on Methodology: Cost Benefit Analysis and Policy Responses.

Pedro, B., Sara, M., Jorge, S., 2011. Health Systems in Transition - Portugal Health System Review, The European Observatory on Health Systems and Policies. WHO Regional Office for Europe, Copenhagen.

Peng, Y., Chang, W., Zhou, H., Hu, H., Liang, W., 2010. Factors associated with health-seeking behavior among migrant workers in Beijing, China. BMC Health Serv. Res. 10, 69.

Phelps, C.E., 2010. Health economics, 4th ed. ed, The Addison-Wesley series in economics. Addison-Wesley, New York.

PRC, 2011. China's Twelfth Five Year Plan (2011-2015) - the Full English Version [WWW Document]. URL http://cbi.typepad.com/china_direct/2011/05/chinas-twelfth-five-new-plan-the-full-english-version.html (accessed 11.14.14).

PRC, 2009. Implementation Plan for the Recent Priorities of the Health Care System Reform (2009-2011) [WWW Document]. URL http://www.china.org.cn/government/scio-press-conferences/2009-04/09/content_17575401.htm (accessed 11.14.14).

Prochaska, J.O., DiClemente, C.C., Norcross, J.C., 1992. In search of how people change: Applications to addictive behaviors. Am. Psychol. 47, 1102–1114. doi:10.1037/0003-066X.47.9.1102

Razum, O., 2006. Commentary: of salmon and time travellers—musing on the mystery of migrant mortality. Int. J. Epidemiol. 35, 919–921.

Razum, O., Zeeb, H., Rohrmann, S., 2000. The "healthy migrant effect"–not merely a fallacy of inaccurate denominator figures. Int. J. Epidemiol. 29, 191–192.

Rodwin, V., 1994. Japan's Universal and Affordable Health Care: Lessons for the United States? Japanese Society, New York.

Roemer, M., 1993. National Health Systems of the World - The issues. Oxford University Press, Oxford.

Scherer, F., 2000. The pharmaceutical industry, in: Handbook of Health Economics. Elsevier, Amsterdam.

Schön, S., Nowak, D., 2002. Medikamentöse Verfahren zur Raucherentwöhnung. Suchtmedizin Forsch. Prax. 4, 189.

Schusdziarra, V., Hausmann, M., 2007. Satt essen und abnehmen - individuelle Ernährungsumstellung ohne Diät. Wissensverlag, Neu Isenburg.

Shapiro, M., Ware, J., Sherbourne, C., 1986. Effects of cost sharing on seeking care for serious and minor symptoms: results of a randomized controled trial. Ann. Intern. Med. 2.

Shih, W., 2011. Chinas's Five-Year Plan, Indigenous Innovation and Technology Transfers and Outsourcing [WWW Document]. URL http://www.uscc.gov/Hearings/hearing-china%E2%80%99s-five-year-plan-indigenous-innovation-and-technology-transfers-and (accessed 11.14.14).

Siu, A., Sonnenberg, F., Manning, W., Goldberg, G., Bloomfield, E., Newhouse, J., Brook, R., 1986. Inappropriate use of hospitals in a randomized trial of health insurance plan. N. Engl. J. Med.

Slaymaker, T., Adank, M., Boelee, E., Hagos, F., Nicol, A., Tafesse, T., Tolossa, D., Tucker, J., 2007. Water, Livelihoods and Growth: Concept paper. Department for International Development, Addis Ababa.

Slovic, P., 1987. Perception of Risk. Science 236, 280–285.

Stearns, S., Wolfe, B., Kindig, D., 1992. Physician responses to fee-for-service and capitation payment. Inquiry.

Stuckler, D., Feigl, A., Basu, S., McKee, M., 2010. The political economy of universal health coverage. Presented at the Global Symposium on Health Systems Research.

Stuecker, H., 2008. Health Care reform and Medical Insurance policies in China. EU-China Social Security Reform Co-operation Project, Beijing, China.

Sun, Q., Santoro, M.A., Meng, Q., Liu, C., Eggleston, K., 2008. Pharmaceutical Policy In China. Health Aff. (Millwood) 27, 1042–1050. doi:10.1377/hlthaff.27.4.1042

Swartz, K., 2010. Cost-sharing: effects on spending and outcomes. Synth. Proj.

Tang, S., Tao, J., Bekedam, H., 2012. Controlling cost escalation of healthcare: making universal health coverage sustainable in China. BMC Public Health 12, S8. doi:10.1186/1471-2458-12-S1-S8

Taylor, R.S., Brown, A., Ebrahim, S., Jolliffe, J., Noorani, H., Rees, K., Skidmore, B., Stone, J.A., Thompson, D.R., Oldridge, N., 2004. Exercise-based rehabilitation for patients with coronary heart disease: systematic review and meta-analysis of randomized controlled trials. Am. J. Med. 116, 682–692. doi:10.1016/j.amjmed.2004.01.009

ten Brink, P., Ljupco, A., Vermoote, S., Bassi, S., Callebaut, K., Lust, A., Hunt, A., 2007. Task 2 - Benefits for the former Yugoslav Republic of Macedonia and other countries of SEE of compliance with the environmental acquis Final Report – Part II : Country.

Tobe, R.G., Xu, L., Zhou, C., Yuan, Q., Geng, H., Wang, X., 2013. Factors affecting patient delay of diagnosis and completion of Direct Observation Therapy, Short-course (DOTS) among the migrant population in Shandong, China. Biosci. Trends 7, 122–128.

Tudor Hart, J., 1971. The inverse care law. The Lancet 297, 405–412. doi:10.1016/S0140-6736(71)92410-X

Tuomilehto, J., Lindström, J., Eriksson, J.G., Valle, T.T., Hämäläinen, H., Ilanne-Parikka, P., Keinänen-Kiukaanniemi, S., Laakso, M., Louheranta, A., Rastas, M., Salminen, V., Aunola, S., Cepaitis, Z., Moltchanov, V., Hakumäki, M., Mannelin,

M., Martikkala, V., Sundvall, J., Uusitupa, M., 2001. Prevention of Type 2 Diabetes Mellitus by Changes in Lifestyle among Subjects with Impaired Glucose Tolerance. N. Engl. J. Med. 344, 1343–1350. doi:10.1056/NEJM200105033441801

UN, 2015. Sustainable Development Goals .:. Sustainable Development Knowledge Platform [WWW Document]. Sustain. Dev. Knowl. Platf. URL https://sustainabledevelopment.un.org/?menu=1300 (accessed 11.14.15).

UN, 2014. World Urbanization Prospects: The 2014 Revision, CD-ROM Edition. [WWW Document]. URL http://esa.un.org/unpd/wup/CD-ROM/WUP2014_XLS_CD_FILES/WUP2014-F05-Total_Population.xls (accessed 11.14.14).

UN, 2012a. United Nations General Assembly Sixty-seventh session 53rd plenary meeting.

UN, 2012b. United Nations General Assembly Distr.: General 14 March 2013 Sixty-seventh session Agenda item 123 Global health and foreign policy.

UN, 2005. A Health Situation Assessment of the People's Republic of China. United Nations Health Partners Group in China, Beijing.

US Census Bureau, 2015. Income, Poverty and Health Insurance Coverage in the U.S.: 2014 [WWW Document]. URL http://census.gov/newsroom/press-releases/2015/cb15-157.html (accessed 11.14.15).

Vail, J., 2009. Managing Infectious Diseases among China's Migrant Populations, in: China's Capacity to Manage Infectious Diseases: Global Implications. Center for Strategic & International Studies, Washington D.C.

von Neumann, J., Morgenstern, O., 1944. Theory of games and economic behavior. Princeton University Press, Princeton.

Wang, X., Wu, S., Song, Q., Tse, L.-A., Yu, I.T.S., Wong, T.-W., Griffiths, S., 2011. Occupational Health and Safety Challenges in China—Focusing on Township-Village Enterprises. Arch. Environ. Occup. Health 66, 3–11. doi:10.1080/19338244.2010.486424

Wang, Y.P., Murie, A., 2011. The New Affordable and Social Housing Provision System in China: Implications for Comparative Housing Studies. Int. J. Hous. Policy 11, 237–254. doi:10.1080/14616718.2011.599130

WHO, 2015. Towards a monitoring framework with targets and indicators for the health goals of the post - 2015 Sustainable Development Goals.

WHO, 2014a. Making fair choices on the path to universal health coverage. World Health Organization, Geneva.

WHO, 2014b. The top 10 causes of death - The 10 leading causes of death by country income group (2012) [WWW Document]. URL http://www.who.int/mediacentre/factsheets/fs310/en/index1.html (accessed 9.1.14).

WHO, 2014c. The top 10 causes of death - Major causes of death [WWW Document]. URL http://www.who.int/mediacentre/factsheets/fs310/en/index2.html (accessed 9.1.14).

WHO, 2014d. Alcohol in the WHO European Region. World Health Organization, Copenhagen.

WHO, 2014e. Global status report on alcohol and health 2014. World Health Organization, Geneva.

WHO, 2013. World health report 2013: research for universal health coverage. World Health Organization, Geneva.

WHO, 2011a. Sustainable health financing structures and universal coverage. World Health Organization, Geneva.

WHO, 2011b. Global status report on noncommunicable diseases: 2010. World Health Organization, Geneva.

WHO, 2011c. Country-specific unit costs [WWW Document]. URL http://www.who.int/choice/country/country_specific/en/ (accessed 12.9.14).

WHO, 2010a. Health systems financing: the path to universal coverage. World Health Organization, Geneva.

WHO, 2010b. Heavy episodic drinking, past 30 days [WWW Document]. Glob. Health Obs. Data Repos. URL http://apps.who.int/gho/data/node.main.A1047?lang=en (accessed 12.7.14).

WHO, 2010c. Alcohol consumers, past 12 months [WWW Document]. Glob. Health Obs. Data Repos. URL http://apps.who.int/gho/data/node.main.A1044?lang=en (accessed 12.8.14).

WHO, 2009. Global health risks: mortality and burden of disease attributable to selected major risks. World Health Organization, Geneva.

WHO, 2008a. Closing the gap in a generation: Health equity through action on the social determinants of health (Final Report of the Commission on Social Determinants of Health). World Health Organization, Geneva.

WHO, 2008b. WHO-China Country Cooperation Strategy 2008-2013. World Health Organization, Geneva.

WHO, 2006. Constitution of the World Health Organisation.

WHO, 2005. Sustainable health financing, universal coverage and social health insurance. World Health Organization, Geneva.

WHO, 1996. Health Care Systems in Transition - Greece. WHO Regional Office for Europe, Copenhagen.

WHO, 1978. Declaration of Alma-Ata. World Health Organization, Alma Ata.

WHO, Lerberghe, W. van., 2008. The world health report 2008 primary health care: now more than ever. World Health Organization, Geneva, Switzerland.

WHO, OECD, 2015. Economic cost of the health impact of air pollution in Europe: Clean air, health and wealth. WHO Regional Office for Europe, OECD, Copenhagen.

Wikipedia, 2012. Equity (economics) [WWW Document]. URL http://en.wikipedia.org/wiki/Horizontal_equity (accessed 3.4.12).

Williamson, D.F., Pamuk, E., Thun, M., Flanders, D., Byers, T., Heath, C., 1995. Prospective Study of Intentional Weight Loss and Mortality in Never-Smoking Overweight US White Women Aged 40–64 Years 141, 1128–1141.

Willinger, M., 2001. Environmental Quality, Health and the Value of Life (No. 7). European Commission, Cambridge.

Woolf, L., 2011. Health Services in Israel. Ministry of Immigrant Absorption, Jerusalem.

Word Bank, 2013. China 2030.

World Bank, 2014a. Out-of-pocket health expenditure (% of total expenditure on health) in selected countries [WWW Document]. World DataBank - World Dev. Indic.

URL   http://databank.worldbank.org/data/views/reports/tableview.aspx#
(accessed 12.17.14).

World Bank, 2014b. Data from database: Health Nutrition and Population Statistics:
Population   estimates   and   projections   [WWW   Document].   URL
http://data.worldbank.org/data-catalog/population-projection-tables   (accessed
11.18.14).

World Bank, 2007. Cost of Pollution in China: Economic Estimates of Physical
Damages. The World Bank, Beijing.

World Bank, 2005. World Development Report 2006 - Equity and well-being. The World
Bank and Oxford University Press, Washington DC.

Wu, W., 2002. Migrant Housing in Urban China: Choices and Constraints. Urban Aff.
Rev. 38, 90–119. doi:10.1177/107808702401097817

Xie, E., 2011. Income-related inequalities of health and health care utilization. Front.
Econ. China 6, 131–156. doi:10.1007/s11459-011-0125-5

Xinhua, 2014. China holds meeting on 13th five-year plan [WWW Document]. URL
http://news.xinhuanet.com/english/china/2014-09/05/c_133621684.htm
(accessed 11.14.15).

Xiong, T., 2011. General practitioner system to take shape in China by 2020.

Yip, W.C.-M., Hsiao, W.C., Chen, W., Hu, S., Ma, J., Maynard, A., 2012. Early appraisal
of China's huge and complex health-care reforms. The Lancet 379, 833–842.
doi:10.1016/S0140-6736(11)61880-1

Yip, W.C.-M., Hsiao, W.C., Chen, W., Hu, S., Ma, J., Maynard, A., 3. Early appraisal of
China's huge and complex health-care reforms. The Lancet 379, 833–842.
doi:10.1016/S0140-6736(11)61880-1

Zhang, L., Chow, E.P., Jahn, H.J., Kraemer, A., Wilson, D.P., 2013. High HIV
prevalence and risk of infection among rural-to-urban migrants in various
migration stages in China: a systematic review and meta-analysis. Sex. Transm.
Dis. 40, 136–147.

Zheng, Z., Lian, P., 2005. Health Vulnerability among Temporary Migrants in Urban
China. International Population Conference, Tours.

Zilanawala, A., Davis-Kean, P., Nazroo, J., Sacker, A., Simonton, S., Kelly, Y., 2015. Race/ethnic disparities in early childhood BMI, obesity and overweight in the United Kingdom and United States. Int. J. Obes. 39, 520–529. doi:10.1038/ijo.2014.171

Zuckerman, S., Holahan, J., 1991. Medicare balance billing: its role in physician payment, in: Regulating Doctors' Fees: Competition, Controls, and Benefits under Medicare. American Enterprise Institute, Washington.

Zweifel, P., Manning, W., 2000. Moral hazard and consumer incentives in health care, in: Handbook of Health Economics. Elsevier, Amsterdam.

人力资源和社会保障部, 卫 生 部, 财 政 部, 2009. 三部门印发流动就业人员医保转移接续暂 行 办 法 [WWW Document]. URL http://www.gov.cn/gzdt/2010-01/19/content_1513824.htm (accessed 11.19.14).

新 华, 2014. 国 家 新 型 城 镇 化 规 划 (2014-2020 年) [WWW Document]. URL http://wenku.baidu.com/link?url=Zg4eap46ZU1s7lUfQ5e3ujwbRTeUa-eVD7uJhDnjjttHaD9yjO98rDSK3QYAj6kR-8a9S7pGOGiQkkQVos9iuFcX4Ep_NnZRK1KZosiA34y (accessed 11.17.14).

黄 赟, 2012. 苏 州 金 阊 医 改 三 年 调 研 报 告 [WWW Document]. URL http://wenku.baidu.com/view/415848838762caaedd33d4d3.html (accessed 11.11.14).

Annexes

Annex 1

Housing Choices for temporary migrants

TABLE 3: Temporary Migrants Have Limited Housing Choices (in percentages)

	Shanghai			Beijing		
	Temporary Migrants (n = 1,789)	Permanent Migrants (n = 80)	Local Residents (n = 137)	Temporary Migrants (n = 927)	Permanent Migrants (n = 145)	Local Residents (n = 154)
Renting private housing	49.0	2.5	3.6	31.9	7.6	2.6
Renting public housing	11.6	33.8	43.8	18.7	26.9	24.7
Dorm/workshed	28.8	3.8	0.0	41.6	11.0	1.3
Staying with local residents	4.6	1.3	2.9	3.9	1.4	0.0
Private housing	0.0	51.3	39.4	0.0	32.4	42.9
Commercial housing	0.7	5.0	10.2	0.4	1.4	2.6
Other[a]	5.4	2.5	0.0	3.3	19.3	26.0
Combined	100.0	100.0	100.0	100.0	100.0	100.0

a. Other housing choices include self-built shed, boat, hotel/inn, living on the street or in a hall-way, and staying in hospital rooms for temporary migrants and include relocation housing and housing sold by work units for permanent migrants and local residents.

Table 42: "Housing Choices for temporary migrants", (Wu, 2002, p. 105).

Annex 2

Housing conditions for temporary migrants

TABLE 5: Housing Conditions of Temporary Migrants Compare Very Unfavorably Against Those of Local Residents Across Geographical Location (in percentages)

	Per Capita Usable Area (m^2)	No Water	No Gas/ Propane	No Kitchen	No Bathroom
Shanghai					
Central city					
Temporary migrants	8.0	3.1	57.1	56.0	59.9
Local residents	12.5	0.4	4.8	50.5	54.6
Inner suburbs					
Temporary migrants	8.4	5.8	68.3	77.6	72.7
Local residents	26.8	1.6	11.4	11.2	39.2
Outer suburbs					
Temporary migrants	12.3	3.8	66.3	71.2	65.2
Local residents	28.0	3.0	19.9	12.6	44.5
Combined					
Temporary migrants	9.0	4.4	63.8	68.4	66.5
Local residents	18.7	1.1	8.7	34.1	48.8
Beijing					
Central city					
Temporary migrants	8.1	14.6	52.8	62.5	80.6
Local residents	14.4	0.1	9.4	19.8	51.1
Inner suburbs					
Temporary migrants	6.7	22.8	66.4	78.3	91.4
Local residents	20.3	0.4	16.0	10.3	26.6
Outer suburbs					
Temporary migrants	9.9	7.0	66.1	73.0	91.3
Local residents	19.2	10.9	53.2	9.0	30.6
Combined					
Temporary migrants	7.5	18.5	63.5	74.1	89.1
Local residents	18.4	1.9	19.7	13.0	34.6

SOURCE: Housing conditions of local residents based on results of the 1995 1% Population Survey in Beijing and Shanghai.

Table 43: "Housing conditions of temporary migrants compare very unfavorably against those of local residents across geographical location (in percentage)" (Wu, 2002, p. 107).

Annex 3

Migration paths in China

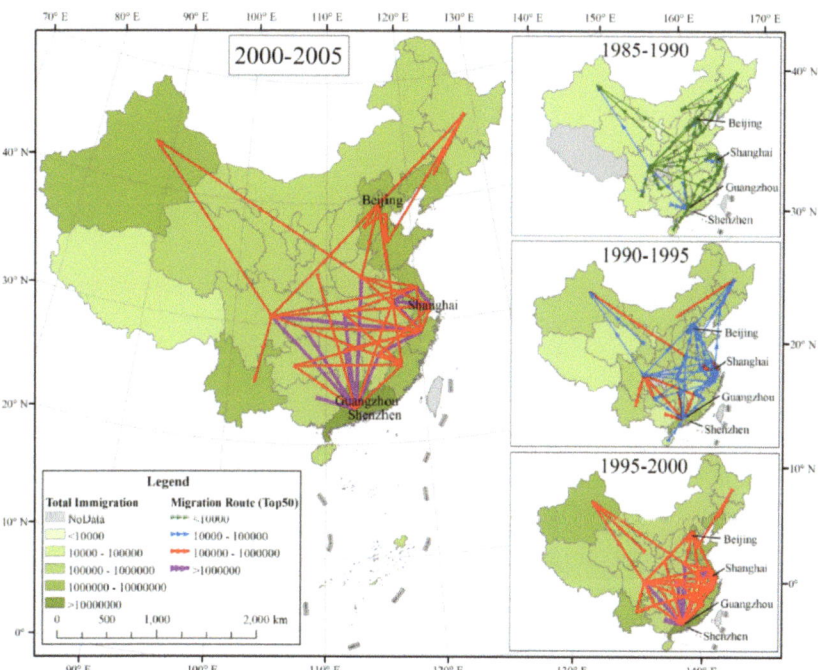

Figure 24: Top 50 cross□provincial population migration paths in China, based on population censes in 1990 and 2000, and the 1% population sampling survey in 1985, 1995 and 2005.3 Background shading represents the total immigration to each province during the interval. Path colors indicate the total number of cross□ provincial migrants moving between provinces in direction of arrow during the time period. The paths shown accounted for 31%, 50%, 66% and 67% of the total migration that occurred in the four time periods, respectively. Data from Wang, Li et al. 2011 (Gong et al., 2012b).

Annex 4

Total Economic Value (TEV)

Health economics possesses an approach to measure the „total economic value" (TEV). The TEV basically consists of three different types of costs (Holland et al., 2014a, 2014b):

$$TEV = medical\ costs + productivity\ costs + welfare\ costs$$

Acknowledging that this sum leads to double counting, the formula can be adapted by including the out of pocket payments that people invest. These payments are paid, and therefore accounted, individually, but they are at the same time included within the total medical costs (compare Figure 25).

$$TEV = medical\ costs + productivity\ costs + welfare\ costs - OOP$$

Medical costs are those costs that are directly incurred with an illness. They are therefore labeled "direct costs of illness" or "direct COI". In Figure 25 below, direct COI include "administration costs" and "costs of medical care" (Figure 25). In open market economies, these costs can relative easily be measured through hospital costs and other health expenditures.

Productivity costs are those costs that are indirectly incurred with illness („indirect COI"). In bellow's Figure 25 they are labeled „Economic production losses". They can be measured through two approaches: Either they are based on employee surveys (CBI, 2013, 2011, 1998) or they are retrieved through macroeconomic modeling (EC, 2013; Holland, 2014). Medical and productivity costs together are measuring the vast share of the „cost borne by society" (Figure 25).

Welfare costs are quantified through individual preferences. This is modeled either by asking the individual „willingness to pay" (WTP) for a certain reduction of the health risk or through the „willingness to accept" (WTA) a certain increase of a health risk. Welfare costs are basically measuring the „costs borne by the victim" (Figure 25).

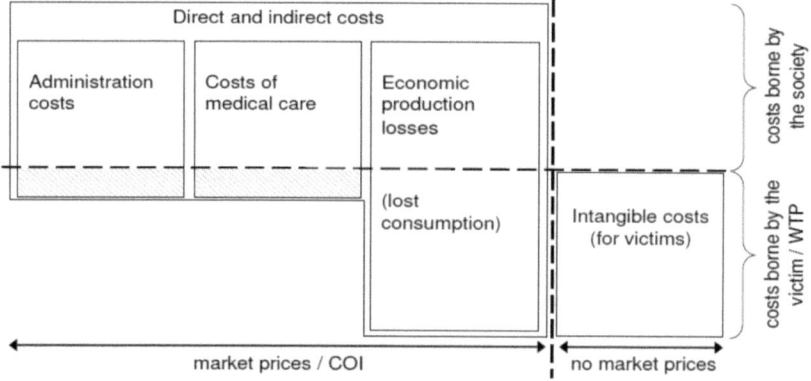

Figure 25: Economic valuation of total health costs by COI and WTP (WHO, 2008c, p. 25).

Annex 5

VSL and Equity

The comparison between different countries easily violates equity if countries are not treated equally. One study in the tradition of environmental health economics where this aspect can be shown are the latest WHO/OECD and OECD publications "Economic cost of the health impact of air pollution in Europe: Clean air, health and wealth" (WHO and OECD, 2015) and "The Cost of Air Pollution: Health Impacts of Road Transport" (OECD, 2014b). In order to measure external costs from human health impacts, the authors use the "value of a statistical life" (VSL) approach. VSL builds on the "willingness to pay" (WTP) method where people are asked to state their preferences in monetary terms for reducing their risk of dying from a certain risk factor (e.g. air pollution). The underlying formula used in this study to calculate VSL is:

$$VSL = WTP * 100{,}000$$

In words: VSL is calculated by deriving the WTP for reducing the risk of dying from air pollution from the rate of $\frac{3}{100{,}000}$ to $\frac{2}{100{,}000}$, and multiplying it by 100,000 in order to receive the amount of money that society is willing to pay to save one statistical life within a group of 100.000 people (OECD, 2014b, p. 17; WHO and OECD, 2015, p. 16).

Although the VSL and WTP approaches are well embedded in classical and current economic theory, they are also target of critique and rejection. This is mainly due to three reasons:

1. The dominance of VSL approaches in CBAs.
2. VSL values are measured different contexts and might therefore provide inaccurate numbers if transferred to other backgrounds.
3. VSL is often misinterpreted as "value of life", whereas it really is the "value of a statistical life". It is not life, but health risks that are measured in this approach (Pearce and Howarth, 2000, p. 43).

Among these three reasons, only the second one might be strong enough to reject the use of VSL. And indeed, the recommended VSL base value from OECD ranges

176

between USD 3 (for OECD countries, in 2010 USD) and USD 3.6 (for EU 27, in 2010 USD) million (OECD, 2014b, 2012; Hunt, 2011; Hunt and Ferguson, 2010; Braathen, 2012; Biausque, 2012; WHO and OECD, 2015) and is consequently up to three times as high as the most common value found in other OECD meta-analysis (Lindhjem et al., 2010) and in projects of the European Commission (Holland et al., 2005; New-Ext, 2004; Chanel, 2011; ten Brink et al., 2007). Therefore, the results of the OECD paper "The Cost of Air Pollution" (OECD, 2014b) – may they be right or wrong – are prone to be criticized with respect to the second argument mentioned above. However, discussions concerning the methodology and the height of the value, should not lead to the conclusion that the OECD findings can be rejected. Independently from the final result, the analysis clearly shows that the societal costs resulting from health impacts of air pollution are enormously high and should not be ignored by policy makers. It is not so much the final magnitude of the results that is important, but the enormity of the problem. For this reason, we conclude that there is no necessity to reject the use of VSL for this analysis or for the environment and health topic *per se*.

As economics is not only a calculation method with the aim of producing numbers, but also a science that analyses and at the same time influences society, the results communicated are not amoral as sometimes stated by economists. The potential society shaping impact of economic research shows with regard to the three points of critique mentioned above:

1. The OECD paper strongly advocates measuring costs by referring to peoples preferences (using the WTP approach) (OECD, 2014b, p. 16) instead of direct costs of medical care and administration (Chanel, 2011, p. 12). They thereby indirectly make a value statement that lost consumption and intangible costs for victims are more important than administrative costs, costs for medical care and economic production costs (Figure 25, Annex 4).
2. By transferring VSL values from environmental areas to the area of NCDs, the implicit statement is made that people value health outcomes from both sources equally.
3. Although based on a misunderstanding, the third point of critique shows that the VSL approach raises ethical questions about valuing people's lives economically.

One of these ethical concerns within the VSL approach is that of equality and equity. Seeking orientation on the constitution of the WHO for this case, equity is closely linked to equality: "The enjoyment of the highest attainable standard of health is one of the fundamental rights of every human being without distinction of (...) economic or social condition." (WHO, 2006, p. 1) Applied to the context of this thesis this means: Any health measurement tool used must ascertain that health is promoted independent from economic or social factors.

The OECD paper does unfortunately not pursue this goal, due to using a different VSL for each analyzed country.[87] Conceptually, the different VSLs are explained by the country specific WTP values (see formula above). As the value of WTP is not only influenced by risk (Alberini et al., 2004;

Pearson Correlation		Spearman Correlation	
2005	0.9982	2005	0.9993
2010	0.9767	2010	0.9725

Table 44: "GDP and VSL correlation", author's calculations.

Chestnut and De Civita, 2009; Cropper et al., 1994; Krupnick, 2007; Krupnick et al., 2002; Slovic, 1987), but also by economic parameters (e.g. income) (Willinger, 2001, p. 8) and social variables (e.g. health, gender, health status) (OECD, 2012, p. 3), such an approach violates the equity and equality request formulated by the WHO (WHO, 2006, p. 1) and adapted for this thesis. Due to the observation that national WTP and VSL are closely related to the countries' economic performances, GDP and VSL data correlate nearly perfectly (Table 44 above and Table 46 in Annex 7)[88].

The use of country specific values is not an equity issue per se, but becomes a matter of concern when individual numbers are added up. Even if the author explicitly states not to make a normative judgment (OECD, 2014b, p. 56), with this methodology in use, he implicitly states that rich nations with high VSL values should be the target of

---

[87] They justify this choice with the observation that health risks are typically socialized at the level of nation-states (OECD, 2014b, p. 55). This justification does however not hold entirely. Firstly, plenty policies in our days are supranational and are funded by and enjoyed by many nation states. Secondly, the original intention of creating country specific VSL values was different. The initial motivation for creating country-specific VSL has been to facilitate national cost-benefit analysis (CBA) in order to give policy recommendations to national governments (OECD, 2012, pp. 13–15) not to take out supranational analysis.
[88] Including calculations for differences in GDP per capita at purchasing power parity (PPP) (10), must not be misinterpreted as a tendency towards equality, because it is used to disaggregate VSL for the EU 27 from 2005 (10,13).

environmental policies before nations with lower income levels and lower VSLs (*ceteris paribus*, other variables are assumed to be equal). This argument becomes clear by looking at the underlying formula (OECD, 2014b, pp. 57–59):

$$Economic\ cost = Mortality\ costs + Morbidity\ costs$$

$$= \sum_{i=1}^{i=34} No.\ of\ deaths\ n_i * VSL_i + 0.1 * No.\ of\ deaths\ n_i * VSL_i$$

$$= \sum_{i=1}^{i=34} No.\ of\ deaths\ n_i * VSL_i * 1.1$$

The economic cost of air pollution in OECD countries, estimated by this analysis, consequently depends on the amount of the country specific VSL values and on the country specific number of deaths. Environmental policy interventions will however hardly influence VSL values, but they will influence mortality rates. Following the economic principle of efficiency, in this case for minimizing the total economic cost, the greatest reduction effect per statistical life saved can be achieved in the country where VSL is highest.

To give two examples: Saving one statistical life in Luxembourg reduces the economic cost by USD 5,779,000 in 2005 and USD 6,283,000 in 2010, while a statistical life saved in Turkey only reduces the cost by USD 1,381,000 in 2005 and USD 2,024,000 in 2010. In economic cost reduction terms, we can therefore state that 4.18 (2005) or 3.10 (2010)[89] statistical lives have to be saved in Turkey to achieve the same economic result than by saving 1 statistical life in Luxembourg. To reach the same amount in cost reduction that can be achieved by saving all 184 (2005) or 150 (2010) statistical lives lost in Luxembourg, 770 (2005) or 466 (2010) statistical lives would have to be saved in Turkey.[90] In economic cost reduction terms, it therefore does not make sense to safe statistical lives in Turkey (or any other country with a VSL lower than that of Luxembourg, compare Annex 4), before all statistical lives are saved in Luxembourg.

The second example: Environmental pollution and the resulting early deaths, are less important in Turkey than in Luxembourg if benefits are calculated with the approach

---

[89] $VSL_{L2005}: VSL_{T2005} = 5,779,000: 1,381,000 = 4.18$
$VSL_{L2010}: VSL_{T2010} = 6,283,000: 2,024,000 = 3.10$
[90] $n_{L2005} * VSL_{L2005}: VSL_{T2005} = 1,063,336,000: 1,381,000 = 769.98$
$n_{L2010} * VSL_{L2010}: VSL_{T2010} = 942,450,000: 2,024,000 = 465.64$

above. On an international basis, the above calculation might suggest that polluting Turkey is, in terms of economic costs, cheaper than polluting Luxembourg. To take the diesel example from the OECD paper, in economic terms, it would make sense to shift all diesel vehicles from rich to poor OECD countries, because this would – without changing the environmental and probably the health situation - reduce the total cost. It might also be possible to buy new non-diesel vehicles for the rich OECD countries, thereby worsening the total environmental and health situation, and still reduce the economic cost.

It might be argued that the ceteris paribus assumption is not realistic, because policy interventions in Luxembourg might, due to several reasons, be more expensive than in Turkey. And indeed this objective must be taken into calculation if a whole CBA is undertaken (Pearce and Howarth, 2000, p. 51). However, even then, a policy maker in Turkey would have to save nearly five (2005) or four (2010) statistical lives for the same cost that would be spent for saving one life in Luxembourg. Only if this ratio is achieved, it makes economically more sense to invest in Turkey instead of Luxembourg following the approach above. Therefore, it can be stated that the inequality problem of accounting statistical lives differently remains, even if the ceteris paribus assumption is dropped and the policy costs for saving one statistical life are different.

It is important to understand that above calculations are not made to suggest such resource allocation methods to any of the international organizations. They are neither made to blame the OECD authors. They are merely undertaken to showcase that economic analysis can convey moral judgments and shape our society towards one or the other direction – be it on purpose or unintended. In this analysis we want to stress the importance to follow the statement of the WHO constitution: "The enjoyment of the highest attainable standard of health is one of the fundamental rights of every human being without distinction of (...) economic or social condition." (WHO, 2006, p. 1)

In order to follow this moral aim, this thesis has, whenever comparing different countries with each other, used one VSL that represents all parties equally. Looking at the formula by which country specific VSLs are derived, we find that it builds on a base value of USD 3 million which is adjusted for differences in per capita GDP at a purchasing power parity (PPP) $(\frac{GDP\ per\ capita_i}{GDP\ per\ capita_{OECD}})$ adapting an income elasticity to the power of 0.8 (β) and (for 2010 values) an adjustment of income growth ($\%\Delta Y_i$) and inflation ($\%\Delta P_i$) also to the power of 0.8 (β) (OECD, 2014b, pp. 54–55):

$$VSL_{i\ 2005} = VSL_{OECD\ 2005} * (\frac{GDP\ per\ capita_i}{GDP\ per\ capita_{OECD}})^\beta$$

$$VSL_{i\ 2010} = VSL_{OECD\ 2005} * (\frac{GDP\ per\ capita_i}{GDP\ per\ capita_{OECD}})^\beta * (1 + \%\Delta P_i + \%\Delta GDP\ per\ capita_i)^\beta$$

Looking at these calculations, it is striking that not country specific WTPs lead to country specific VSLs, but that a common VSL value ($VSL_{OECD\ 2005}$) has been adapted to the country's specific economic situation. As discussed above, this has been done due to two reasons: 1. Health risks are typically socialized at the level of nation-states (OECD, 2014b, p. 55). 2. Facilitate national cost-benefit analysis (CBA) for national governments (OECD, 2012, pp. 13–15). While both reasons are strong and logic to argue for country specific VSL estimates, they do explain why and how an economic cost analysis may use country specific VSL values to come up with a total cost. Although, there is no reason given why individual VSLs cannot be used on the level of individual countries, e.g. for cost benefit analysis, they lead to unwanted implications if they are summed up to a total cost (see section above). A possible approach towards a more equal calculation could for example rely on average OECD data:

$$VSL_{i\ 2005} = VSL_{OECD\ 2005}$$

$$VSL_{i\ 2010} = VSL_{OECD\ 2005} * (1 + \%\Delta P_{OECD} + \%\Delta GDP_{OECD})^{\beta OECD}$$

Other scholars even propose to use the same procedure that is used on the country level to gain an average VSL on an international level if VSL values differ beforehand (Pearce and Howarth, 2000, p. 51). This step is not necessary for the OECD analysis, but shows the importance of using the same VSL values when comparing different countries.

The importance of using a single WTP to calculate the value of a statistical life (VSL) and calculate the welfare costs per 100,000 inhabitants has clearly been shown in the paragraphs before and will be adapted for the first approach in this section. In the second approach, the calculations will be adapted to the Chinese economic situation in order to avoid overestimating the economic burden and later on the benefits. Consequently, the WTP value used before will be adapted through the China specific GDP per capita and consumer price index. This approach has also been discussed through the specific country calculations above.

It is furthermore important to know that health effects of the interventions are only measured in the reduction of the death rate and only for a few illnesses. Morbidity issues will only be taken into account as an estimate of making up 10% of mortality figures. It has however to be kept in mind that using the VSL approach includes the assumption that morbidity "only" account for 10% of mortality. One reason for this might be that the VSL approach excludes "costs paid by third parties (e.g., insurance paid medical costs)" (Chestnut et al., 2000) and consequently understates the benefits made by the reducing morbidity.

Annex 6

The Chinese situation in comparison with Europe and the USA

Comparing China, Europe and the USA, the most obvious finding is that the situation for the risk factors tobacco use, diet and physical inactivity is better in China than in Europe or the USA. For the risk factor alcohol, China is still doing better than Europe, however as bad as the US (Table 45, Figure 26-Figure 29). Unlike Europe and the USA, China is however steadily worsening the situation concerning dietary risks and physical activity and only slightly getting better for tobacco and alcohol in recent years (Table 45, Figure 26-Figure 29).

		Tobacco				Alcohol			
		Deaths (mortality per 100.000)	DALY (mortality & morbidity per 100.000)	Mio. US$ (mortality)	Mio. US$ (mortality & morbidity)	Deaths (mortality per 100.000)	DALY (mortality & morbidity per 100.000)	Mio. US$ (mortality)	Mio. US$ (mortality & morbidity)
1990	China	87.57	2,430.18	$318.43	$350.27	30.50	1,117.43	$110.91	$122.00
	Europe	209.29	4,435.61	$761.05	$837.16	51.37	1,824.78	$186.82	$205.50
	USA	193.43	4,154.59	$703.39	$773.73	29.94	1,300.72	$108.87	$119.76
2005	China	100.60	2,296.36	$365.80	$402.38	32.65	1,169.82	$118.73	$130.60
	Europe	166.31	3,418.59	$604.77	$665.24	47.31	1,638.72	$172.02	$189.23
	USA	157.49	3,301.63	$572.70	$629.97	27.74	1,154.67	$100.89	$110.97
2010	China	100.45	2,206.51	$365.28	$401.81	28.20	1,013.35	$102.55	$112.80
	Europe	160.50	3,222.94	$583.64	$642.01	44.21	1,485.68	$160.75	$176.82
	USA	149.13	3,099.98	$542.28	$596.51	28.37	1,141.83	$103.17	$113.48

		Diet				Physical inactivity			
		Deaths (mortality per 100.000)	DALY (mortality & morbidity per 100.000)	Mio. US$ (mortality)	Mio. US$ (mortality & morbidity)	Deaths (mortality per 100.000)	DALY (mortality & morbidity per 100.000)	Mio. US$ (mortality)	Mio. US$ (mortality & morbidity)
1990	China	145.60	3,199.08	$529.47	$582.42				
	Europe	340.70	5,742.59	$1,238.91	$1,362.80				
	USA	287.08	4,829.97	$1,043.91	$1,148.30				
2005	China	182.25	3,806.96	$662.74	$729.02	34.02	805.97	$123.70	$136.07
	Europe	278.02	4,399.67	$1,010.98	$1,112.08	94.18	1,597.88	$342.46	$376.71
	USA	225.92	3,873.82	$821.53	$903.69	77.03	1,429.72	$280.09	$308.10
2010	China	186.97	3,801.99	$679.88	$747.86	36.42	841.18	$132.45	$145.70
	Europe	273.33	4,176.94	$993.92	$1,093.31	93.40	1,542.17	$339.65	$373.61
	USA	217.23	3,683.20	$789.91	$868.90	74.95	1,384.77	$272.54	$299.79

Table 45: "Welfare costs of the 'deadly quartet', 1990-2010", per 100.000 inhabitants, in 2010 million US$, health data from IHME (IHME, 2014b), author's calculations.

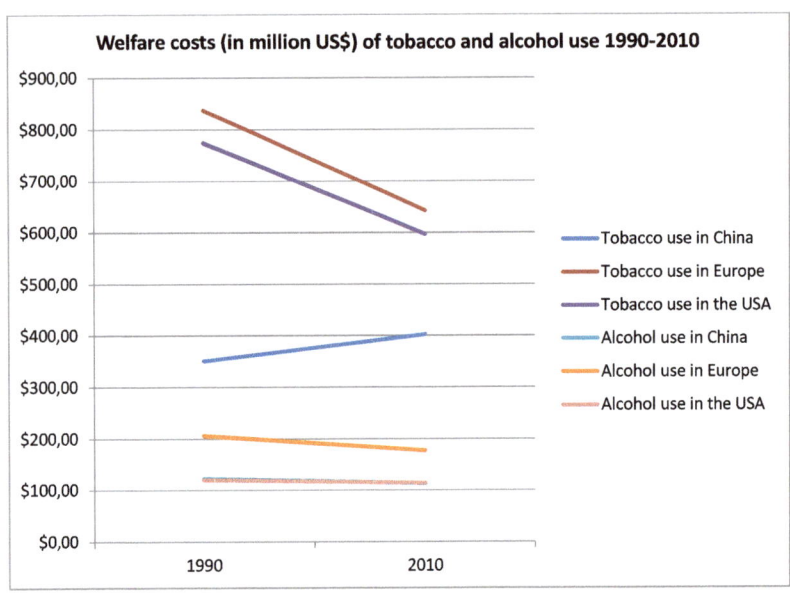

Figure 26: "Welfare costs (in million US$) of tobacco and alcohol use 1990-2010", health data from IHME (IHME, 2014b), author's calculations.

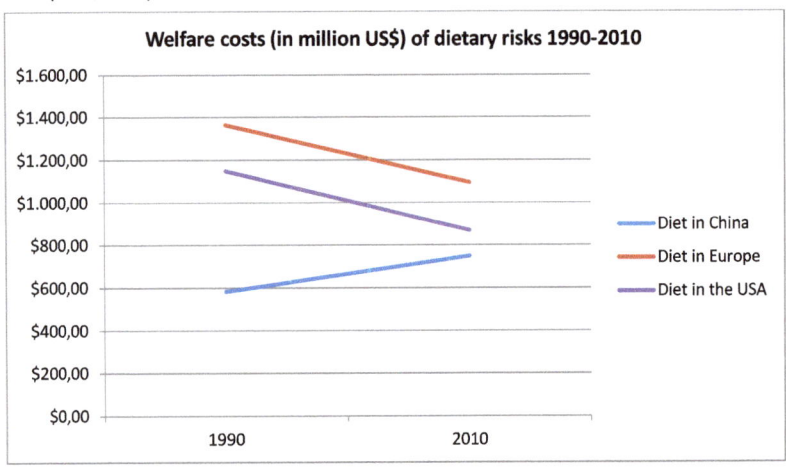

Figure 27: "Welfare costs (in million US$) of dietary risks 1990-2010", health data from IHME (IHME, 2014b), author's calculations.

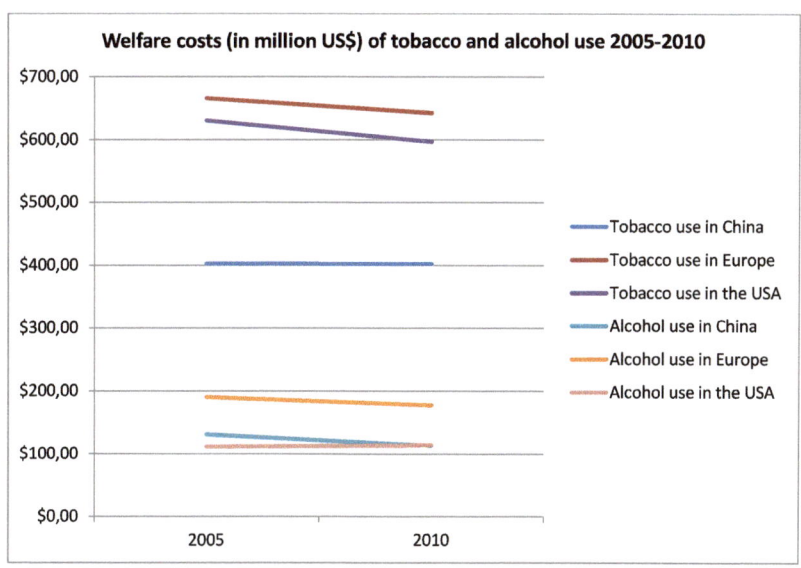

Figure 28: "Welfare costs (in million US$) of tobacco and alcohol use 2005-2010", health data from IHME (IHME, 2014b), author's calculations.

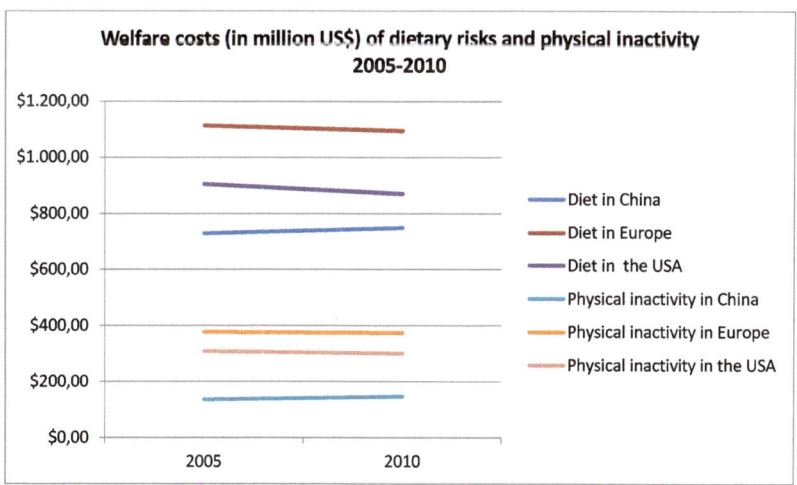

Figure 29: "Welfare costs (in million US$) of dietary risks and physical inactivity 2005-2010", health data from IHME (IHME, 2014b), author's calculations.

GDP, VSL and Correlations

Dataset: Gross domestic product (GDP) and value of statistical life (VSL) values (OECD data and author's calculations)

Contry	Rank	GDP 2005	Rank	VSL 2005	Rank	GDP 2010	Rank	VSL 2010
Australia	8	35004.958	9	3380	6	36592.995	5	3925
Austria	10	33636.816	10	3283	9	35321.994	9	3670
Belgium	14	32203.541	14	3170	12	32885.052	12	3504
Canada	6	36048.004	6.5	3397	7	32680.916	10	3657
Chile	32	12689.734	32	1505	32	14511.089	33	1923
Czech Republic	27	21268.021	27	2275	26	23625.407	26	2749
Denmark	12	33195.883	12	3248	15	32327.701	15	3456
Estonia	29	16530.731	29	1860	31	16612.084	30	2269
Finland	16	30707.922	16	3052	16	31321.397	16	3319
France	18	29554.47	18	2960	18	29635.744	17	3155
Germany	15	31116.576	15	3085	11	33519.884	14	3480
Greece	22	24372.639	22	2535	25	24328.724	25	2824
Hungary	28	16974.56	28	1899	30	16928.317	29	2316
Iceland	9	34991.781	8	3388	14	32758.893	4	4456
Ireland	4	38761.346	4	3677	8	35490.161	8	3751
Israel	23	24143.767	24	2440	19	27854.015	23	2922
Italy	19	28279.691	19	2857	20	27059.089	21	2995
Japan	17	30445.637	17	3031	17	30866.127	18	3068
Korea	25	22783.217	25	2404	22	26773.815	20	3027
Luxembourg	1	68210.629	1	5779	1	67669.446	1	6263
Mexico	33	12341.515	33	1483	33	12741.46	34	1811
Netherlands	7	35111.416	6.5	3397	5	36995.731	7	3761
New Zealand	21	25382.343	21	2621	23	25352.755	22	2937
Norway	2	47639.583	2	4337	2	46776.314	2	4650
Poland	31	13784.16	31	1608	29	17195.814	31	2098
Portugal	26	21368.959	26	2284	27	21779.646	27	2499
Slovak Republic	30	16174.534	30	1828	28	20167.127	28	2418
Slovenia	24	23471.598	23	2462	24	25008.942	24	2898
Spain	20	27392.007	20	2785	21	26906.957	19	3059
Sweden	13	32701.433	13	3210	10	34123.988	13	3502
Switzerland	5	36647.53	5	3516	4	39235.831	6	3851
Turkey	34	11394.035	34	1381	34	12520.897	32	2024
United Kingdom	11	33318.026	11	3258	13	32770.36	11	3554
United States	3	44242.262	3	4088	3	43888.63	3	4498

	Pearson Correlation	Spearmann Correlation
2005	0.9981673	0.9993124
2010	0.9767277	0.9724981

GDP data extracted on 08 Jun 2014 16:30 UTC (GMT) from OECD.Stat (http://stats.oecd.org/index.aspx?queryid=9185#)
VSL values extracted from OECD (2014),The Cost of Air Pollution: Health Impacts of Road Transport, OECD Publishing.http://dx.doi.org/10.1787/97

Table 46: "Dataset: Gross domestic product (GDP) and value of statistical life (VSL) values", (OECD, 2014b, 2014c) and author's calculations.

Annex 8

Explanation of economic values used for calculations

Abbreviation	Explanation
$VSL_{OECD\ 2005}$	The Value of a Statistical Life (VSL) of the average of the 34 OECD countries. According to OECD (2012). The best estimate of the VSL is USD 3.0 million, with the range of USD 1.5-4.5 million (in 2005).
GDP per capita$_i$	Country specific Gross Domestic Product (GDP) per capita at the purchasing power parity (PPP). The GDP is converted to international dollars using the PPP rates.
GDP per capita$_{OECD}$	The average GDP per capita of the 34 OECD countries at PPP. This value equals USD 32 220, in 2011.
β	Income elasticity of VSL. It measures the percentage increase in VSL for a percentage increase in income. The maximum value estimate is 0.8 and the minimum value estimate is 0.4.
PPP	Purchasing power parity-adjusted exchange rate, in 2005. PPP is the number of units of a country's currency required to buy the same amounts of goods and services in the domestic markets as US dollar would buy in the US.
%ΔP	The percentage increase in consumer price from year 2005 to 2010. This is measured by consumer price index (CPI) that reflects the inflation or changes in the cost to the average consumer of acquiring a basket of goods and services.
%Δ GDP per capita$_i$	The percentage change in real GDP per capita growth from year 2005 to 2010. This is derived from real GDP per capita annual growth.

Table 47: "Explanation of economic values used for calculations.", (OECD, 2014a; WHO and OECD, 2015), authors' adjustments.

Annex 9

Proposed targets and indicators for SDG goal 3.8

Targets:

- By 2030, all populations, independent of household income, expenditure or wealth, place of residence or sex, have at a minimum 80% essential health services coverage.
- By 2030, everyone has 100% financial protection from out-o-pocket payments for health services (WHO, 2015, p. 15)

Indicators:

Health services coverage

- Prevention: coverage with a set of tracer interventions for prevention services.
  - o Equity: a measure of prevention service coverage as described above, stratified by wealth quintile, place of residence and sex
  - o The proposed tracer indicators include (effective) coverage family planning, antenatal care (4 or more visits), immunization coverage (full or DTP3), non-tobacco use, and adequate water source and sanitary facilities. The latter two indicators are covered under another goal.
- Treatment: coverage with a set of tracer interventions for treatment services
  - o Equity: a measure of treatment service coverage as described above, stratified by wealth quintile, place of residence and sex
  - o The proposed tracer indicators include skilled birth attendance, (effective) coverage of TB treatment, ARV therapy, diabetes treatment and hypertension treatment.

Financial protection coverage

- Impoverishing expenditure
  - o Aggregate: fraction of the population protected against impoverishment by out-of-pocket health expenditures, comprising two types of household: families already below the poverty line on the basis of their consumption and who incur out-of-pocket health expenditures that push them deeper into poverty; and families for which out-of-pocket spending pushes them below the poverty line.
  - o Equity: fraction of households protected against impoverishment or further impoverishment by out-of-pocket health expenditures, stratified by wealth quintile, place of residence and sex.
- Catastrophic expenditure
  - o Aggregate: fraction of households protected from incurring catastrophic out-of-pocket health expenditure.
  - o Equity: fraction of households protected from incurring catastrophic out-of pocket health expenditure stratified by wealth quintile, place of residence and sex. (WHO, 2015, p. 15)

Herstellung und Verlag: BoD – Books on Demand, Norderstedt

ISBN 978-3-7322-3958-0